WOODSMITH CUSTOM WOODWORKING

Gift Projects

WOODSMITH CUSTOM WOODWORKING

Gift Projects

By the editors of Woodsmith magazine

Gift Projects

Kaleidoscope

Holiday Lantern

KEEPSAKES   88

Candle Centerpiece

ESPECIALLY FOR KIDS

Toys like these will never go out of style. That's good, because they're also built to last longer than the years of childhood. And unlike today's electronic toys, they'll only run out of power when the kids do.

Our biplane has a spinning propeller and turning wheels. All that's needed is a youngster to make engine noises as it rolls down the runway and lifts off the ground.

When play time is more "down-to-earth," the toy truck is the ticket. This one doubles as a bank. Even better, it features a secret, hidden release to get the money out.

For those rare moments when they sit still, the child's rocker will withstand some "rough riding" and you can build a matching table to make a set. Although it's made from round stock, store-bought dowels mean you don't need a lathe to build it. And little mommies will love the doll cradle that will last through years of lullabies.

Kaleidoscopes have always fascinated inquisitive minds. Ours uses a wide-angle lens to give an entirely different look to the everyday world. Kids may have trouble getting its showcase of mirrors and illusions away from the grown-ups.

Biplane

Take off to the shop and turn out a replica of an old-time flying machine. The spinning propeller and wheels make this a toy that will be prized by a child or even a grown-up who loves classic aircraft.

For years I've wondered why anyone would name an airplane the "Sopwith Camel," especially one as romantic as a classic World War I biplane.

I found the answer to my question when I began investigating designs for a toy plane and ran across a book that explained the history of old airplanes. It turns out that Sopwith is the name of the company that made it. Okay, I guess that can't be changed. The "camel" part is a nickname this plane got because of the hump in front of the cockpit where twin machine guns were mounted.

On my toy version, the machine guns are gone. But the sound effects will always be present as soon as someone picks it up and dives out of the clouds in a surprise attack on the Red Baron.

DETAILS. This toy is built tough enough to take a few "crash landings," plus it still has plenty of authentic details that are true to the original airplane.

For example, the wings are tapered on both faces for a realistic airfoil profile. The propeller is "twisted," just like the real thing, and it actually spins. (The wheels turn too.) I even figured out how to stagger the wings so the top one extends in front of the lower one.

The great thing is that it's not difficult to build in these details. Some time at the band saw and disc sander are all it takes to create these shapes.

TOY PARTS. Although I made the propeller myself, I used some ready-made toy pieces for other parts of the airplane (the wheels, and wood pins used for the axles and propeller shaft). You might find these (or suitable substitutes) at a local hobby or craft store. If not, a list of mail order sources can be found on page 126.

THIN LUMBER. The wings and propeller are $1/4$"-thick hardwood. It's not always possible to find lumber this thin, so I resaw and plane my own from thicker stock. The Technique article on page 65 explains how to do this.

EXPLODED VIEW

OVERALL DIMENSIONS:
10½"W x 8⅝"D x 4⅛"H

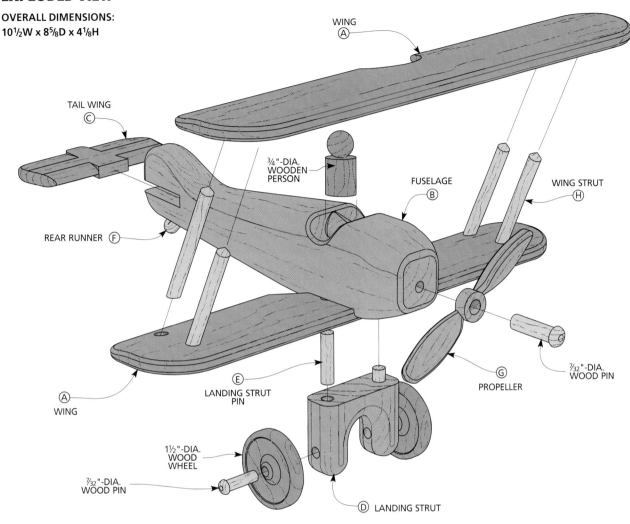

WING
Ⓐ

TAIL WING
Ⓒ

¾"-DIA.
WOODEN
PERSON

FUSELAGE
Ⓑ

WING STRUT
Ⓗ

REAR RUNNER Ⓕ

⁷⁄₃₂"-DIA.
WOOD PIN

PROPELLER
Ⓖ

Ⓐ
WING

Ⓔ
LANDING STRUT
PIN

1½"-DIA.
WOOD
WHEEL

⁷⁄₃₂"-DIA.
WOOD PIN

Ⓓ LANDING STRUT

MATERIALS LIST

WOOD
A Wings (2)   ¼ x 2 - 10½
B Fuselage (1)   1¾ x 1½ - 7⅞
C Tail Wing (1)   ¼ x 1⅜ - 3½
D Landing Strut (1)   ¾ x 2 - 1½
E Landing Strut Pins (2) ¼ dowel x ¾
F Rear Runner (1)   ⁵⁄₁₆ dowel x 1⅜
G Propeller (1)   ¼ x ¾ - 4
H Wing Struts (4)   ¼ dowel x 2¾ rgh.

HARDWARE SUPPLIES
(2) 1½"-dia. wood wheels
(3) ⁷⁄₃₂"-dia. wood pins, 1¼" long
(1) ¾"-dia. wooden person (optional)

CUTTING DIAGRAM

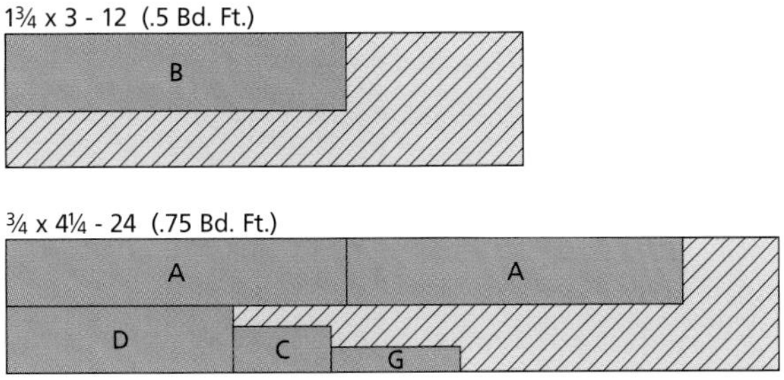

1¾ x 3 - 12 (.5 Bd. Ft.)

B

¾ x 4¼ - 24 (.75 Bd. Ft.)

A   A
D   C   G

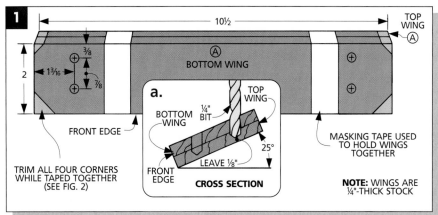

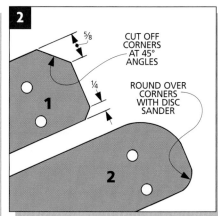

WINGS

After building several prototypes to work out the final design, I discovered that the key to building this Biplane is to start with the wings.

RESAW WINGS. To form the wings (A), first resaw and plane two strips $1/4$" thick. (Resawing is nothing more than ripping on edge. See the Technique article on page 65.) Then cut them to size (Fig. 1).

These two wings are connected with struts ($1/4$" dowels). But I wanted to make the wings just like the ones on the real plane — with the top wing canted out in front of the bottom wing.

DRILL HOLES FOR STRUTS. After a little experimenting, I finally figured out that this can be done by drilling the holes for the struts at an angle of 25° (Fig. 1a).

To do this, fasten the two wings together with masking tape and mark the positions of the holes (Fig. 1). Then tilt the drill press table to 25° and clamp the wings in position. (Or place a wedge under the workpieces.) Now you can drill a hole all the way through the bottom wing and stop when you're halfway through the top wing (Fig. 1a). Then do the same thing for the remaining holes.

SHAPE THE WINGS. After the holes are drilled, the shaping process on the wings can begin. While the wings are still taped together, use a band saw to cut off the corners (Step 1 in Fig. 2). Then gently round these corners on a disc sander (Step 2).

To form the wing flaps, cut a 13° bevel on the trailing edge of each wing, leaving a thickness of $1/8$" (Fig. 3).

Safety Note: Install a zero-clearance insert in your table saw.

NOTCH ON BOTTOM WING. Next, an angled notch is cut on the back edge of the bottom wing (Fig. 4). This notch should be deep enough to remove the beveled portion of the wing (the flap).

NOTCH ON TOP WING. On the top wing, cut a half-circle notch centered on the length of the wing (Fig. 5). I cut this $5/8$" radius to rough shape on a band saw and smoothed it with a small drum sander chucked in the drill press.

SAND TO SHAPE. Now the wings can be sanded to final shape. Start by rounding over the front edge of both wings (Fig. 6).

Then sand a slight bevel on the bottom side of each wing (below the bevel cut that was made on the table saw). What you're after here is to narrow the trailing edge of the wing flap to about $1/16$" thick.

Finally, sand all surfaces smooth. I used a sanding block when sanding the bevel so I wouldn't remove the crisp angle that forms the flaps.

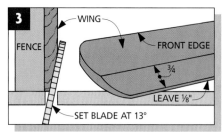

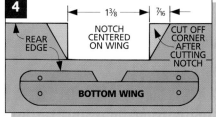

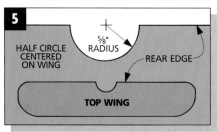

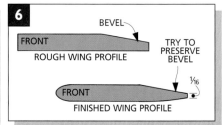

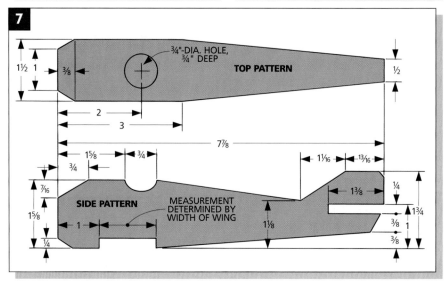

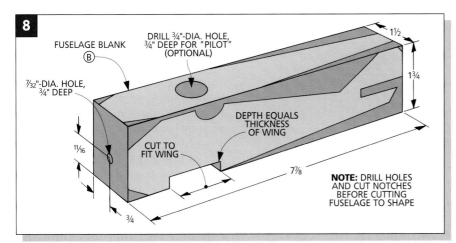

8

FUSELAGE BLANK
Ⓑ

DRILL ¾"-DIA. HOLE,
¾" DEEP FOR "PILOT"
(OPTIONAL)

7⁄32"-DIA. HOLE,
¾" DEEP

1½

1¾

DEPTH EQUALS
THICKNESS
OF WING

11⁄16

CUT TO
FIT WING

7⁄8

¾

NOTE: DRILL HOLES
AND CUT NOTCHES
BEFORE CUTTING
FUSELAGE TO SHAPE

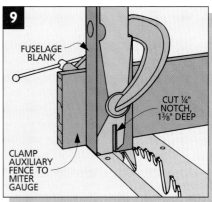

9

FUSELAGE
BLANK

CUT ¼"
NOTCH,
1⅜" DEEP

CLAMP
AUXILIARY
FENCE TO
MITER
GAUGE

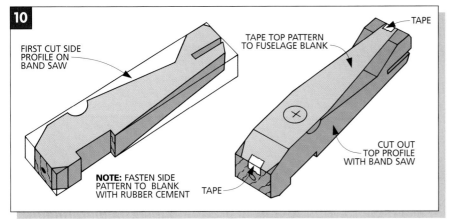

10

TAPE

FIRST CUT SIDE
PROFILE ON
BAND SAW

TAPE TOP PATTERN
TO FUSELAGE BLANK

CUT OUT
TOP PROFILE
WITH BAND SAW

NOTE: FASTEN SIDE
PATTERN TO BLANK
WITH RUBBER CEMENT

TAPE

FUSELAGE

Now the fuselage (B) can be formed. It all starts with a blank *(Fig. 8)* and a couple of patterns: one for the side view of the fuselage, and one for the top view *(Fig. 7)*.

Once you have the patterns transferred to a piece of paper, the side pattern can be fastened directly to the block of wood for the fuselage.

Note: I used rubber cement (available at art supply stores) to fasten the pattern to the wood.

DRILL HOLES. Before cutting the fuselage to shape, two holes can be drilled.

The first hole is optional. It holds a toy wooden "person" for a pilot. (You can see the top of his head in the photo on page 8. Sources of wooden people are listed on page 126.) This hole is on top of the fuselage block *(Fig. 8)*. The second hole is on the front of the fuselage for the propeller shaft.

NOTCHES. Next, two notches are cut in the fuselage block. The first is on the bottom of the block to fit the notched area of the bottom wing *(Fig. 8)*. This notch can be cut by making multiple passes on the table saw.

A second notch is cut on the end of the block for the tail wing. To make this cut, attach an auxiliary fence to the miter gauge and clamp the fuselage to this fence *(Fig. 9)*. Use the pattern as a guide to cut a ¼"-wide notch, 1⅜" deep.

CUT TO SHAPE. Now the fuselage can be cut to rough shape on a band saw. First, cut the side profile to form the shape of the tail section, the recessed section for the cockpit, and the nose *(Fig. 10)*.

Next, the fuselage is tapered from the cockpit back to the tail. To make these cuts, tape the top pattern to the top of the fuselage *(Fig. 10)*. Then make the cuts on the band saw so the blade just skims the edge of the pattern. Also trim the corners of the nose area.

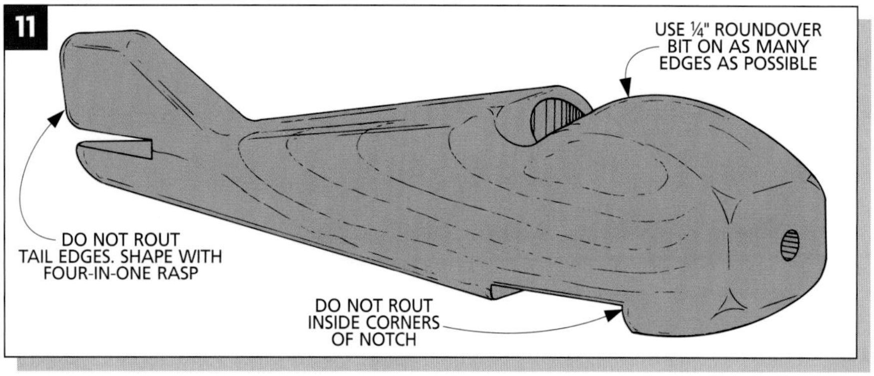
11
USE ¼" ROUNDOVER BIT ON AS MANY EDGES AS POSSIBLE
DO NOT ROUT TAIL EDGES. SHAPE WITH FOUR-IN-ONE RASP
DO NOT ROUT INSIDE CORNERS OF NOTCH

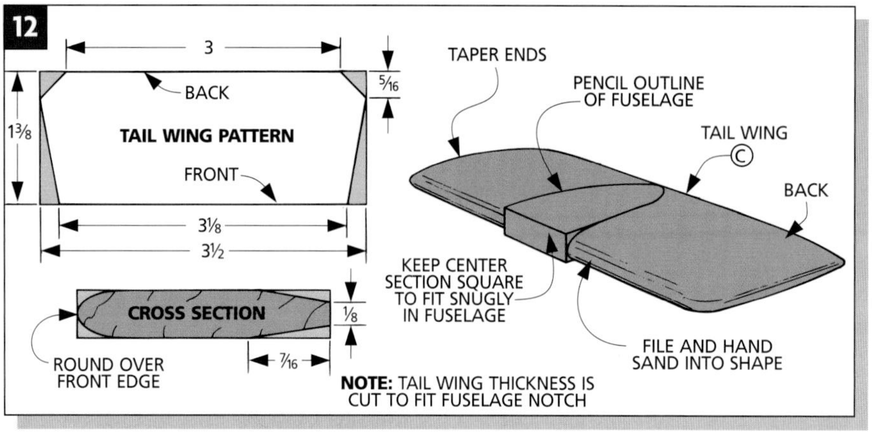
12
3
BACK
TAIL WING PATTERN
FRONT
1⅜
5⁄16
3⅛
3½
CROSS SECTION
⅛
7⁄16
ROUND OVER FRONT EDGE
TAPER ENDS
PENCIL OUTLINE OF FUSELAGE
TAIL WING
C
BACK
KEEP CENTER SECTION SQUARE TO FIT SNUGLY IN FUSELAGE
FILE AND HAND SAND INTO SHAPE
NOTE: TAIL WING THICKNESS IS CUT TO FIT FUSELAGE NOTCH

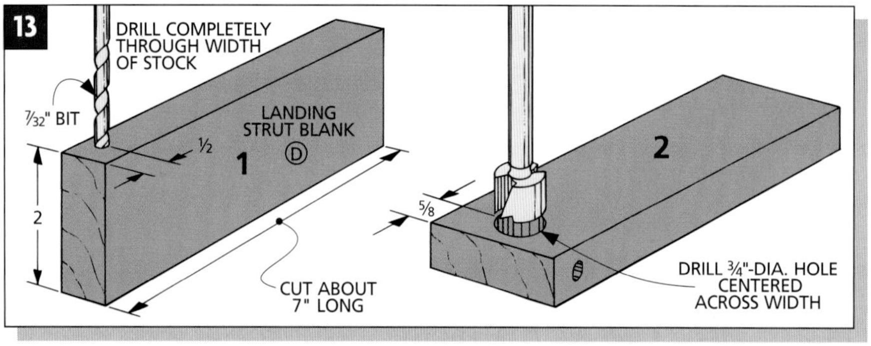
13
DRILL COMPLETELY THROUGH WIDTH OF STOCK
7⁄32" BIT
LANDING STRUT BLANK
D
½
1
2
CUT ABOUT 7" LONG
⅝
2
DRILL ¾"-DIA. HOLE CENTERED ACROSS WIDTH

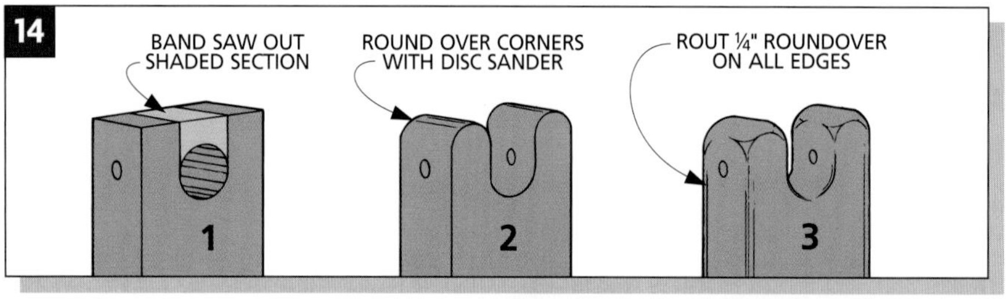
14
BAND SAW OUT SHADED SECTION
ROUND OVER CORNERS WITH DISC SANDER
ROUT ¼" ROUNDOVER ON ALL EDGES
1
2
3

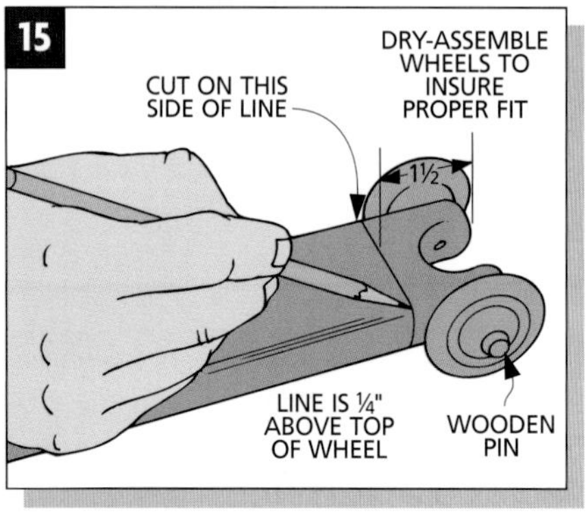
15
CUT ON THIS SIDE OF LINE
DRY-ASSEMBLE WHEELS TO INSURE PROPER FIT
1½
LINE IS ¼" ABOVE TOP OF WHEEL
WOODEN PIN

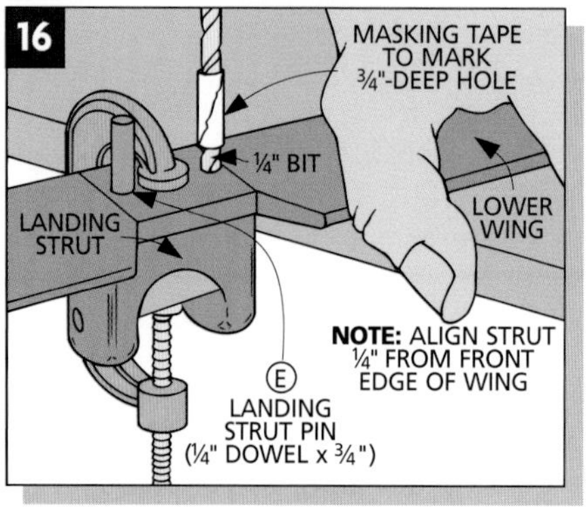
16
MASKING TAPE TO MARK ¾"-DEEP HOLE
¼" BIT
LANDING STRUT
LOWER WING
NOTE: ALIGN STRUT ¼" FROM FRONT EDGE OF WING
E
LANDING STRUT PIN (¼" DOWEL x ¾")

SMOOTH THE FUSELAGE. After the fuselage is cut to rough shape, some sanding will remove the band saw marks.

Then all the edges are rounded over. I did this with a ¼" roundover bit on the router table to get to as many edges as possible. However, there are two areas you *don't* want to rout: the end of the tail (which could be chipped off too easily), and the inside corners of the notch for the bottom wing *(Fig. 11)*.

To round the edges of the tail to match the routed edges, I used a four-in-one hand rasp. (There's more about this tool in the Shop Info box on page 11.)

TAIL WING

The next piece to work on is the tail wing (C). First, plane a piece of stock so it fits into the notch in the tail of the fuselage. (You want a snug fit because it can't be clamped when the glue is applied.) Then cut the wing to size *(Fig. 12)*.

Next, slide the wing into the notch and mark the outline of the fuselage on both the top and bottom.

Now to shape the wing, first trim the corners on a band saw *(Fig. 12)*. Then use a file and sandpaper to round over the front edge and taper the trailing edges without sanding the outlined area.

LANDING GEAR

The landing strut is a small piece that needs a fair amount of work on it. So I shaped the landing strut (D) at the end of a larger blank to make it easier to handle.

The first thing to do is to drill a hole to accept the axle pins, ½" from the end of the blank *(Step 1 in Fig. 13)*.

SHAPE THE STRUTS. Next, the end of the block is divided to form the two landing struts. First, bore a ¾"-dia. hole centered ⅝" from the end of the block *(Step 2 in Fig. 13)*. Then cut out the end section on a band saw to form the two struts *(Step 1 in Fig. 14)*, and sand the ends of the struts round *(Step 2)*. Finally, round over all the edges with a ¼" roundover bit on the router table *(Step 3)*.

CUT TO LENGTH. After routing the edges, dry-assemble the wheels and axles to make sure the wheels spin freely. With the wheels mounted to the struts, mark the final length of the strut ¼" above the tops of the wheels *(Fig. 15)*. Then remove the wheels and cut the strut to length.

MOUNT TO WING. Now the landing strut can be mounted to the bottom wing.

First. clamp the landing strut to the wing *(Fig. 16)*. (I cut a $^3/_4$" dowel in half to fit inside the strut as a pad for the clamp.) Then drill two $^1/_4$" holes through the wing and into the strut, and glue two landing strut pins (E) into the holes. After the glue dries, cut the dowels off and sand them flush with the top of the wing.

ASSEMBLY. At this point, the wing and landing strut assembly and the tail wing can be mounted to the fuselage *(Fig. 17)*. A couple of clamp pads make this easier.

When the glue is dry on the tail wing, drill a hole at a 45° angle at the bottom of the tail section for the rear runner (F) *(Fig. 18)*. Then round off the end of a $^5/_{16}$" dowel and glue it in place.

PROPELLER

I wanted to make the propeller as close to the real thing as possible. This meant sanding a very small piece of wood.

The propeller starts as a $^1/_4$"-thick blank with a hole centered on its length and width *(Fig. 19)*. The hole is $^1/_{16}$" larger than the diameter of the wooden pin that's used as the propeller shaft.

Once the hole is drilled, cut the blank to rough shape *(Step 1 in Fig. 19)*. Then, on a disc sander, gently sand the edges to the rounded shape *(Step 2)*.

Now, rough-sand half of the front side of each blade to a sharp angle *(Step 3)*. Then sand the other half at a gentle angle, and also sand the back side of the blade at a gentle curve to complete the shape *(Step 4)*. Refine this shape so the edges feather to a point *(Step 5)*.

MOUNT PROPELLER. Before mounting the propeller to the fuselage, cut the shaft (a wooden pin) to final length and test the propeller on the end of the shaft to make sure it spins freely. (A little wax helps here.) Then mount the propeller on the shaft, put a small dab of glue in the fuselage hole, and push the shaft in place.

MOUNT WINGS & STRUTS

The last step is to mount the top wing. Cut four wing struts (H) from a $^1/_4$" dowel and glue them into the holes in the top wing *(Fig. 21)*. Then put a dab of glue in each hole in the bottom wing, and slide the struts through these holes. Cut off the excess length and sand the struts flush.

FINISHING. For a finish, I applied three coats of tung oil to all the pieces. And then for a final touch, I placed my wooden "pilot" in the cockpit.

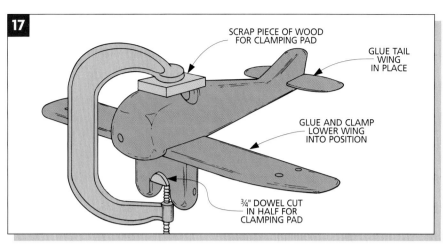

17

SCRAP PIECE OF WOOD FOR CLAMPING PAD

GLUE TAIL WING IN PLACE

GLUE AND CLAMP LOWER WING INTO POSITION

¾" DOWEL CUT IN HALF FOR CLAMPING PAD

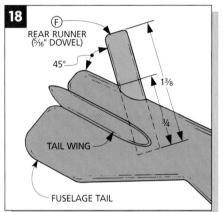

18

(F) REAR RUNNER (⁵/₁₆" DOWEL)

45°

1³/₈

³/₄

TAIL WING

FUSELAGE TAIL

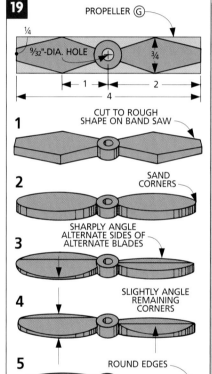

19

PROPELLER (G)

¼

⁹/₃₂"-DIA. HOLE

¾

1

2

4

1 CUT TO ROUGH SHAPE ON BAND SAW

2 SAND CORNERS

3 SHARPLY ANGLE ALTERNATE SIDES OF ALTERNATE BLADES

4 SLIGHTLY ANGLE REMAINING CORNERS

5 ROUND EDGES

TAPER ENDS

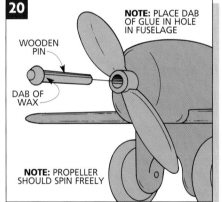

20

NOTE: PLACE DAB OF GLUE IN HOLE IN FUSELAGE

WOODEN PIN

DAB OF WAX

NOTE: PROPELLER SHOULD SPIN FREELY

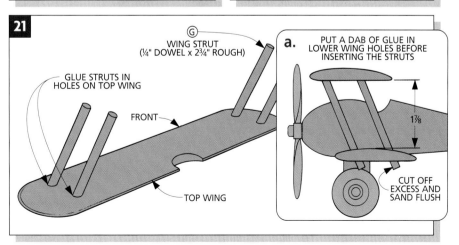

21

(G) WING STRUT (¼" DOWEL x 2¾" ROUGH)

GLUE STRUTS IN HOLES ON TOP WING

FRONT

TOP WING

a. PUT A DAB OF GLUE IN LOWER WING HOLES BEFORE INSERTING THE STRUTS

1⅞

CUT OFF EXCESS AND SAND FLUSH

Doll Cradle

A few pine boards and a weekend are all it takes to make this simple cradle for a little girl's treasured baby. It's perfectly sized, lightweight and includes handles, so even a small child can move it around.

This is truly a one-weekend project. If you glue up the panels on Friday night, you can cut them to size and shape on Saturday, and have the Doll Cradle assembled and a finish applied before Sunday evening.

The reason this project can be built so quickly is that it consists of just five pieces: two sides and a bottom that are joined to the headboard and footboard.

Obviously, the Doll Cradle is designed to be a fairly simple piece. It uses basic joinery techniques. The headboard and footboard are joined to the sides with butt joints reinforced with screws. And a dado in each side accepts the bottom.

WOOD MOVEMENT. Even with a simple project like this, there are still some basics that have to be considered in the design process. The main one is how wood movement affects the joinery. For example, the grain on the headboard, footboard, and sides runs horizontally. Since these pieces will expand and contract in the same direction, they can be glued and screwed together.

However, the bottom panel "floats" between the sides. That's because if it were glued in, it would force the sides apart as it expanded across the grain.

TEMPLATE. There are a lot of curves in the cradle: from the broad curves of the

rockers on the bottom of the headboard and footboard, to the smaller, decorative curves that add "character."

While the headboard and footboard look the same, the headboard is actually wider (taller). But by using a template, it's easy to lay out both pieces so that the curves at the top and bottom match.

MATERIALS. I used ponderosa pine to keep the cradle light enough that even a two-year-old can carry it around the house. For the finish, I chose a tung oil varnish for a couple of reasons. First, it gives the pine an attractive hue, and second, it provides some protection against the inevitable nicks and dings.

EXPLODED VIEW

OVERALL DIMENSIONS:
16W x 19½D x 14H

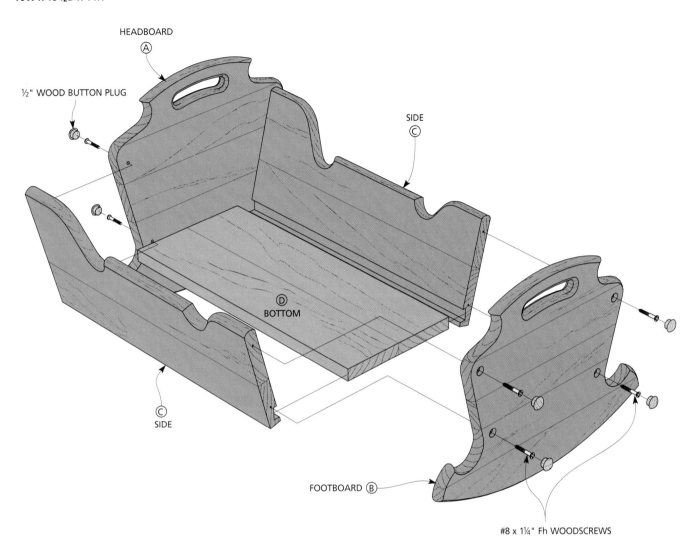

HEADBOARD Ⓐ

½" WOOD BUTTON PLUG

SIDE Ⓒ

BOTTOM Ⓓ

SIDE Ⓒ

FOOTBOARD Ⓑ

#8 x 1¼" Fh WOODSCREWS

CUTTING DIAGRAM

MATERIALS LIST

WOOD

A	Headboard (1)	¾ x 15 rgh. - 17 rgh.
B	Footboard (1)	¾ x 15 rgh. - 17 rgh.
C	Sides (2)	¾ x 8 - 18
D	Bottom (1)	¾ x 7¾ - 18

HARDWARE SUPPLIES
(8) No. 8 x 1¼" Fh woodscrews
(8) ½" button plugs

¾ x 7¼ - 60 (3.1 Bd. Ft.)

A	A	A
A	A	D

B	B	B
B	B	D

¾ x 5½ - 48 (1.8 Bd. Ft.)

C	C

C	C

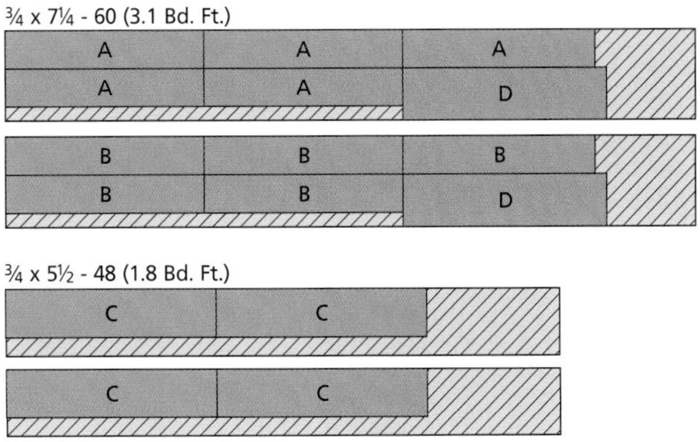

TEMPLATE

To make the template, I started by cutting a piece of ¼"-thick hardboard to a size of 16" by 18½" *(Fig. 1)*.

CENTERLINE. The key to laying out the profile is the vertical centerline *(Fig. 1)*.

Once this line is drawn, the rest of the profile is centered around it.

DIAGONALS AND ARCS. Start by drawing two diagonals *(Fig. 1)*.

After the sides had been drawn, I marked the top arc. To do this, first locate point "A" on the centerline, 3½" from the bottom edge. Then draw a 10½"-radius arc *(Fig. 1)*.

Note: I used a simple beam compass to draw the arcs *(Fig. 4)*.

The bottom arc is drawn the same way: Locate point "B" on the centerline 18" from the bottom edge and draw an 18"-radius arc *(Fig. 1)*.

CURVES. Once these two arcs are drawn, locate the center points for the four curves at the top. These curves define the outside edges of the handle and the shoulders of the cradle *(Fig. 2)*.

After the curves are drawn, you can complete the shoulder by drawing a line connecting the two arcs on each side.

To complete the outline of the template, lay out the two 1" and 2"-radius arcs near the bottom of the template to form the ends on the rocker.

HANDLE. At this point, the template is taking shape. All that remains is to lay out the handle. First, find the centerline by drawing a 9⅛"-radius arc from point "A" *(Fig. 3)*. Then locate and draw the ¾"-dia. end holes on this arc. The last thing to do is to connect the top and bottom edges on the two end holes with arcs.

SCREW HOLES. The template is complete now, except for six holes that are used later to locate the screw holes for attaching the headboard and footboard to the cradle sides *(Fig. 3)*.

After these points are located, drill ⅛" pilot holes in the template so the location of the holes can be transferred onto the headboard and footboard.

CUTTING. There's just one last thing to do before cutting out the profile. That's to bore the radius corners and handle holes with a drill bit or hole saw.

Once the corners are drilled out, use either a band saw or jig saw to cut out the remaining profile. (To cut out the handle, I used a jig saw and hand-filed the edges smooth.) Then sand the edges of the template smooth. I used a sanding block to smooth the outside edges and a drum sander for smoothing each of the radii.

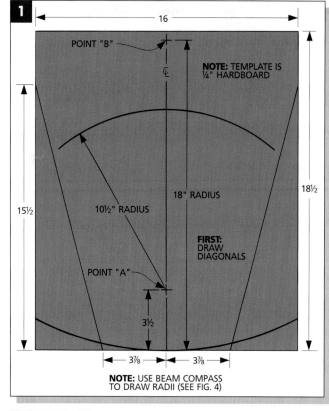

1

16

POINT "B"

NOTE: TEMPLATE IS ¼" HARDBOARD

C⃠L

18" RADIUS

18½

15½

10½" RADIUS

FIRST: DRAW DIAGONALS

POINT "A"

3½

3⅞ — 3⅞

NOTE: USE BEAM COMPASS TO DRAW RADII (SEE FIG. 4)

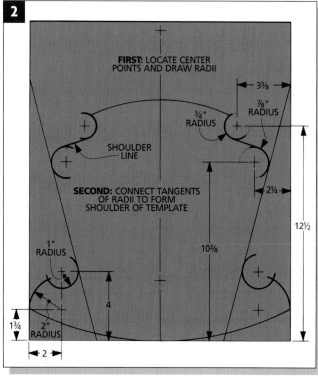

2

FIRST: LOCATE CENTER POINTS AND DRAW RADII

3⅜

⅞" RADIUS

¾" RADIUS

SHOULDER LINE

SECOND: CONNECT TANGENTS OF RADII TO FORM SHOULDER OF TEMPLATE

2¼

12½

1" RADIUS

10⅜

4

1¾

2" RADIUS

2

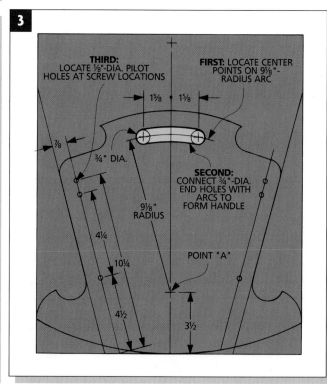

3

THIRD: LOCATE ⅛"-DIA. PILOT HOLES AT SCREW LOCATIONS

FIRST: LOCATE CENTER POINTS ON 9⅛"-RADIUS ARC

1⅝   1⅝

⅞

¾" DIA.

SECOND: CONNECT ¾"-DIA. END HOLES WITH ARCS TO FORM HANDLE

9⅛" RADIUS

4¼

10¼

POINT "A"

4½

3½

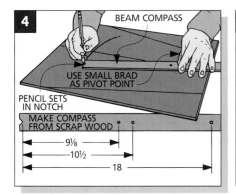

4 USE SMALL BRAD AS PIVOT POINT — BEAM COMPASS — PENCIL SETS IN NOTCH — MAKE COMPASS FROM SCRAP WOOD

9⅛ — 10½ — 18

5 LINE UP CENTERLINES — TEMPLATE — (A)

TRACE OUTLINE OF TEMPLATE ONTO HEADBOARD PANEL

6 SCREW HOLES — 8d FINISH NAIL

BEFORE MOVING TEMPLATE, USE 8d FINISH NAIL TO MARK TOP AND BOTTOM SCREW HOLES

HEADBOARD & FOOTBOARD

With the template complete, the next step is to use it to build the headboard (A) and footboard (B). Start by gluing up two panels of ¾"-thick pine, 15" wide and 17" long. After these panels are planed and sanded smooth, draw a vertical centerline on each one to align the template.

HEADBOARD. To trace the profile on the headboard, position the template so the centerlines on both pieces line up and they are flush at the bottom. Then trace the outline of the template *(Fig. 5)*. With the template still in position, mark the location of the top and bottom screw holes (not the middle one) with an 8-penny finish nail *(Fig. 6)*.

FOOTBOARD. A slightly different procedure is required to trace the profile on the footboard because it's 1½" shorter than the headboard.

Just as before, the first step is to position the template on the footboard so the centerlines line up, and the bottom edges are flush *(Fig. 7)*. Then trace the bottom half of the template, only up to the shoulders near the handle.

With the template still in this position, mark the location of the lower two screw holes with an 8-penny finish nail.

To complete the layout of the footboard, lift up the template and mark a point on the centerline of the panel 12½" from the bottom edge *(Fig. 8)*. Then reposition the template so the top of the handle is flush with this mark, and the centerlines on both pieces are aligned.

Now hold the template steady and trace the top half (including the handle) down to where it intersects the lower portion of the profile *(Fig. 8)*.

You'll notice that, because the template has been shifted down, the radius at the shoulders doesn't line up properly where the upper and lower profiles meet.

To produce a smooth corner between the two profiles, use a compass to draw a

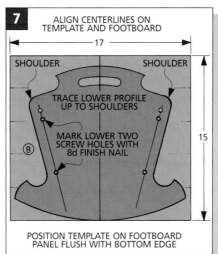

7 ALIGN CENTERLINES ON TEMPLATE AND FOOTBOARD — 17 — SHOULDER — SHOULDER — TRACE LOWER PROFILE UP TO SHOULDERS — MARK LOWER TWO SCREW HOLES WITH 8d FINISH NAIL — (B) — 15

POSITION TEMPLATE ON FOOTBOARD PANEL FLUSH WITH BOTTOM EDGE

8 REPOSITION TOP OF TEMPLATE FLUSH WITH LINE — KEEP TEMPLATE ALIGNED WITH CENTERLINE — SHOULDER — SHOULDER — TRACE HANDLE, AND UPPER PROFILE TO SHOULDERS — 12½ — (B)

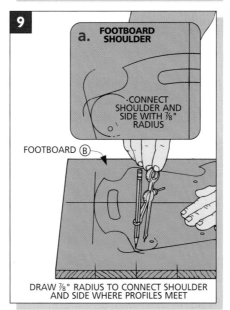

9 **a. FOOTBOARD SHOULDER** — CONNECT SHOULDER AND SIDE WITH ⅞" RADIUS — FOOTBOARD (B)

DRAW ⅞" RADIUS TO CONNECT SHOULDER AND SIDE WHERE PROFILES MEET

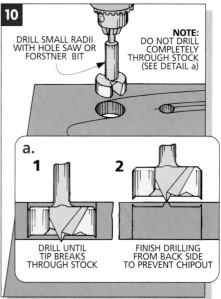

10 DRILL SMALL RADII WITH HOLE SAW OR FORSTNER BIT — **NOTE:** DO NOT DRILL COMPLETELY THROUGH STOCK (SEE DETAIL a)

a. 1 DRILL UNTIL TIP BREAKS THROUGH STOCK — **2** FINISH DRILLING FROM BACK SIDE TO PREVENT CHIPOUT

new ⅞" radius connecting the shoulder line and the side of the footboard *(Fig. 9)*.

DRILL CORNERS. After the profiles for the headboard and footboard have been laid out, drill all the radius corners, just as you did on the template *(Fig. 10)*.

Note: To prevent chipout on the back side of the workpiece, stop drilling as soon as the centerpoint of the bit breaks

through the back *(Step 1 in Fig. 10a)*. Then flip the workpiece over, and finish drilling from the back side *(Step 2)*.

The remaining profile is cut out on a band saw (or with a jig saw). I again used a sanding block and a drum sander to sand the edges smooth. Finally, use a jig saw to cut out the handle, and then smooth the edges with a file.

Once the headboard and footboard are completed, the next step is to cut the cradle sides and the bottom. Glue up enough $3/4$"-thick pine for the sides (C) and the bottom (D) *(Figs. 11 and 13)*. Then plane or sand the panels smooth and trim the sides to size *(Fig. 11)*.

ANGLED GROOVE. The sides of the cradle are joined to the bottom with a groove angled at 15°. This angle cants the cradle sides out so they match the sides of the headboard and footboard.

To cut the groove, I used a dado blade on the table saw *(Fig. 12)*. I made several trial cuts, adjusting the number of chippers and shims in the dado set until the width of the groove matched the thickness of the bottom. Then I set the blade to cut $3/16$" deep, as measured to the low side of the blade *(Fig. 12)*.

When the blade is set, adjust the fence to cut a groove $1/4$" from the bottom edge of the cradle sides.

After the grooves are cut, lay out the profile on the cradle sides *(Fig. 11)*. Then cut out the profile, drilling the radius corners first, and sanding the profile smooth with a drum sander.

DRILL PILOT HOLES. To join the sides to the headboard and footboard, first drill counterbores and shank holes in the headboard and footboard for No. 8 woodscrews and $1/2$" button plugs *(Fig. 14)*.

To drill the pilot holes on the ends of the cradle sides, draw a line centered on the ends and mark the location of the bottom holes *(Fig. 11)*. Measure up to the top holes using exactly the same spacing as the pilot holes on the headboard and footboard. Finally, drill $3/32$" pilot holes $3/4$" deep in the ends of the cradle sides.

CUT BOTTOM. When the pilot holes are drilled, dry-assemble the sides to the headboard and footboard to determine the final width of the bottom. With these pieces screwed together, trace the outline of the angled grooves on the headboard and footboard. Then disassemble the pieces and measure between the grooves to determine the final width of the bottom. Allow about $1/8$" for expansion *(Fig. 13)*.

ROUNDING EDGES. The last step is to round over all the edges of the headboard and footboard, and the top edges on the sides. I used a $1/2$" roundover bit set to a depth of $5/16$" to produce a softened bullnose profile *(Fig. 15)*.

Note: As I was routing the headboard, the first couple of times I came to one of

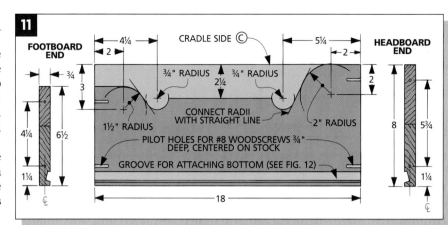

11

FOOTBOARD END · CRADLE SIDE (C) · HEADBOARD END · $4\frac{1}{4}$ · 2 · $3/4$" RADIUS · $3/4$" RADIUS · $5\frac{1}{4}$ · 2 · $3/4$ · 3 · $2\frac{1}{4}$ · 2 · $4\frac{1}{4}$ · $6\frac{1}{2}$ · CONNECT RADII WITH STRAIGHT LINE · $1\frac{1}{2}$" RADIUS · 2" RADIUS · 8 · $5\frac{3}{4}$ · $1\frac{1}{4}$ · PILOT HOLES FOR #8 WOODSCREWS $3/4$" DEEP, CENTERED ON STOCK · GROOVE FOR ATTACHING BOTTOM (SEE FIG. 12) · $1\frac{1}{4}$ · 18

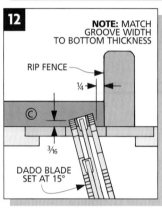

12

NOTE: MATCH GROOVE WIDTH TO BOTTOM THICKNESS · RIP FENCE · $1/4$ · (C) · $3/16$ · DADO BLADE SET AT 15°

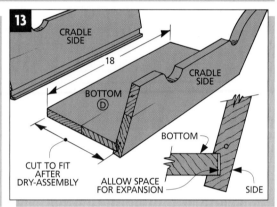

13

CRADLE SIDE · 18 · CRADLE SIDE · BOTTOM (D) · BOTTOM · CUT TO FIT AFTER DRY-ASSEMBLY · ALLOW SPACE FOR EXPANSION · SIDE

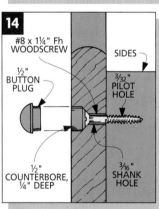

14

#8 x $1\frac{1}{4}$" Fh WOODSCREW · SIDES · $1/2$" BUTTON PLUG · $3/32$" PILOT HOLE · $1/2$" COUNTERBORE, $1/4$" DEEP · $3/16$" SHANK HOLE

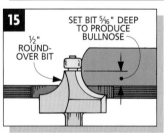

15

SET BIT $5/16$" DEEP TO PRODUCE BULLNOSE · $1/2$" ROUND-OVER BIT

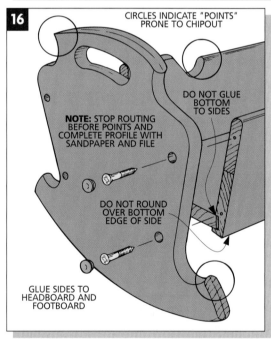

16

CIRCLES INDICATE "POINTS" PRONE TO CHIPOUT · DO NOT GLUE BOTTOM TO SIDES · NOTE: STOP ROUTING BEFORE POINTS AND COMPLETE PROFILE WITH SANDPAPER AND FILE · DO NOT ROUND OVER BOTTOM EDGE OF SIDE · GLUE SIDES TO HEADBOARD AND FOOTBOARD

the "points" on the profile where the grain direction made an abrupt change, the wood tended to chip out *(Fig. 16)*. To prevent this, I stopped just short of the remaining points, and rounded over this area by hand with a file and sandpaper.

ASSEMBLY. Now the cradle is ready to assemble. First, insert the bottom in the sides, but don't glue it in place. (It needs to be able to expand and contract.) Then apply glue to the ends of the sides and screw the headboard and footboard in place. (The sides, footboard, and headboard will all expand and contract together in the same direction.)

Lastly, glue button plugs into the screw holes *(Fig. 14)*. I finished the cradle with three coats of tung oil varnish. ∎

Child's Rocker

You won't need a lathe to build this chair — the round stock used for the frame is all regular dowels.
A standard router bit and a simple drill press jig make it easy to cut the round mortises and tenons.

Although this rocker is made with lots of round stock, you don't have to spend time at the lathe trying to turn sets of identical parts.

Instead, I used common dowels for the frame. So cutting the stock to size meant just cutting the dowels to length.

Using dowels also makes it easy to create strong joints. The rocker is held together with mortise and tenon joints. But they're not cut like typical mortises and tenons. The round tenons are shaped first on the router table. And the mortises are drilled on the drill press with the help of a shop-made jig.

BUILDING SEQUENCE. There's another thing that simplifies this rocker — the building sequence.

Usually, I work on one sub-assembly, making and adding each part until the sub-assembly is complete. And then I work on the next sub-assembly.

But this chair is different. Instead of building individual pieces for just one section of the frame, I found it was faster to work on all the dowels at once — cutting, routing, drilling, and assembling.

When I was done working on the dowels, the frame of the chair was complete. The only remaing pieces were the seat, arms, and rockers.

MATCHING TABLE. A child's room isn't complete without a table. So I designed one using the same concepts used to build the chair. The Designer's Notebook on page 26 shows how to build it.

EXPLODED VIEW

OVERALL DIMENSIONS:
17W x 22D x 25½H

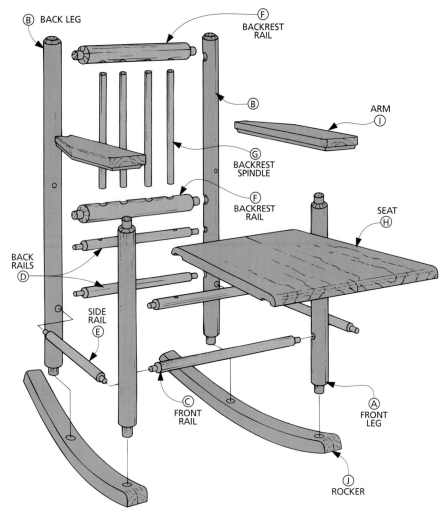

Labels in exploded view:
- (B) BACK LEG
- (F) BACKREST RAIL
- (B)
- (ARM) (I)
- (G) BACKREST SPINDLE
- (F) BACKREST RAIL
- (SEAT) (H)
- BACK RAILS (D)
- SIDE RAIL (E)
- (C) FRONT RAIL
- (A) FRONT LEG
- (J) ROCKER

When working with dowels, you have to select them carefully. The dowels must be straight (especially for the back legs). And they must be truly round and consistent in diameter. If not, you'll have a hard time fitting tenons into their matching mortises.

DOWEL GAUGE. To avoid these problems, I use a gauge to help select the dowels. The gauge is simply a block with holes drilled in it to match the size of the dowels needed. Then I take this block with me when buying dowels.

Note: I used maple dowels for the Child's Rocker. See Sources on page 126.

CUT DOWELS. Once you have all the dowels selected, you can start on the frame of the rocker. The first step is easy.

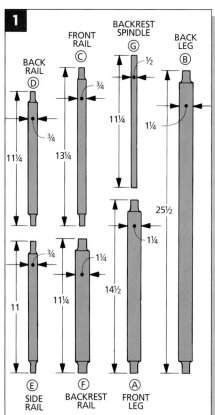

CUTTING DIAGRAM

¾ x 7¼ - 48 (2.5 Bd. Ft.)

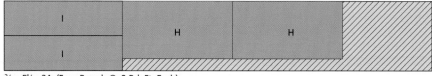

¾ x 5¼ - 24 (Four Boards @ .9 Bd. Ft. Each)

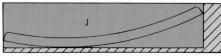

ALSO NEED:
2 - 1¼"-DIA. x 48" MAPLE DOWELS
1 - 1¼"-DIA. x 36" MAPLE DOWEL
1 - ¾"-DIA. x 48" MAPLE DOWEL
1 - ¾"-DIA. x 36" MAPLE DOWEL
1 - ½"-DIA. x 48" MAPLE DOWEL

MATERIALS LIST

WOOD

A	Front Legs (2)	1¼ dowel x 14½
B	Back Legs (2)	1¼ dowel x 25½
C	Front Rails (2)	¾ dowel x 13¼
D	Back Rails (2)	¾ dowel x 11¼
E	Side Rails (2)	¾ dowel x 11
F	Backrest Rails (2)	1¼ dowel x 11¼
G	Backrest Spindles (4)	½ dowel x 11¼
H	Seat (1)	¾ x 11½ - 12
I	Arms (2)	¾ x 3½ - 13 rgh.
J	Rockers (2)	1½ x 4¾ - 22

HARDWARE SUPPLIES

(4) No. 8 x 1" Fh woodscrews
(6) No. 8 x 1¼" Fh woodscrews
(2) ⅜"-dia. dowel plugs

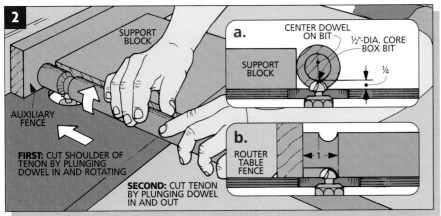

FIRST: CUT SHOULDER OF TENON BY PLUNGING DOWEL IN AND ROTATING

a. CENTER DOWEL ON BIT / ½"-DIA. CORE BOX BIT / SUPPORT BLOCK / ¼

b. ROUTER TABLE FENCE / 1

SECOND: CUT TENON BY PLUNGING DOWEL IN AND OUT

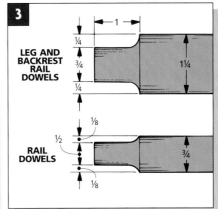

LEG AND BACKREST RAIL DOWELS — 1 / ¼ / ¾ / ¼ / 1¼

RAIL DOWELS — ⅛ / ½ / ⅛ / ¾

Just cut all the dowels for parts A through G to length *(Fig. 1)*.

Safety Note: Dowels tend to twist or roll when being cut. Be sure to clamp or hold your dowels securely while cutting.

TENONS

After the dowels are cut to length, tenons can be routed on the ends of all the dowels, except the backrest spindles (G). (Set them aside for now.) All these pieces start with the same *length* tenons on both ends *(Fig. 3)*. But the 1¼"-dia. dowels (A, B, F) have larger *diameter* tenons than the ¾"-dia. dowels (C, D, E).

CORE BOX BIT. I routed the tenons with a special setup on the router table and a ½"-dia. core box bit *(Fig. 2)*.

To create the tenons on the legs (A, B) and backrest rails (F), set the bit ¼" high *(Figs. 2a and 3)*. Reset the bit to ⅛" above the table to cut the ½"-dia. tenons on the front, back and side rails (C, D, E).

SET FENCE. Next, clamp an auxiliary fence to the router table fence to cover the opening for the bit *(Fig. 2)*. Then position the auxiliary fence 1" from the outside edge of the bit *(Fig. 2b)*.

SUPPORT BLOCK. To keep the dowel centered over the bit, clamp a support block to the router table *(Fig. 2a)*.

Note: Before routing any tenons, first test the setup using a scrap piece of dowel. Adjust the height of the router bit until each tenon fits perfectly in a ¾" (or ½") hole drilled in a piece of scrap wood.

ROUT TENONS. To rout the tenons, hold the dowel against the support block and slowly push the end into the spinning router bit. Keep pushing until the dowel bottoms out against the auxiliary fence *(Fig. 2)*. Now, form the shoulder of the tenon by rotating the dowel clockwise against the auxiliary fence. Then back the dowel out.

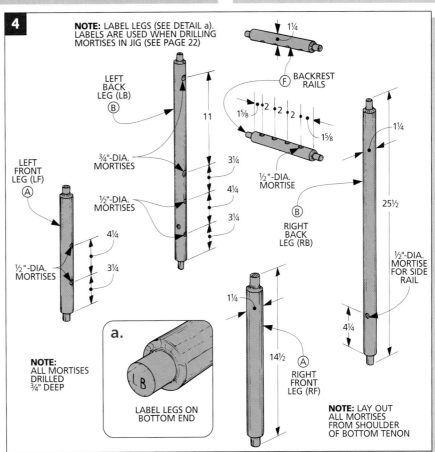

NOTE: LABEL LEGS (SEE DETAIL a). LABELS ARE USED WHEN DRILLING MORTISES IN JIG (SEE PAGE 22)

LEFT BACK LEG (LB) (B)

LEFT FRONT LEG (LF) (A)

BACKREST RAILS (F)

RIGHT BACK LEG (RB) (B)

RIGHT FRONT LEG (RF) (A)

¾"-DIA. MORTISES / ½"-DIA. MORTISES / ½"-DIA. MORTISES

11 / 3¼ / 4¼ / 3¼ / 4¼ / 3¼

1¼ / 1⅝ / 2 / 2 / 2 / 1⅝ / ½"-DIA. MORTISE

25½ / 1¼ / ½"-DIA. MORTISE FOR SIDE RAIL / 4¼

1¼ / 14½

NOTE: ALL MORTISES DRILLED ¾" DEEP

a. LABEL LEGS ON BOTTOM END

NOTE: LAY OUT ALL MORTISES FROM SHOULDER OF BOTTOM TENON

Next, remove the remaining waste around the tenon in small bites. To do this, push the dowel in against the auxiliary fence and pull it straight out *(Fig. 3)*. Rotate the dowel slightly and repeat this procedure until each tenon is complete.

MORTISES

After the tenons are routed, the mortises can be cut to fit the tenons. Since the tenons are round, these mortises are simply drilled out using the drill press.

It sounds easy enough, and in fact, most of the mortises in the legs are drilled

in line with each other. But there's one on each leg that's not — the mortise for the side rail. This hole has to be positioned at an odd angle in relation to the others. And there's a good reason for this.

Like many chairs, the sides on this one aren't parallel. The seat is wider at the front than at the back. (It makes the rocker easier to get in and out of.) This means the holes in the legs aren't positioned 90° to each other.

If this sounds difficult, don't worry. I designed a jig to help position the dowels properly while drilling the mortises. (See the Shop Jig on the next page.)

This dowel mortising jig has only two parts — a base and an end cap.

BASE. The base (a 2x4 ripped 3" wide) has a V-shaped trough to support the dowel and center the hole *(Fig. 1)*. To cut the trough, make two passes, flipping the piece between passes *(Fig. 1a)*.

END CAP. The ³⁄₄"-thick end cap serves as a guide for locating the holes. First,

draw a centerline on it from top to bottom *(Fig. 2)*. Next, lay out and label two more lines *(Fig. 2a)*. These lines will be used to position the legs so the holes will be drilled at the correct angle to each other.

To hold the leg tenon, drill a ³⁄₄"-dia. hole in the end cap where all three lines intersect *(Fig. 2)*. Next, cut a kerf down the centerline to the hole with a hand

saw *(Fig. 3)*. (By pinching the kerf with a clamp, the tenon is locked securely.)

The end cap is held to the base by a couple of 1" screws *(Fig. 3)*. To position the cap on the base, insert a leg tenon in the end cap and set the leg on the base. Now, screw the end cap in place.

Note: The bottom edges of the cap and the base won't be flush.

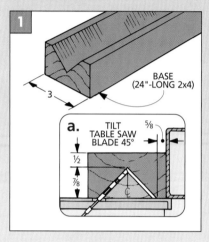

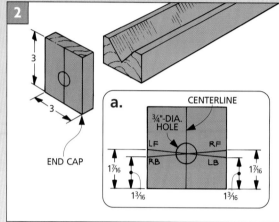

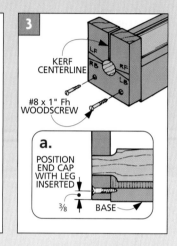

DRILLING THE MORTISES

Now that the mortising jig is built, you can begin drilling. But it helps to get the pieces organized first.

MARK LEGS. To keep everything straight, orient the four legs as they will be when the chair is complete (refer to *Fig. 4* on page 21). Then label the bottom end of each leg and mark the locations of the mortises. Measure all the holes from the shoulder of the bottom tenon.

POSITION THE JIG. Next, position the jig on the drill press table. To do this, chuck a small-diameter bit into the drill press and lower the bit into the kerf on the end cap. Then clamp a fence to the table and against the jig *(Fig. 5)*.

DRILL MORTISES. I started drilling the mortises in the back legs (B). First, place

one of the back legs in the jig. Then clamp the end cap to lock the tenon in position *(Fig. 5)*. Now you're set to drill the mortises in a line at the marked positions.

Note: On each back leg there are two sizes of holes to be drilled. Two ³⁄₄"-dia. holes for the backrest rails. And two ¹⁄₂"-dia. holes for the back rails.

MARK TENON. Before removing the dowel from the jig, draw on the tenon an arrow that points up to the kerf *(Fig. 6)*. This will serve as a reference line when positioning the hole for the side rail.

REPOSITION DOWEL. To drill the ¹⁄₂"-dia. hole for the side rail, loosen the clamp and rotate the leg. The arrow should point to the line labeled the same as the leg you're working on *(Fig. 7)*.

Here's where the lines and labels on the end cap begin to make sense. They

show just how far (and in which direction) to rotate each leg. This way, the mortise for the side rail will be drilled at the proper angle in relation to the first set of holes you drilled in each leg.

DRILL MORTISE FOR SIDE. Once the leg is positioned correctly, retighten the clamp. You should already have a layout line on the leg, so just drill the mortise for the side rail to complete the leg *(Fig. 6)*.

With one leg completed, repeat the procedure with the remaining legs.

Note: The front legs (A) only have ¹⁄₂"-dia. mortises drilled in them.

BACKREST MORTISES. Finally, the mortising jig can be used again to hold the backrest rails (F) while the mortises are drilled in them. The backrest rails each have four ¹⁄₂"-dia. mortises to accept the backrest spindles (G).

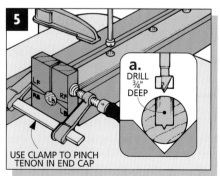

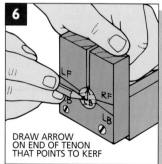

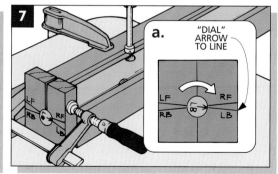

ASSEMBLY

Before assembling the frame, there are a few final steps to take care of.

TRIM TENONS. First, the tenons on both the front and back legs need to be trimmed $3/4$" long *(Fig. 8)*. (They started out 1" long to fit in the mortising jig.)

The tenons on the tops of the back legs aren't really needed, but I thought a decorative shoulder would look nice. So I trimmed these tenons to $1/4$" *(Fig. 8)*.

SHANK HOLES. Also, you'll need to screw the seat down later. So drill shank holes in one front and back rail *(Fig. 9a)*.

FRAME ASSEMBLY

Now you're ready to glue up the frame. To do this, I glued the dowels into sub-assemblies. Then I glued these units together to complete the frame.

BACKREST. Begin with the backrest, sandwiching the backrest spindles (G) between the backrest rails (F) *(Fig. 9)*.

BACK LEGS. Next, glue the backrest assembly and the back rails (D) between the back legs (B) *(Fig. 9)*. To attach the seat later, the back rail with the holes must be on top, with the holes facing up.

FRONT LEGS. Now, glue and clamp the front rails (C) and front legs (A) together *(Fig. 10)*. Again, the rail with the holes must be on top with the holes facing up.

FRAME ASSEMBLY. Once the glue dries, glue the side rails (E) between the assemblies to complete the frames *(Fig. 10)*.

Note: To position the legs correctly, I made a plywood base with holes drilled in it to hold the leg tenons *(Fig. 10)*.

SEAT

While the frame dries, begin work on the seat. First, glue up $3/4$"-thick hard maple for the oversize seat blank *(Fig. 11)*. Then cut the seat (H) to finished length.

GROOVES FOR SEAT. Two $3/4$"-dia. grooves routed across the bottom of the seat blank help position it on the rails. Instead of buying a larger core box bit, I used the same $1/2$" core box bit used to rout the tenons *(Fig. 12)*. To rout a $3/4$"-wide groove, I just made several passes.

TAPER SEAT. With the grooves routed, measure between the legs to find the width of the seat. (Allow $1/16$" between the seat and each leg.) Since the front of the chair is wider than the back, the sides of the seat will be tapered *(Fig. 11)*.

ROUND OVER EDGES. After cutting the seat to width, flip it over and rout a $1/2$" roundover on each end *(Fig. 13a)*. Then soften all the edges of the seat, using a $1/8$" roundover bit *(Fig. 13)*.

ATTACH SEAT. Now you're ready to put the seat in place and mark the location of the pilot holes on the bottom. (You can use a brad point bit to mark them.)

Once the pilot holes have been drilled, go ahead and screw the seat to the rails *(Figs. 13 and 13a)*. (I used a stubby screwdriver to reach between the rails.)

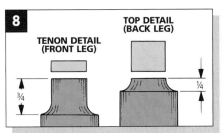

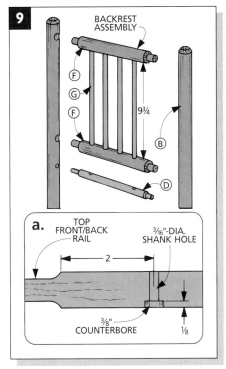

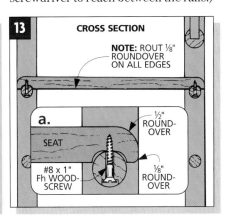

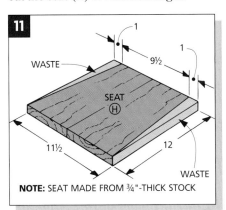

After the seat has been screwed to the frame of the rocker, the arm rests are the next pieces to be added.

LAY OUT SHAPE. Each arm rest starts out as an oversize blank of ³⁄₄"-thick maple *(Fig. 14)*. The first step is to lay out the shape of the arm on the blank.

DRILL LEG RELIEF. The arm is screwed through the back leg. To get the arm to wrap around the leg with a tight fit, an arc must be cut out of the blank.

The best way to do this is to drill a 1¹⁄₄"-dia. hole to match the diameter of the back legs *(Figs. 14 and 15)*.

Note: If you don't have a drill bit this size, you could use a jig saw with a very fine blade to cut the arc. Then sand the arc smooth with a drum sander.

Now you can cut the arms (I) to finished size and shape *(Fig. 14)*. Then, remove the sharp edges by sanding a ³⁄₈" radius on the corners. (Don't round the corners formed by the arc.)

DRILL MORTISE. The arm is glued on top of the tenon on the front leg. To do this, you'll have to drill a ³⁄₄"-dia. mortise, ¹⁄₂" deep. Be sure to drill the mortise on the bottom side of the arm 1" from the inside edge *(Fig. 14)*.

SHAPE EDGES. There are just a couple more steps to take care of before the

arms can be attached. Since this rocker is for children, I wanted to be sure to remove all the sharp edges.

So I began by routing the bottom edges of the arms using a ¹⁄₄"-radius cove bit *(Fig. 16a)*. (Don't rout the arcs where the arms are connected to the back leg.)

Note: If you don't have a cove bit, a ¹⁄₂"-dia. core box bit will also work. You'll have to bury the bit in the router table fence. To complete the cove, you'll need to file and sand the corners by hand.

Next, I routed a ¹⁄₈" roundover along the top edge of each arm *(Fig. 16b)*.

(Again, don't rout the arcs where the arms are connected to the back leg.)

ATTACH ARM. To attach each arm, position an arm on the front leg. Then cut a spacer to fit between the arm and seat *(Fig. 17)*. This spacer will hold the arm at the proper position on the back leg. This way, you can mark the position of the counterbored pilot hole that is drilled through the back legs *(Fig. 17a)*.

After drilling the pilot holes, glue the arm to the front leg. Then screw and glue the arm to the back leg *(Fig. 18)*. Use a ³⁄₈"-dia. plug to fill the hole in the back leg.

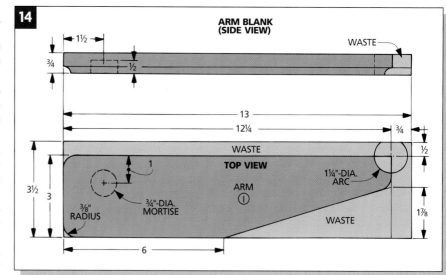

14 ARM BLANK (SIDE VIEW)

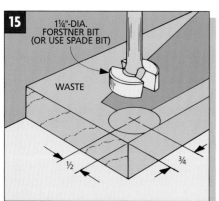

15

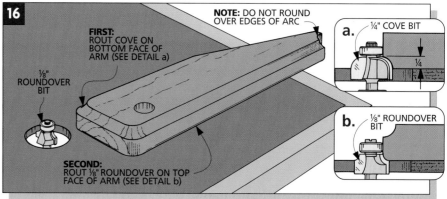

16

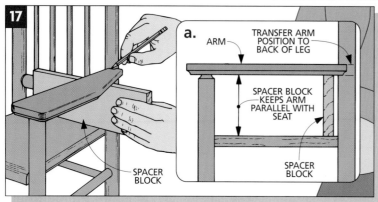

17

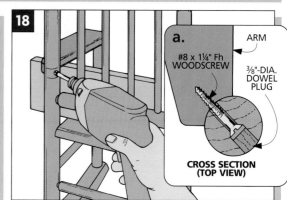

18

The rockers might look like they've been steam-bent to shape. But they're really cut from oversize blanks.

LAMINATE BLANKS. To make the blanks for each rocker (J), just glue together two ³/₄"-thick pieces of maple *(Fig. 19).* Then lay out the shape of the rocker on the face of each blank.

MAKE COMPASS. I used a shop-built beam compass to lay out the shape of the rockers. This compass is made from a piece of scrap that's a few inches longer than the largest radius (33"). Drill a hole at one end to hold a nail that will act as a pivot point. Then drill two more holes near the other end — one 32" from the pivot point and the other 33".

Before drawing the arcs, the compass needs to be elevated to the same height as the rocker blank *(Fig. 20).* Just fasten two boards together with double-sided tape to make a base for the compass.

To get the arcs in the correct position on the rocker blanks, the beam compass must be nailed to the base exactly 6³/₄" from the end *(Fig. 20).*

LAY OUT ROCKER ARCS. Now clamp the base of the compass to your workbench so it's flush with the edge *(Fig. 20).* Do the same with the rocker blank. (The hole for the 33" radius should just touch the bottom edge of the rocker blank 6³/₄" in from the end.) Now you're ready to draw both arcs on each blank.

DRILL MORTISES. Before cutting out the rockers, I drilled the mortises for the legs. But I couldn't drill through 4" of

wood to make a ³/₄"-deep mortise. So I cut a notch out of the rocker blank *(Fig. 21).*

To drill the mortises, stand the blank on the drill press and set the depth of the hole 1" above the bottom of the blank *(Fig. 21a).* Then drill the mortises to match the diameter of the leg tenons.

CUT OUT ROCKERS. Next, I cut out the rockers (J) on my band saw, cutting a little wide of the layout lines. Then I mounted a drum sander in my drill press and sanded to the lines. (Check to make

sure both rockers are the same shape.) To complete the rockers, I softened all the edges with a ¹/₈" roundover bit *(Fig. 22).*

ATTACH ROCKERS. Drill shank holes in from the top through the mortises *(Fig. 19).* Next, counterbore the holes from the bottom. Then drill pilot holes in the ends of the legs. Finally, glue and screw the rockers to the legs *(Fig. 23).*

FINISH. All that's left is to apply a finish. You might consider paint or a bright, colored stain for a fun look. ∎

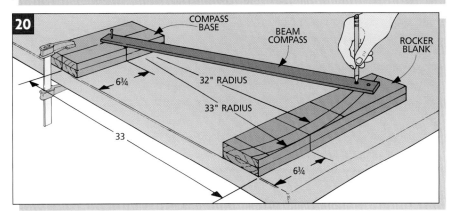

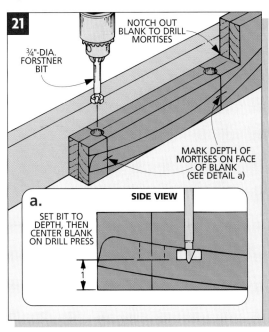

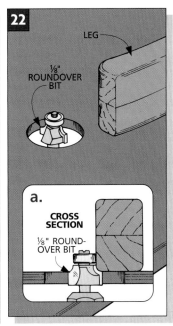

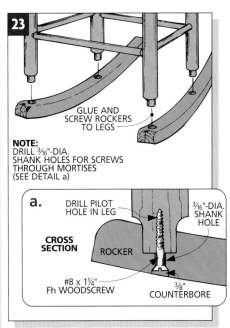

DESIGNER'S NOTEBOOK

A table built to be "kid high" will give little ones a place of their own to color, create, and serve tea. The same techniques used to build the rocker are used to build this matching table.

CONSTRUCTION NOTES:

■ Start by cutting the legs (K) to length from 2"-dia. dowels *(Fig. 1)*.

■ Before drilling holes in the legs to accept the tenons on the rails, you'll need to modify the dowel mortising jig used on the rocker. A new end cap is needed with a larger hole to accept the legs *(Fig. 1)*. On this end cap, cut a kerf down the centerline as before. Then draw a line 90° to the kerf centered on the diameter of the hole.

■ Now lay out the locations of the mortises on the legs and drill $3/4$"-dia. holes, $3/4$" deep on the marks *(Figs. 1 and 1b)*.

■ Finally, rout a $1/8$" roundover around the bottom of each leg.

■ The next pieces to work on are the skirt plates (L). Rip the plates to finished width from $3/4$"-thick stock and crosscut them to rough length *(Fig. 2)*.

■ Before mitering the skirt plates to finished length, rout a $1/4$" cove along the bottom outside edge of each piece.

■ Now miter the skirt plates to a finished length of $24 1/2$" *(Fig. 2)*.

■ The next step is to lay out the positions of the holes for the skirt spindles. Start at the centerline of each skirt plate and work out to the ends *(Fig. 2)*.

■ Once the holes are laid out, you can drill $1/2$"-dia. holes, $1/2$" deep at the marks.

■ At this point, it's a good idea to also lay out and drill countersunk shank holes for attaching the legs and the tabletop later *(Figs. 2 and 2a)*. Note that the holes are countersunk on opposite faces.

■ The next pieces to work on are the skirt rails (M). These pieces form the bottom of the skirt assemblies. Cut them to length from $1 1/4$"-dia. dowels *(Fig. 3)*.

■ Just as with the chair, tenons are routed on each end of the rails. The setup will be similar, using a $1/2$"-dia. core box bit to make rounded shoulders. But here, the tenons are only $7/8$" long *(Fig. 3a)*.

■ The holes in the rails need to align with those on the skirt plate. So again, I started from the center of each rail and worked toward the ends *(Fig. 3)*.

■ Before drilling the holes in the skirt rails, you'll need to reattach the original end cap to the mortising jig (the one with

CHILD'S TABLE

MATERIALS LIST

NEW PARTS

K	Legs (4)	2 dowel x 20
L	Skirt Plates (4)	$3/4$ x $2 1/4$ - $24 1/2$
M	Skirt Rails (4)	$1 1/4$ dowel x 21
N	Skirt Spindles (36)	$1/2$ dowel x 4
O	Top Panel (1)	$3/4$ ply - $23 1/2$ x $23 1/2$
P	Top Frame (4)	$3/4$ x 1 - $25 1/2$

HARDWARE SUPPLIES

(8) No. 8 x $1 1/4$" Fh woodscrews
(8) No. 8 x 2" Fh woodscrews

1

DRILL $3/4$"-DIA. HOLES, $3/4$" DEEP

ROUT $1/8$" ROUNDOVER ON LEG BOTTOM

LEG (K)

20

$3 3/8$

NOTE: MAKE NEW END CAP FOR JIG TO ACCCEPT 2"-DIA. LEGS

a. END VIEW

DRILL FIRST MORTISE, THEN ROTATE LEG 90°

LEG

2

b.

SECTION VIEW

$3/4$" FORSTNER BIT

$3/4$

$3/4$

$3/4$

the $\frac{7}{8}$"-dia. hole). Then, with a rail clamped in the jig, drill $\frac{3}{4}$"-deep holes.

■ The last pieces to make for the skirt assemblies are the skirt spindles (N). These are just 4" lengths of $\frac{1}{2}$"-dia. dowel *(Fig. 3)*. Since there are so many of these (36), I attached an auxiliary fence to the miter gauge of my table saw. Then I clamped on a stop block to make it easier to cut them all to the same length quickly.

■ After all the spindles were cut to length, I sanded a slight chamfer on each end of each one, so they would easily slip into the holes in the rails and skirts.

■ With the spindles ready to go, I dry-assembled the base to check the fit. (Band clamps will help hold everything together.) While the base is temporarily assembled, drill pilot holes into each leg using the skirt plate shank holes as a guide *(Fig. 4a)*. These holes will pass through the tenons of the skirt rails. That way the screws help lock the base assembly together.

■ When you're ready to glue up the base of the table, there are a lot of pieces to keep straight. So I followed this procedure: First, I glued up the four skirt assemblies, placing the spindles in the mortises between the skirt rails and skirt plates. Then I glued a leg to each end of two skirts to form leg assemblies *(Fig. 4)*.

■ Next, I joined the two leg assemblies by gluing the remaining skirt assemblies between them. After checking for square, drive the screws into each leg *(Fig. 4)*.

■ While the glue on the base dries, you can turn your attention to the tabletop. This is just a panel of $\frac{3}{4}$" plywood edged with hardwood. Start by cutting the top panel (O) to size *(Fig. 5)*.

■ The top panel is trimmed with four top frame pieces (P). These pieces are cut from $\frac{3}{4}$"-thick stock to finished width and rough length *(Fig. 5)*.

■ Next, carefully miter the frame pieces to fit around the panel.

■ Once the frame has been glued in place around the top panel, you can plane and sand it flush with the top and bottom faces of the top panel.

■ The last thing to do is to ease the top and bottom edges of the frame by routing $\frac{1}{8}$" roundovers *(Fig. 5)*.

■ To attach the top, turn it upside down. Then center the base on it and drill pilot holes into the top panel, using the shank holes in the skirt plate as a guide. Use a depth stop on the drill bit so you don't drill through the top of the table.

■ Now glue and screw the tabletop to the base and apply a finish.

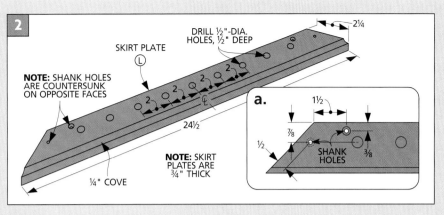

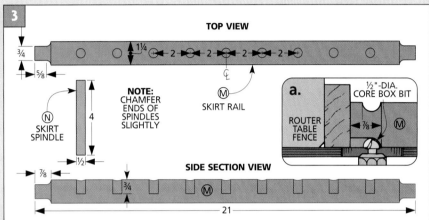

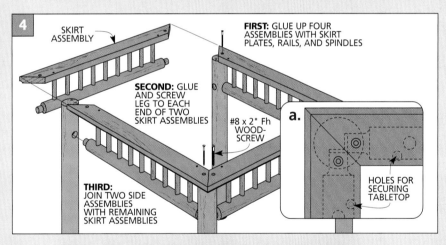

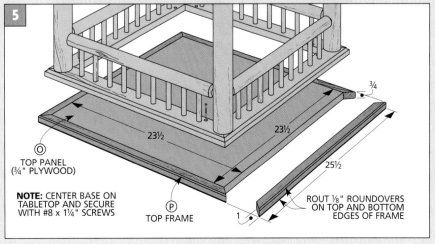

Toy Truck Bank

It may not be an armored truck, but your money will still be safe and secure in this bank. Only those who know how to release a secret mechanism will be able to get this truck to give up its cargo.

This old-time delivery truck is a dual-purpose gift. First, it's a toy truck with rolling wheels, solid enough to take a few knocks against walls or table legs. And the cargo box actually holds cargo — in this case, pocket change. Which is a clue to the truck's second purpose: it serves as a bank.

MAKING WITHDRAWALS. The biggest problem with toy banks is how to get your money out when you want it. The usual solution is to drill a hole in the bottom of the bank and use a cork stop. Pull out the stop and out comes your money. But that's too easy. Anybody could get to your hard-earned cash.

I thought the challenge of building a toy bank would be to figure out a secret, hidden release to get the money out. And I came up with a simple shop-built mechanism that works beautifully.

WINDOWS. Besides the secret release, one thing you may wonder about is how the windows in the cab were made. It doesn't involve any tricky carving or chiseling. Instead, a dado is cut across each of two blocks. Then, when the blocks are glued together to form the cab, these dadoes form the side windows. And before the pieces are glued up, the windshield is created by simply drilling starter holes and sawing out the waste.

CUSTOMIZING. Although there's nothing sporty about this truck, there are still a few ways to add some "custom touches" to dress it up. For example, all it takes to add some snappy "pinstripes" to the cargo box is to cut a couple of saw kerfs in each of the side panels.

An even more special way to personalize the truck is to add the name of the person you're building it for (as if they had their own trucking company). Or add a company or team logo. This is easy to do with a photocopy of the image and a woodburning pen or clothes iron. The details about this are in the Designer's Notebook on page 35.

EXPLODED VIEW

OVERALL DIMENSIONS:
4W x 11⅛D x 6¼H

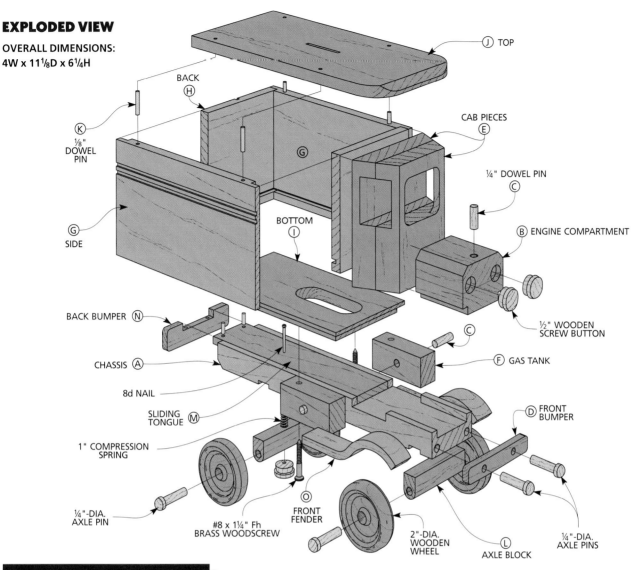

- J — TOP
- BACK — H
- K — ⅛" DOWEL PIN
- CAB PIECES — E
- ¼" DOWEL PIN — C
- G — SIDE
- B — ENGINE COMPARTMENT
- BOTTOM — I
- ½" WOODEN SCREW BUTTON
- BACK BUMPER — N
- CHASSIS — A
- 8d NAIL
- C
- F — GAS TANK
- SLIDING TONGUE — M
- 1" COMPRESSION SPRING
- D — FRONT BUMPER
- ¼"-DIA. AXLE PIN
- O
- #8 x 1¼ Fh BRASS WOODSCREW
- FRONT FENDER
- 2"-DIA. WOODEN WHEEL
- L — AXLE BLOCK
- ¼"-DIA. AXLE PINS

MATERIALS LIST

WOOD

A	Chassis (1)	¾ x 2 - 9⅞
B	Engine Cmprt. (1)	1½ x 2¼ - 6
C	¼" Dowel Pins (5)	¼ dowel x 1⅜ rgh.
D	Front Bumper (1)	¼ x ½ - 3
E	Cab Pieces (2)	¾ x 3½ - 4
F	Gas Tanks (2)	¾ x 1 - 2¼
G	Sides (2)	⅜ x 3¾ - 6¾
H	Front/Back (2)	⅜ x 3¾ - 3⅜
I	Bottom (1)	⅜ x 3⅜ - 6¼
J	Top (1)	⅜ x 4 - 10 rgh.
K	⅛" Dowel Pins (6)	⅛ dowel x 1½ rgh.
L	Axle Blocks (2)	½ x ¾ - 2½
M	Sliding Tongue (1)	½ x 1½ - 7
N	Back Bumper (1)	¾ x 3 - ¼
O	Front Fenders (2)	¾ x 1 - 3½

HARDWARE SUPPLIES

- (2) No. 8 x 1¼" Fh brass woodscrews
- (1) 8d finish nail
- (1) 1" compression spring
- (3) ½" wooden screw buttons
- (6) ¼"-dia. axle pins
- (4) 2"-dia. wooden wheels

CUTTING DIAGRAM

¾ x 4½ - 36 (1.1 Bd. Ft.)

½ x 4 - 12 (.3 Sq. Ft.)

ALSO NEED:
¼" DOWEL 12" LONG FOR PART C AND
⅛" DOWEL 12" LONG FOR PART K

⅜ x 4½ - 48 (1.5 Sq. Ft.)

CHASSIS

The first part to make on the truck is the chassis, since all the other assemblies are fastened to it. I started by cutting the chassis (A) to finished length and a rough width of 2½" *(Fig. 1)*.

DADOES. The next step is to cut three dadoes across the workpiece — two narrow ones on the bottom of the chassis for a couple of axle blocks and a wider dado on the top for the cab.

Although these three dadoes (and the groove that's cut later) can be cut with a dado set, it would leave a slightly irregular bottom. Instead, I cut these dadoes on the router table using a ½" straight bit to get a smooth bottom.

Before cutting the dadoes, clamp an auxiliary fence to the router table fence to cover the bit opening *(Fig. 2)*. Then, use a push board (a piece of ¾" plywood works well) to guide the narrow workpiece along the fence and through the bit *(Fig. 2)*. Note that each of the axle block dadoes are ⅛" deep and the dado for the cab is ¼" deep *(Fig. 1)*.

TRIM TO WIDTH. After the three dadoes are routed, the chassis can be trimmed to a final width of 2". (Trim off both edges to clean up any chipout caused when cutting the dadoes.)

CENTER GROOVE. Next, a groove is routed down the center of the chassis to hold the engine compartment and also the secret sliding mechanism *(Fig. 1)*.

There's a simple procedure I used to rout this groove so it's centered. Start by setting the router table fence so the bit is near the center of the workpiece. Make a pass with one edge of the workpiece against the fence. Then flip the chassis end for end and make a pass with the other edge against the fence *(Fig. 3)*.

To widen the groove, move the fence away from the bit and continue with this procedure until the groove is 1½" wide.

Safety Note: Feed the workpiece from right to left and adjust the fence so the bit is cutting the shoulder that's *farthest* from the fence. This way, the shoulder being cut is fed *against* the rotation of the bit. If you rout the shoulder nearest the fence, the bit will "grab" the workpiece. The effect is like kickback, except the piece is thrown forward.

CHAMFER END. After the center groove is completed, rout a chamfer on the rear end of the chassis *(Fig. 1)*. As before, use a push board to back up the piece and help prevent chipout.

COIN REMOVAL HOLE. The last step on the chassis is to cut the coin removal hole. Start by drilling two 1"-dia. holes *(Fig. 1a)*. Then use a jig saw to cut out the slot between the holes. To sand the edges smooth, I used a drum sander chucked in a drill press.

ENGINE COMPARTMENT

At this point, the chassis is pretty much complete. Now it's just a matter of building and adding the remaining pieces to it. I started at the front, with the engine compartment *(Fig. 4)*.

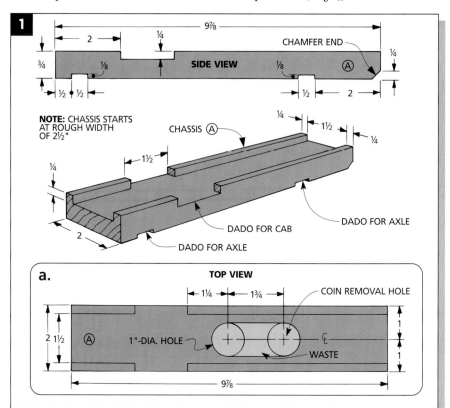

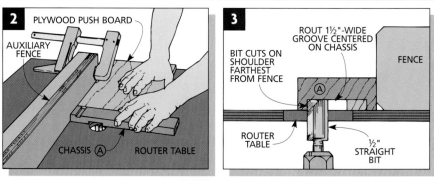

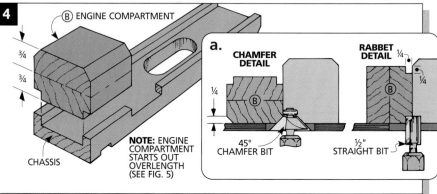

The engine compartment (B) starts out as an overlength blank of two pieces of $3/4$" stock laminated together. The blank is about 6" long and trimmed to width to equal the width of the chassis.

RABBETS AND CHAMFERS. Next, rout rabbets on the bottom edges of this block to produce a wide tongue that fits snugly in the groove in the chassis *(Fig. 4a)*.

To complete the engine compartment, I routed 45° chamfers on the top edges. These chamfers are $1/4$" deep *(Fig. 4a)*.

MOUNT TO CHASSIS. After the rabbets and chamfers are cut, the engine compartment can be glued and clamped to the chassis. The only problem you might find here is that the block tends to slide on the glue as it's clamped in place.

To make this alignment automatic, I cut a piece of scrap to width to fit in the cab dado. That way, the engine block could be butted against this block as the clamp is tightened *(Fig. 5)*.

Note: Once the engine compartment is clamped in place, remove the scrap block. This way, if any excess glue has seeped out, the scrap won't get glued into the dado.

When the glue is dry, trim off the front end of the engine compartment so it's flush with the front of the chassis *(Fig. 6)*.

DRILL HOLES. The last thing to do on the engine compartment is to lay out the positions of the holes for the headlights, radiator cap, and front bumper.

The headlights are wood buttons. They fit into $1/2$"-dia. holes about $3/16$" deep *(Fig. 7)*. The radiator cap is a $1/4$" dowel pin (C) that fits in a hole on the top of the engine block. It sticks $3/16$" above the top of the compartment.

And finally, the front bumper (D) is cut to size *(Fig. 7)*. It's mounted with two $1/4$" axle pins *(Fig. 7a)*. Mark these holes on the front end of the chassis and, as you drill them, make sure you don't drill into the axle dado.

CAB

The challenge in building the cab is how to make the windows. The solution turned out to be kind of like the theory behind carving — you cut away everything that doesn't look like a window.

The way to do this is to cut dadoes in two $3/4$"-thick cab pieces (E) and glue these two pieces together *(Fig. 9)*. However, I found it was easier to start by working with one longer piece rather than two short pieces *(Fig. 8)*.

I cut a dado $1/2$" from each end of this workpiece. This can be done on the table saw with an auxiliary fence on the miter gauge *(Fig. 8)*. To establish the edges of the dadoes, I clamped a stop block to the auxiliary fence. The rip fence served as a stop for the other edge of the dado.

CUT TO SIZE. After the dadoes are cut, trim the workpiece to a final width of $3\frac{1}{2}$" to remove any chipout along the edges.

Then cut off the two blocks (E) that will become the cab *(Fig. 9)*.

FRONT WINDOW. The dadoes you just cut produce the side windows when the blocks are laminated. To make the front window, all you have to do is drill holes in one of the pieces *(Fig. 9)*. (The edges of the holes align with the edges of the dado.) Then remove the waste with a coping saw or jig saw.

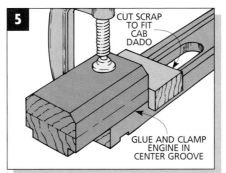

CUT SCRAP TO FIT CAB DADO

GLUE AND CLAMP ENGINE IN CENTER GROOVE

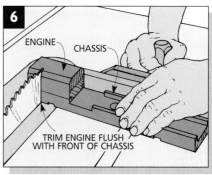

ENGINE   CHASSIS

TRIM ENGINE FLUSH WITH FRONT OF CHASSIS

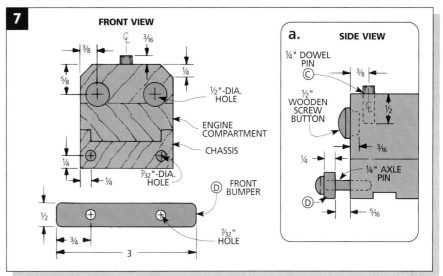

FRONT VIEW

$3/8$ — $3/16$ — $1/4$

$5/8$

$1/2$"-DIA. HOLE

ENGINE COMPARTMENT

CHASSIS

$1/4$ $1/4$

$7/32$"-DIA. HOLE

FRONT BUMPER

$1/2$ $3/4$ 3

$7/32$" HOLE

a.   SIDE VIEW

$1/4$" DOWEL PIN (C) $3/8$

$1/2$" WOODEN SCREW BUTTON

$1/2$ $3/16$

$1/4$

$1/4$" AXLE PIN   (D) $5/16$

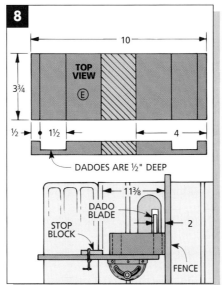

TOP VIEW (E)

$3\frac{3}{4}$ 10

$1/2$ $1\frac{1}{2}$ 4

DADOES ARE $1/2$" DEEP

$11\frac{3}{8}$

DADO BLADE

STOP BLOCK   2

FENCE

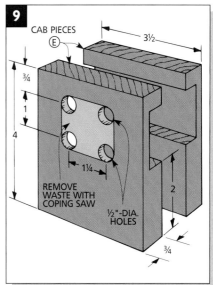

CAB PIECES (E) $3\frac{1}{2}$

$3/4$ 1   4 $1\frac{1}{4}$

REMOVE WASTE WITH COPING SAW

$1/2$"-DIA. HOLES

2    $3/4$

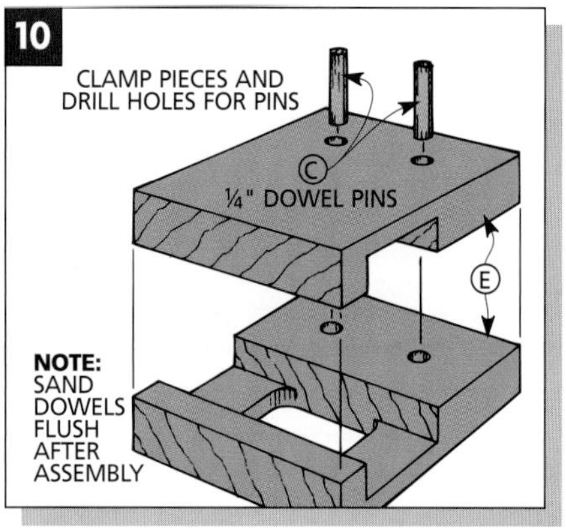
10
CLAMP PIECES AND DRILL HOLES FOR PINS
¼" DOWEL PINS
C
E
NOTE: SAND DOWELS FLUSH AFTER ASSEMBLY

LAMINATE PIECES. With the front window completed, I dry-clamped the pieces together and drilled holes for two 1/4" dowel pins (C) *(Fig. 10)*. Thcsc pins prevent the blocks from sliding out of alignment during glue-up. After the holes are drilled, glue the pieces together.

BEVEL EDGES. When the glue is dry, bevel the edges of the cab at 22° to leave a 1/4"-wide "pillar" on each side of the front window and 1/8"-wide shoulders on each side of the engine compartment *(Figs. 11, 12, and 13)*.

After the bevels are cut, sand the cab and glue it into the chassis *(Fig. 13)*.

GAS TANKS. Next, cut two gas tanks (F) to size *(Fig. 13)* and clamp them in place flush with the top of the chassis *(Fig. 13a)*. Then drill a hole through the tank and into the chassis. Glue and clamp the tanks in place with 1/4" dowel pins (C) sticking out 1/8" to create "gas caps."

BANK COMPARTMENT

The bank compartment is a box made from 3/8"-thick stock.

CUT TO SIZE. Start by ripping the stock for the sides (G), front (H), and back (H) to width to fit between the chassis and the top of the cab *(Figs. 13a and 14)*.

Next, cut the sides to length so they're 3/8" longer than the distance between the cab and the end of the chassis.

PIN STRIPES. At this point, you can cut a couple of kerfs 1/16" deep to add the look of "pinstripes" to the box *(Fig. 14b)*. And a kerf in the back piece creates a couple of "doors" *(Fig. 14)*.

JOINERY. The sides are joined to the front and back with simple rabbet joints *(Fig. 14a)*. I cut these rabbets in the sides at the router table. The sides, front, and back are joined to the bottom (I) with a tongue and groove joint *(Fig. 14c)*. To make this joint, cut a groove on the inside face of the sides, front, and back pieces.

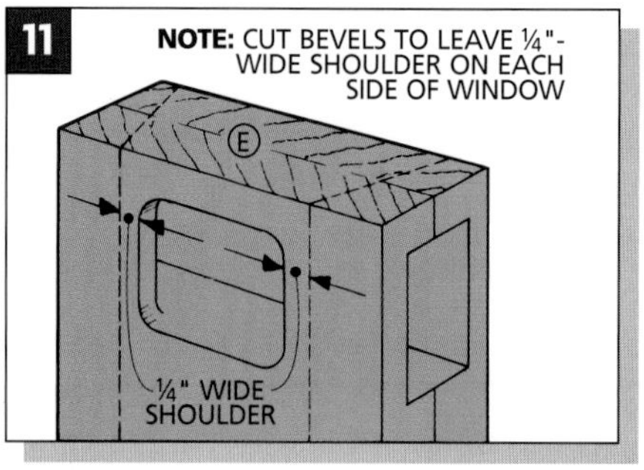
11
NOTE: CUT BEVELS TO LEAVE ¼"-WIDE SHOULDER ON EACH SIDE OF WINDOW
E
¼" WIDE SHOULDER

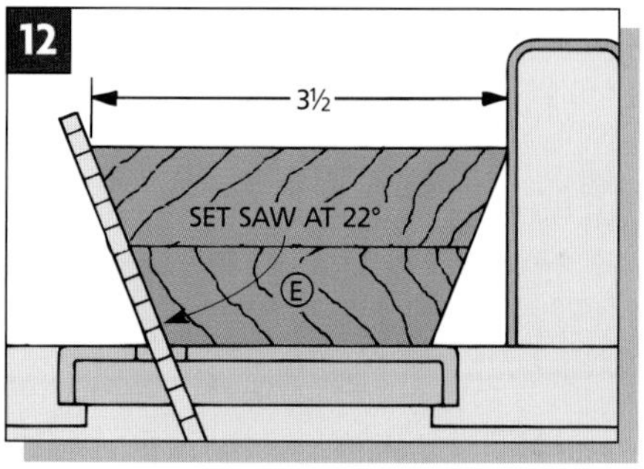
12
3½
SET SAW AT 22°
E

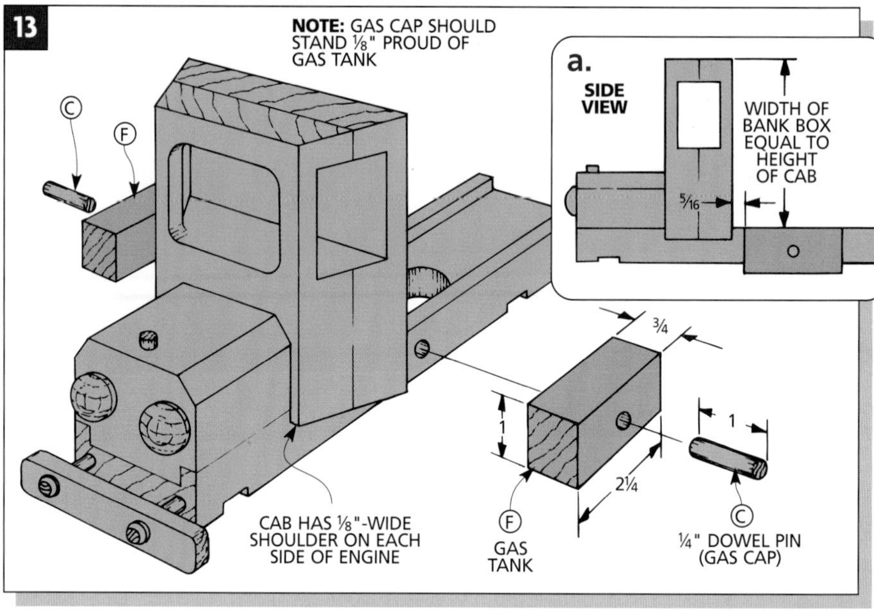
13
NOTE: GAS CAP SHOULD STAND ⅛" PROUD OF GAS TANK
C
F
a. SIDE VIEW
WIDTH OF BANK BOX EQUAL TO HEIGHT OF CAB
5⁄16
¾
1
2¼
1
CAB HAS ⅛"-WIDE SHOULDER ON EACH SIDE OF ENGINE
F
GAS TANK
C
¼" DOWEL PIN (GAS CAP)

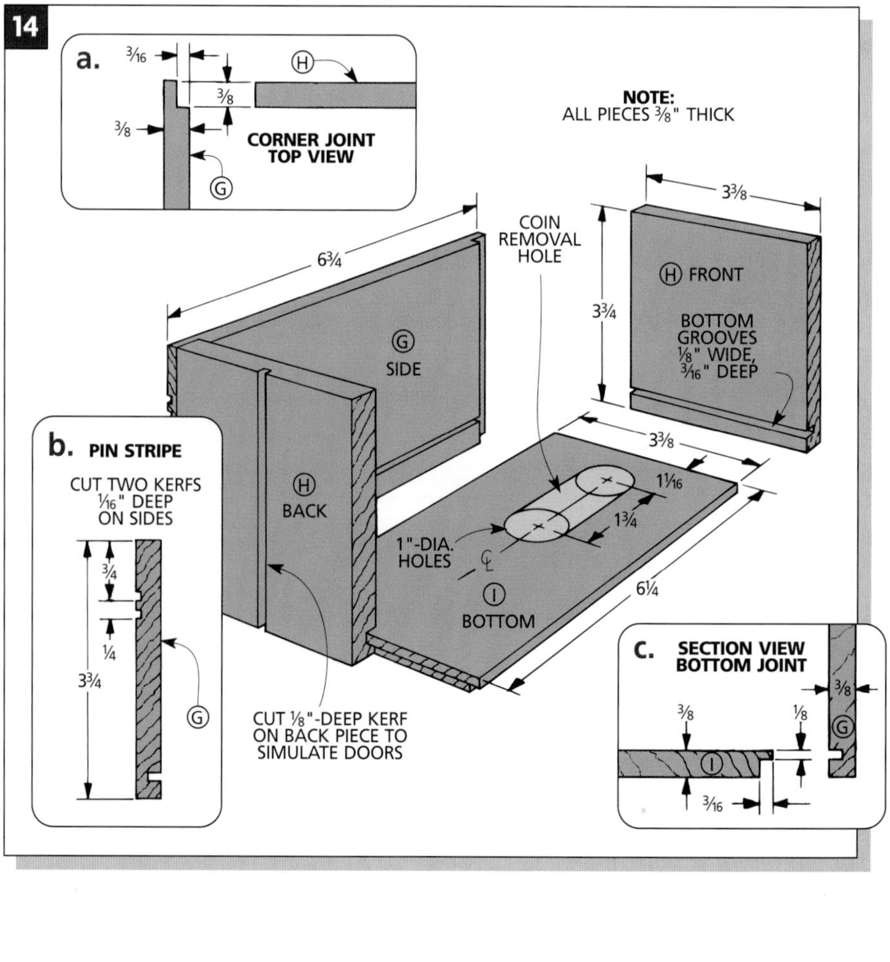
14
a.
3⁄16
⅜
⅜
H
CORNER JOINT TOP VIEW
G
NOTE: ALL PIECES ⅜" THICK
6¾
COIN REMOVAL HOLE
3⅜
H FRONT
3¾
BOTTOM GROOVES ⅛" WIDE, 3⁄16" DEEP
G SIDE
3⅜
1 1⁄16
1¾
1"-DIA. HOLES
6¼
I BOTTOM
H BACK
b. PIN STRIPE
CUT TWO KERFS 1⁄16" DEEP ON SIDES
¾
¼
3¾
G
CUT ⅛"-DEEP KERF ON BACK PIECE TO SIMULATE DOORS
c. SECTION VIEW BOTTOM JOINT
⅜
⅜
⅛
G
I
3⁄16

FRONT AND BACK. Now the front and back pieces (H) can be cut to length (3³⁄₈") *(Fig. 14)*. This makes the outside width of the assembled box ¹⁄₄" wider than the back of the cab *(Fig. 17)*.

BOTTOM. To get the final size of the bottom, dry-assemble the box and measure the inside dimensions, adding ³⁄₈" for the tongues. Then cut rabbets on all four edges to leave tongues to fit snugly in the grooves *(Fig. 14c)*.

Then make a coin removal hole just as you did in the chassis *(Fig. 14)*.

Now the sides, front, and back can be glued and clamped to the bottom.

Note: If you'd like to add a logo to your truck, it's easiest to do that before assembly. Refer to the Designer's Notebook on page 35.

TOP. To complete the box, the top (J) is cut to size so it's ¹⁄₄" wider than the box and 8³⁄₄" long *(Fig. 15)*.

Next, set up the table saw to cut the coin slot in the top.

To do this, mark the location of the slot centered on the length and width of the top (J) *(Fig. 15)*. Then place the top next to the blade and adjust the blade height until the teeth align with the marks on the top face *(Fig. 15)*. Now transfer the marks to the saw table top *(Fig. 16)*.

Lower the blade and use a block to clamp the top on the marks *(Fig. 16)*. Now turn on the saw and raise the blade, stopping when the kerf touches the lines.

Once the slot is cut, chamfer the front edge of the top and round the front corners to a 1" radius *(Fig. 17)*.

MOUNT TOP. Finally, dry-clamp the top in place and drill holes for the four ¹⁄₈" dowel pins (K). Then glue in the pins, and clamp the top in place.

AXLES

Before mounting the bank box to the chassis, the axle blocks (L) are cut to size and mounted. I started with an over-length blank, planed to fit the dadoes on the bottom of the chassis *(Fig. 18)*.

First, rout ¹⁄₄" roundovers on one edge of the blank *(Fig. 18b)*. Then cut two axle blocks to length so they're ¹⁄₂" longer than the width of the chassis.

HOLES FOR AXLE PINS. In order to mount the wheels to these blocks, ⁷⁄₃₂"-dia. holes are drilled for axle pins.

Note: I notched a piece of scrap to hold the blocks while drilling *(Fig. 19)*.

After the holes are drilled, glue the axle blocks in the dadoes in the chassis.

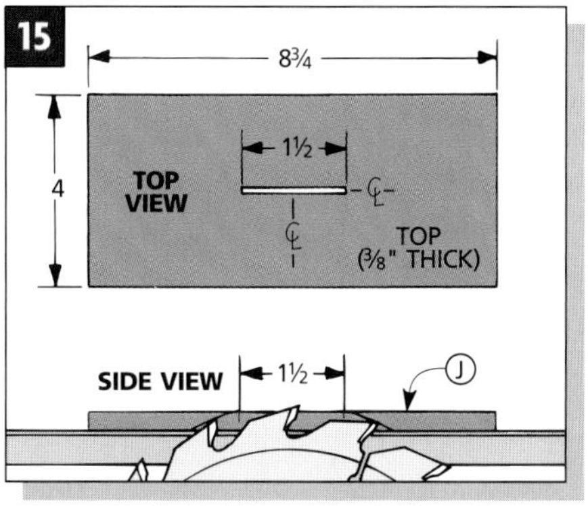
15
8¾
4
1½
TOP VIEW
℄
TOP (⅜" THICK)
SIDE VIEW
1½
J

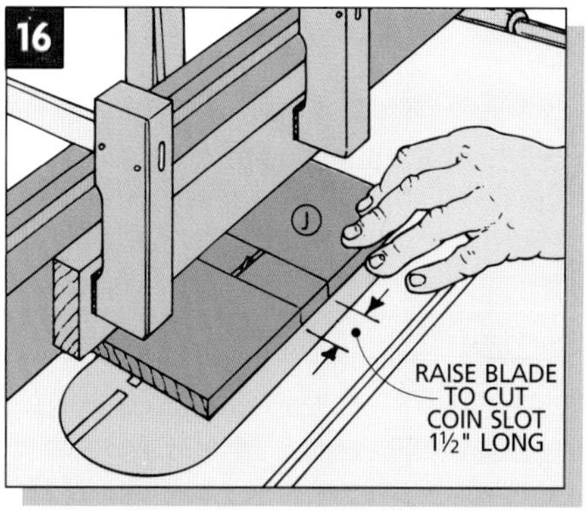
16
J
RAISE BLADE TO CUT COIN SLOT 1½" LONG

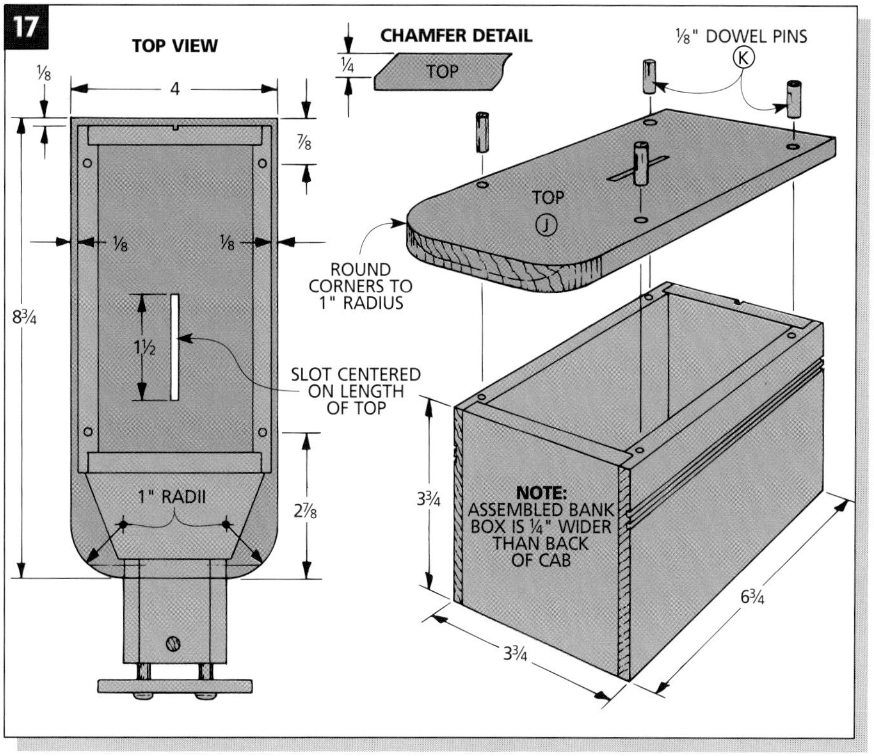
17
TOP VIEW
⅛
4
⅞
⅛
⅛
8¾
1½
1" RADII
2⅞
CHAMFER DETAIL
¼
TOP
⅛" DOWEL PINS
K
TOP
J
ROUND CORNERS TO 1" RADIUS
SLOT CENTERED ON LENGTH OF TOP
3¾
NOTE: ASSEMBLED BANK BOX IS ¼" WIDER THAN BACK OF CAB
3¾
6¾

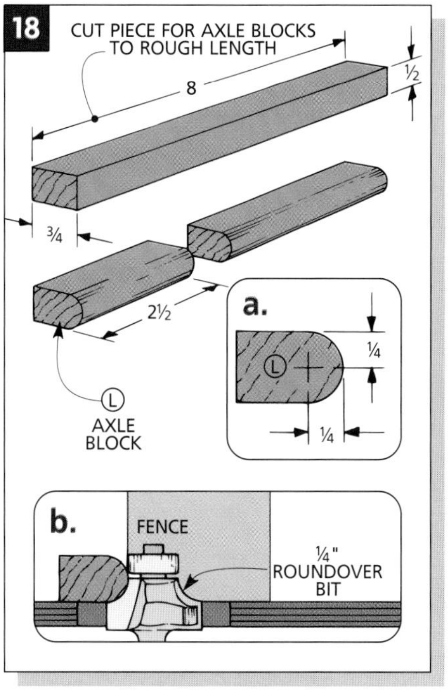
18
CUT PIECE FOR AXLE BLOCKS TO ROUGH LENGTH
8
½
¾
2½
L
AXLE BLOCK
a.
L
¼
¼
b.
FENCE
¼" ROUNDOVER BIT

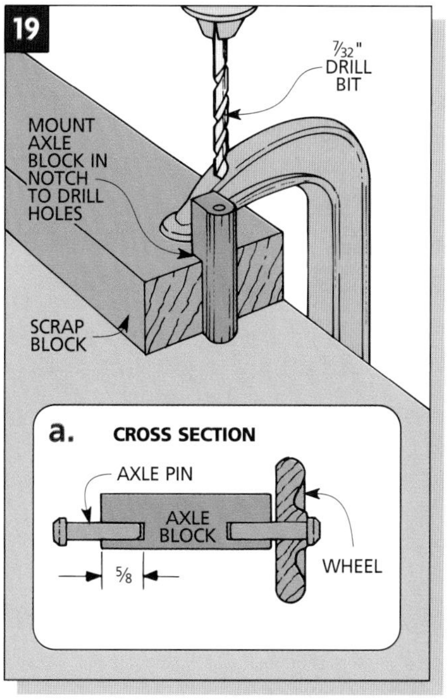
19
⁷⁄₃₂" DRILL BIT
MOUNT AXLE BLOCK IN NOTCH TO DRILL HOLES
SCRAP BLOCK
a. CROSS SECTION
AXLE PIN
AXLE BLOCK
WHEEL
⅝

The secret to getting your money out of this bank is the sliding tongue that covers the hole in the chassis. The tongue slides in the groove in the chassis. And the rear bumper serves as a handle.

TONGUE. The sliding tongue (M) is cut to width so it slides easily in the groove in the chassis *(Fig. 20)*. And it's $\frac{1}{4}$" longer than the bank box (7" for me).

BUMPER. After the tongue is cut to size, the back bumper (N) can be added. Start with an oversize piece of $\frac{3}{4}$"-thick scrap *(Fig. 20)*. Then cut a dado across the center of this piece to fit the tongue.

Now trim off a $\frac{1}{4}$"-long piece for the bumper and glue it to the tongue, flush with the end. To reinforce the joint, I drilled a couple of holes and glued in a couple of $\frac{1}{8}$" dowel pins (K) *(Fig. 20)*.

RELEASE PIN. To keep the tongue from sliding out, a spring-release pin goes through the rear axle block and into the tongue to serve as a catch *(Fig. 24)*. The pin is an 8d finish nail, and the small spring is from an old ball-point pen.

Note: Before drilling the holes for this pin, it's best to have the nail and spring in hand to get the right dimensions for the holes.

The first thing to do is drill a hole for the spring, centered on the chassis and

axle block *(Fig. 21)*. The depth of this hole should be enough to hold the head of the nail and the spring when it's fully compressed *(Fig. 24)*.

Then drill a hole all the way through the axle for the finish nail *(Fig. 22)*.

HOLE IN CHASSIS. After these holes are drilled, mark on the bottom of the sliding tongue the position of the catch hole that traps the head of the nail.

To do this, place the tongue in the "closed" position on the chassis, and tap an 8d nail through the hole in the axle

block *(Fig. 23)*. Then remove the tongue and drill a $\frac{1}{8}$"-deep hole at this point.

BUTTON. After the catch hole is drilled, cut the 8d nail to length so it extends $\frac{1}{2}$" below the axle block, and epoxy a wood button to the end of the nail *(Fig. 24)*.

FRONT FENDERS

Next, the front fenders (O) are cut to shape. (The pattern shown in *Fig. 25* is full size.) I laid out both fenders on one blank with their bottom edges aligned.

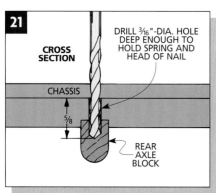

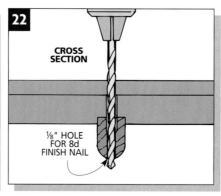

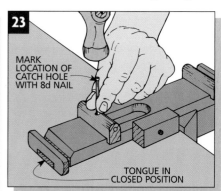

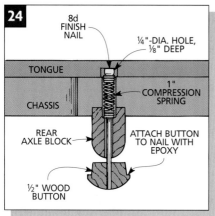

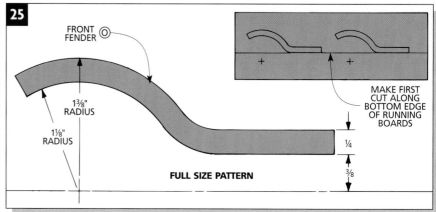

That way, I could rip along the bottom of the running boards to get a straight edge.

Then I cut out the rest of the profile on the band saw, staying a little to the outside of the marked lines.

To smooth the cut edges, I mounted a drum sander in the drill press and sanded to the marked lines.

Before mounting the fenders, temporarily mount the wheels to the axles and insert the axles in the axle blocks. Then glue and clamp the fenders in place with their bottom edges flush with the bottom of the chassis. And check that the fenders clear the wheels.

MOUNT BANK BOX. The next step is to mount the bank box to the chassis. However, before assembly, I clamped a piece of scrap over the chassis to test the sliding mechanism *(Fig. 26)*. (To make it slide easily, wax the center groove.)

After testing the sliding mechanism, I clamped the bank box to the chassis and drilled shank holes through each gas tank. Then you can attach the bank box using a screw through each gas tank *(Fig. 27a)*. Don't glue the bank box — just in case you need to repair the spring-release pin sometime in the future.

MOUNT THE WHEELS. Now all four wheels can be mounted permanently. Put a wheel on each axle, then apply a dab of glue in the hole in the axle block. To pre-

vent the wheels from binding, I used a piece of posterboard to set the space between the inside of the wheel and the end of the axle block *(Fig. 27)*.

FINISH. To complete the truck, I sanded all the surfaces, slightly rounding the edges and corners. Then I finished the truck with tung oil. ■

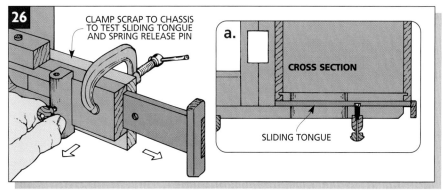

26 CLAMP SCRAP TO CHASSIS TO TEST SLIDING TONGUE AND SPRING RELEASE PIN

a. CROSS SECTION

SLIDING TONGUE

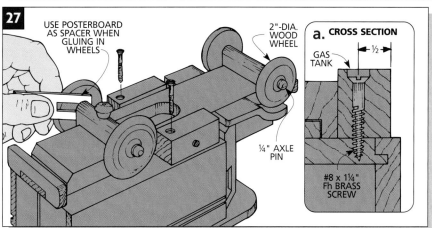

27 USE POSTERBOARD AS SPACER WHEN GLUING IN WHEELS

2"-DIA. WOOD WHEEL

¼" AXLE PIN

a. CROSS SECTION

GAS TANK

½

#8 x 1¼" Fh BRASS SCREW

DESIGNER'S NOTEBOOK

Personalize the bank with a child's name or a company logo.

CONSTRUCTION NOTES:

■ You can use a woodburning pen with a temperature control to transfer a photocopied design to wood. (A clothes iron will also work.) But first, you need a backward (mirror image) copy of the design.
■ You can make the backward copy in one of two ways. The easiest is to make a copy on acetate (a clear plastic sheet).

Then you can quickly make backward copies by turning the acetate over in the photocopier to get the mirror image copy.
■ The other way is to make a standard photocopy of the design first.
■ Then transfer this copy to another piece of paper with a woodburning pen (or iron). Use a series of light passes with the pen on the back of the photocopy with the tool set for a medium heat. This produces a mirror image on the transfer sheet.
■ Now take the backward copy to the photocopier and make a fresh, toner-rich copy of it. When this backward copy is transferred onto the wood project, the logo will once again appear correct.

LOGO TRANSFER

Woodsmith

■ When transferring the copies to wood, tape down the photocopy along one edge so you can check the progress of the image periodically (see drawing). If an area isn't dark enough, keep working over it with the pen until more toner is released. It takes a little practice to find the right amount of heat and time to keep the pen from burning the paper or wood.

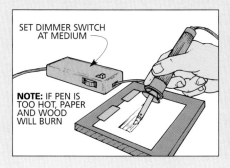

SET DIMMER SWITCH AT MEDIUM

NOTE: IF PEN IS TOO HOT, PAPER AND WOOD WILL BURN

Kaleidoscope

This elegant eyepiece puts a new twist on kaleidoscopes and turning. You don't need a lathe to turn the ends round. And an easy-to-install lens gives the world around you a new look.

When I was a little kid, Santa Claus stuffed my stocking with a cardboard tube that made an intriguing rattle as my hands trembled with excitement. When I looked inside to see what was making the noise, I was amazed to find thousands of pebbles floating in a vast array of colorful geometric shapes. I knew it must be magic.

Now that I'm a somewhat older kid, I've had a chance to make another kind of Kaleidoscope. This one doesn't rely on pebbles for effects. Instead, it alters the view of the real world. It's still amazing, but of course, I realize it's not magic. It's simply done with mirrors.

TUNNEL VISION. The inside of a kaleidoscope body is lined with three slender mirrors fastened edge-to-edge to form a triangle. When looking through this mirror tunnel, the reflections of objects are reflected again and again by the mirrors. In my childhood kaleidoscope, these multiple reflections are what transformed a few pebbles into thousands.

LENS. The Kaleidoscope shown here doesn't use pebbles. Instead, I used a wide-angle lens to slightly distort incoming images of the real world. These images are reflected in the mirrors to form an array of triangular forms as beautiful as any collection of pebbles.

TURNING WITHOUT A LATHE. The Kaleidoscope body is a hollow wooden hexagon. The ends are turned round to accept brass rings that hold the lens and an eyepiece. While that may mean this is a candidate for a lathe project, it's even easier to make with a router mounted in a special turning jig. (See page 42 for more on how to make this jig.)

Note: *Woodsmith Project Supplies* offers a hardware kit that includes the lens and brass rings. See page 126 for details and ordering information.

WOOD. I used maple for the body of the Kaleidoscope with padauk accent strips for contrast.

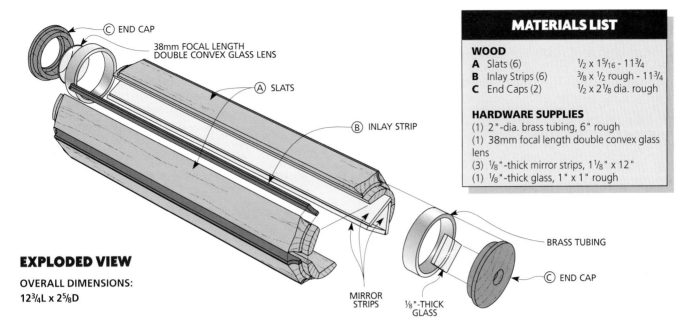

© END CAP

38mm FOCAL LENGTH
DOUBLE CONVEX GLASS LENS

Ⓐ SLATS

Ⓑ INLAY STRIP

BRASS TUBING

© END CAP

MIRROR
STRIPS

⅛"-THICK
GLASS

EXPLODED VIEW

OVERALL DIMENSIONS:
12¾"L x 2⅝"D

MATERIALS LIST

WOOD

A	Slats (6)	½ x 1⁵⁄₁₆ - 11¾
B	Inlay Strips (6)	⅜ x ½ rough - 11¾
C	End Caps (2)	½ x 2⅛ dia. rough

HARDWARE SUPPLIES
(1) 2"-dia. brass tubing, 6" rough
(1) 38mm focal length double convex glass
lens
(3) ⅛"-thick mirror strips, 1⅛" x 12"
(1) ⅛"-thick glass, 1" x 1" rough

BODY

To start, the hexagonal body of the Kaleidoscope has to be made.

SLATS. The slats (A) start with 12"-long blanks of ½"-thick stock. (Mine are maple.) Begin by tilting the blade to 30°. Next, adjust the fence so the width from the point of the bevel to the fence is 1½". Then rip the bevel on one side of all six slats (Step 1 in Fig. 1).

SECOND PASS. To bevel the opposite edge, move the fence so the outside face of the slat (point to point) is 1⁵⁄₁₆" wide. Then make this second cut on all six pieces (Step 2 in Fig. 1).

GLUE BODY. After all the slats are beveled on both edges, the angled edges are glued together to form the hexagonal body. Since this is an unusual shape, I had some rubber bands on hand to clamp the parts together (Fig. 2).

The easiest way to assemble the body is to apply glue to one surface of all six slats. Next, stand the slats on end to roughly align the outside edges.

Note: It's not critical to make the joints absolutely perfect. Any imperfections will be corrected in the next step.

After the glue dries, cut off the ends so the body is 11¾" long (Fig. 2).

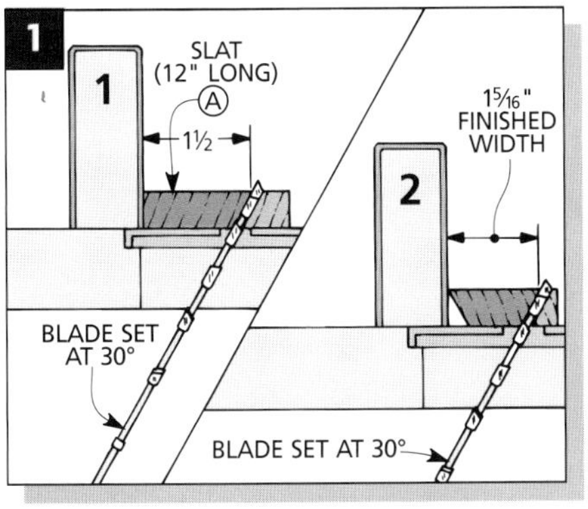

INLAY STRIPS

The next step is to inlay contrasting hardwood accent strips into the corners where the slats join. When the Kaleidoscope is finished these will look like evenly-spaced, ⅛"-wide inlays (and completely conceal any gaps in the glue joints).

KERFING JIG. To make sure the kerfs for the inlay strips are cut straight into the joint lines, a simple jig is needed. The base of the jig is about 2" wide and has a 30° bevel on one side (Fig. 3). This piece is screwed to a second piece to form an "L"-shaped jig that can be clamped to the rip fence of the table saw.

POSITION JIG. To position the jig so the blade cuts a kerf centered on the glue line, the lower edge of the jig's base has to be under-cut slightly at 30° (Fig. 3a).

Now the jig is aligned by holding the Kaleidoscope body against the jig. First, adjust the rip fence and jig until the blade is centered on a glue line. Then adjust the saw blade to cut ⅜" deep (Fig. 3a). Now cut a kerf in all six joints.

INSTALL STRIPS. After the kerfs are cut, you can rip inlay strips (B) from ½"-thick stock to fit the kerfs. (I used padauk to contrast with the maple.)

Now glue the strips into the kerfs. Once the glue dries, plane and sand the strips flush with the slats (Fig. 4).

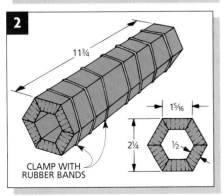

1

SLAT
(12" LONG)
Ⓐ

1½

1⁵⁄₁₆"
FINISHED
WIDTH

2

BLADE SET
AT 30°

BLADE SET AT 30°

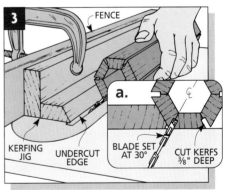

2

11¾

1⁵⁄₁₆

2¼

½

CLAMP WITH
RUBBER BANDS

3

FENCE

a.

₵

KERFING
JIG

UNDERCUT
EDGE

BLADE SET
AT 30°

CUT KERFS
⅜" DEEP

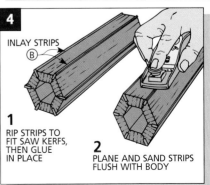

4

INLAY STRIPS
Ⓑ

1

RIP STRIPS TO
FIT SAW KERFS,
THEN GLUE
IN PLACE

2

PLANE AND SAND STRIPS
FLUSH WITH BODY

RINGS & ROUNDING

Now the real fun begins — turning the ends of the body, without a lathe. The ends have to be turned to fit brass rings. Since these rings determine the outside diameter of the ends, I made them first.

RINGS. The 1/2"-long rings that fit over the ends of the body are cut from 2"-dia. brass tubing. (Brass tubing is available at plumbing supply shops. *Woodsmith Project Supplies* also offers a kit with the brass rings and the convex lens. See page 126 for information.)

To cut the rings, I secured the tube in a simple miter box with a wedge to keep it from turning *(Fig. 5)*. After cutting off the first ring, smooth the sawn end with a file using the miter box end as a guide *(Fig. 6)*. Then saw off the second ring.

CENTERING PLUG. Now you can get ready to turn the ends of the body. To do this, you'll need to make a centering plug that will serve as a pivot on the router turning jig. (See page 42 for details about the jig.) First, resaw a hardwood scrap so its thickness is the same as the width of the inside face of the slats *(Fig. 7)*. Next, rip the piece to width so it will fit between two opposite walls of the body. Then cut the piece about 2" long.

INSTALL CENTER. The block spins on a short length of 1/2" dowel. So bore a 1/2" hole in the center of the block and insert the dowel so it projects 3/16" *(Fig. 7)*.

ROUTER TABLE TURNING

Now the ends of the body can be turned on the router turning jig in two steps.

RING SHOULDER. The first step is turning straight shoulders on each end to hold the brass rings. Begin by mounting a 1/4" straight bit in the router so it projects 1/4" above the top of the jig. Next, set the end of the dowel into a hole in the sliding adjustable center on the turning jig *(Fig. 8)*. Then fine-tune the position of the adjustable center so the corners of the body just miss the bit.

ROUT SHOULDER. Next, turn on the router and move the sliding center until the bit takes a light cut off one of the corners. Then rotate the body clockwise to make the first pass *(Figs. 9 and 10)*.

Now move the sliding arm toward the bit slightly *(Fig. 9)*. Repeat until the brass ring slips tightly onto the end *(Fig. 11)*.

SET DEPTH STOP. When the ring fits, set the depth stop on the sliding center and repeat the sequence on the other end.

COVE CONTOUR. After the ring shoulders are routed, a cove is routed to blend the ring shoulder into the flat sides of the body. To do this, mount a 3/4" core box bit in the router so it projects 5/8" above the table surface. Then make progressively deeper passes until the shoulder at the base of the cove matches the thickness of the brass ring *(Fig. 12)*.

Before making the other parts for the Kaleidoscope, I sanded the body and finished it with two coats of tung oil.

END CAPS

While the finish on the body was drying, I turned my attention to the inner workings. The first step was making the end caps that fit into the brass rings and hold the eyepiece glass and lens.

CAP DISKS. The end caps (C) start out as two oversized discs cut from 1/2"-thick stock. Begin by drawing two 2 1/8"-dia. circles *(Fig. 13)*. Next, bore a 1/2" hole

5
WEDGE
BRASS TUBE
1/2
HACK SAW

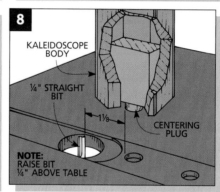

6
WEDGE
NOTE: FILE END OF TUBE SQUARE BEFORE NEXT CUT, USE MITER BOX AS A GUIDE

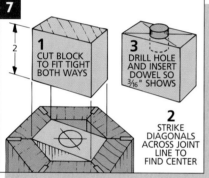

7
2
1 CUT BLOCK TO FIT TIGHT BOTH WAYS
3 DRILL HOLE AND INSERT DOWEL SO 3/16" SHOWS
2 STRIKE DIAGONALS ACROSS JOINT LINE TO FIND CENTER

8
KALEIDOSCOPE BODY
1/4" STRAIGHT BIT
1 1/8
CENTERING PLUG
NOTE: RAISE BIT 1/4" ABOVE TABLE

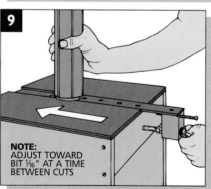

9
NOTE: ADJUST TOWARD BIT 1/16" AT A TIME BETWEEN CUTS

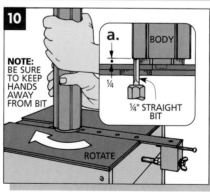

10
NOTE: BE SURE TO KEEP HANDS AWAY FROM BIT
a. BODY
1/4
1/4" STRAIGHT BIT
ROTATE

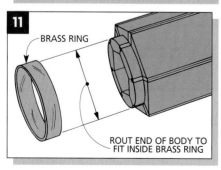

11
BRASS RING
ROUT END OF BODY TO FIT INSIDE BRASS RING

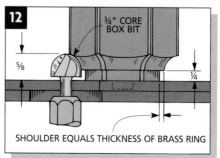

12
3/4" CORE BOX BIT
5/8
1/4
SHOULDER EQUALS THICKNESS OF BRASS RING

through the centerpoint of each circle. Then cut the discs to rough size.

TURNING HANDLE. The end caps are "turned" to finished size with the same technique used to round the ends of the body. To do this safely, I made a 6"-long handle ripped to $1\frac{1}{4}$" square *(Fig. 14)*.

Next, stick the disc to the handle with a piece of carpet tape. Then insert a short length of $\frac{1}{2}$" dowel into the hole in the end cap to act as a turning center.

SIZE DISK. Now the end cap is reduced to the same diameter as the *outside* diameter of the brass rings. Begin by setting the router so a $\frac{1}{4}$" straight bit projects about $\frac{1}{8}$" higher than the thickness of the end cap. Then set the sliding center so the edge of the end cap just clears the

bit (about 1" between the edge of the bit and the centering hole) *(Fig. 15)*.

Now turn on the router and slowly twist the handle while adjusting the sliding center toward the bit. When the bit starts to cut the edge, take a light cut off the edge of the end cap *(Fig. 16)*. Keep making adjustments until the end cap diameter matches the outside diameter of the brass rings *(Fig. 17a)*.

TURN SHOULDER. Next, a shoulder is turned to fit the *inside* diameter of the rings. To do this, first lower the bit so it projects $\frac{1}{4}$" (one half the thickness of the end cap). Then adjust the center and turn the end caps until the shoulder fits tightly into the ring *(Fig. 17)*.

FITTING THE LENS

When the end caps fit the rings, they're drilled to hold the lenses. Although Forstner bits would be excellent for this, I didn't have the large sizes needed. So I did this with spade bits and the help of a jig on the drill press (see page 40).

EYEPIECE. The eyepiece doesn't need a lens. Instead it has a flat piece of glass (mainly to keep dust out). To bore the recess for this piece of glass, first place a centering dowel on the drill press jig *(Fig. 18)*. Then use a $1\frac{1}{2}$" spade bit to bore the recess in the eyepiece $\frac{5}{16}$" deep.

LENS CAP. The lens cap has a larger opening than the eyepiece to admit light through the lens. And the inside surface is recessed to hold the viewing lens. This hole and recess are bored in four steps.

The smaller ($1\frac{1}{4}$") outside opening is bored first. To do this, place a new centering dowel in the jig. Then bore the hole $\frac{1}{4}$" deep *(Fig. 19)*.

Now, to bore the $1\frac{1}{2}$" lens recess on the inside surface, put another centering dowel in the jig. Flip the lens cap over and place it over the dowel. To keep the cap from spinning, grip it with adjustable pliers (see page 40), and bore $\frac{3}{8}$" deep to leave a shoulder for the lens *(Fig. 20)*.

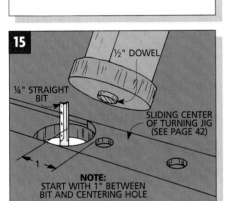

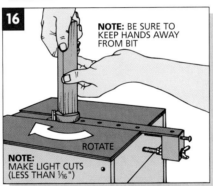

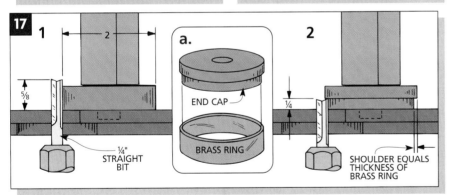

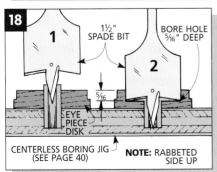

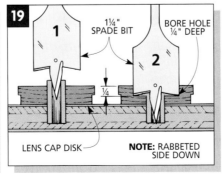

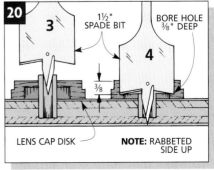

Counterboring a hole so the diameter steps down from larger to smaller (as when counterboring a screw hole) is normally done in what seems to be a reverse sequence. The larger hole is bored part way through the wood first. Then the smaller bit is started on the center mark left by the larger bit to make sure the holes are concentric.

But when counterboring the recesses for the lenses in the end pieces for the Kaleidoscope, that technique won't work. The centers were already bored out to accommodate the turning centers of the router turning jig.

TEMPORARY CENTER. This meant there was no stock to guide the point of the spade bit used to counterbore the recess. To solve this problem, I came up with a drill press jig with temporary centering dowels for the bit.

The temporary center is a short length of dowel with a pilot hole bored through the center. The pilot hole helps guide the spade bit. Without it, the spade bit point would wander badly when starting to bore into the end grain. A brad point bit wanders less, so it's used to get the spade bit off on a straight course.

PILOT HOLE JIG

The pilot hole in the dowel has to be perfectly centered. To locate the centerpoint for the pilot hole, I made a simple jig to hold the dowel on the drill press while drilling the pilot hole. The jig is just a scrap of wood about 2" wide with a hole drilled in it and a kerf cut in the end.

The first step is to use a square to scribe two perpendicular lines near the end of the jig (*Fig. 1*). Next, bore a ½" hole through the jig at the intersection of these lines. Then, to make the jig act as a clamp so it will grip the dowel, saw a kerf to the hole from one end.

MARK CENTER. Now insert the dowel in the hole so its end is flush with the surface. Next, use the square to continue the lines on the jig across the end of the dowel (*Fig. 2*). Finally, to guide the drill bit, mark the centerpoint with an awl.

BORE CENTER. To bore the center, first push the dowel up so its lower end is flush with the bottom of the jig. (This is so it will rest flat on the drill press table.) Then use a small clamp to grip the dowel in the jig (*Fig. 3*) and bore into the center.

Note: Although I needed three temporary centers for the Kaleidoscope, I made extras just in case.

BORING JIG

Now that the temporary centers are made, you can move on to making the jig that is used when drilling the end caps. And this jig couldn't be much simpler. It's just a piece of ¾" plywood clamped to the drill press table. After it's clamped in place, drill a ⅝"-deep hole in the plywood to accept the temporary centers (*Fig. 4*).

POSITION WORKPIECE. When you're ready to drill the end caps, place a temporary center in the jig. (No glue. You'll need to insert a new center for each drilling operation.) Press the workpiece to be counterbored over the centering dowel (*Fig. 5*). As the lens recess is counterbored, the dowel is also cut away.

FIRM GRIP. There was one problem using this technique on the end pieces for the Kaleidoscope. The friction of the spade bit as it scraped out the recess spins the workpiece. To keep it from spinning (without getting my fingers near the bit), I gripped it with a pair of adjustable pliers (*Fig. 6*).

Note: To prevent the jaws of the pliers from marring the end piece, I put two layers of masking tape over each jaw.

BORING SEQUENCE. When you need to drill two different sized holes (like the recess for the lens and the lens opening on the lens end piece), the smaller opening should be bored first.

Then, when the larger recess is bored from the opposite side, the edges of the bit are still supported and don't rattle around (which ruins the workpiece) when the two holes meet in the center (refer to *Fig. 20* on page 39).

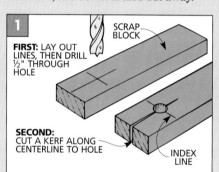

1 **FIRST:** LAY OUT LINES, THEN DRILL ½" THROUGH HOLE — SCRAP BLOCK — **SECOND:** CUT A KERF ALONG CENTERLINE TO HOLE — INDEX LINE

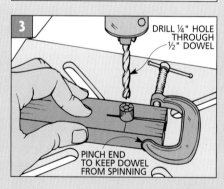

2 ALIGN SQUARE WITH INDEX LINE — STRIKE CROSS LINES TO LOCATE CENTER POINT OF DOWEL — PUNCH CENTER OF DOWEL WITH AWL

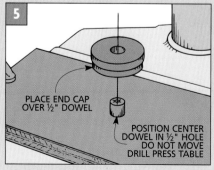

3 DRILL ¼" HOLE THROUGH ½" DOWEL — PINCH END TO KEEP DOWEL FROM SPINNING

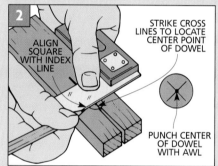

4 CLAMP ¾" PLYWOOD BASE TO DRILL PRESS TABLE — DRILL ½" CENTER HOLE ⅝" DEEP

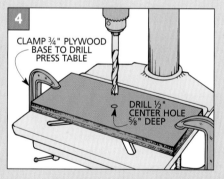

5 PLACE END CAP OVER ½" DOWEL — POSITION CENTER DOWEL IN ½" HOLE DO NOT MOVE DRILL PRESS TABLE

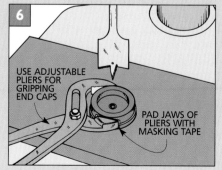

6 USE ADJUSTABLE PLIERS FOR GRIPPING END CAPS — PAD JAWS OF PLIERS WITH MASKING TAPE

CONTOUR CAPS. Now the edges of the caps can be contoured. To do this, begin by scribing a line around the rim of each cap ⅛" from the outside edge *(Fig. 21)*. Then round the caps from the edge of the holes to these lines *(Fig. 22)*.

INSTALL LENSES. After the caps are contoured the lenses can be glued in place. Apply a small dab of clear silicone sealant to four points on the edges and press the lenses into the caps *(Fig. 23)*.

INSTALL RINGS. I used silicone to install the rings *(Fig. 24)*. It holds if the caps shrink in the rings.

MIRROR TUNNEL

All the external parts of the Kaleidoscope are now complete. Next, I turned to making the mirror tunnel that lines the body. I began by cutting three 12"-long mirror strips from a larger panel.

CUTTING JIG. To cut the mirror strips uniformly, I made a simple jig out of two pieces of ¼" hardboard. Begin by gluing a narrow strip to a wide piece to create a step as wide as the mirror strip, less the thickness of the cutter *(Fig. 25)*.

Note: This measurement was 1¹⁄₁₆" for my Kaleidoscope. To determine the width for other sizes, measure between the inside walls, then subtract ³⁄₁₆" (a little more than the thickness of the mirror, plus a little extra for the thickness of the cutter) *(Fig. 28)*.

SCORE MIRROR. To use the jig for scoring, lay it on the mirror (with the glass side up) so the step butts the edge of the mirror. Then make one smooth stroke along the edge with a glass cutter to score a break line *(Fig. 26)*.

BREAK ON LINE. To break the mirror on the line, place the scored line over the edge of a piece of hardboard *(Fig. 27)*. Then hold the mirror with one hand and press down on the jig with the other. The mirror will snap cleanly on the break line.

ASSEMBLE MIRRORS. After the mirror strips are cut, they're taped together. I used duct tape and made sure all three edges lapped the same way *(Fig. 28)*.

FINAL ASSEMBLY. Now all that's left is putting the parts together. Put a bead of silicone along each edge where the mirrors are taped together. Then slip the mirror assembly into the body. Finally, put a few dabs of silicone on the inside edges of the brass rings to glue the end caps to the body *(Fig. 29)*.

Now you can take a magical look at the world. And it's all done with mirrors. ∎

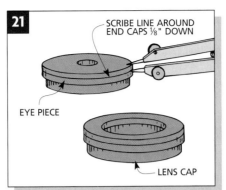

21 SCRIBE LINE AROUND END CAPS ⅛" DOWN
EYE PIECE
LENS CAP

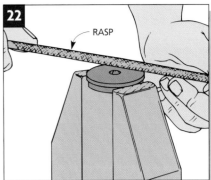

22 RASP

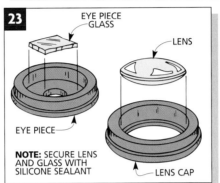

23 EYE PIECE GLASS
LENS
EYE PIECE
NOTE: SECURE LENS AND GLASS WITH SILICONE SEALANT
LENS CAP

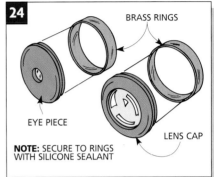

24 BRASS RINGS
EYE PIECE
LENS CAP
NOTE: SECURE TO RINGS WITH SILICONE SEALANT

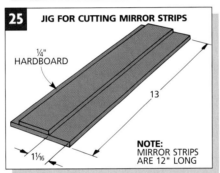

25 JIG FOR CUTTING MIRROR STRIPS
¼" HARDBOARD
13
1¹⁄₁₆
NOTE: MIRROR STRIPS ARE 12" LONG

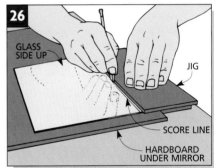

26 GLASS SIDE UP
JIG
SCORE LINE
HARDBOARD UNDER MIRROR

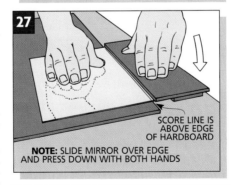

27 SCORE LINE IS ABOVE EDGE OF HARDBOARD
NOTE: SLIDE MIRROR OVER EDGE AND PRESS DOWN WITH BOTH HANDS

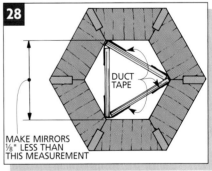

28 DUCT TAPE
MAKE MIRRORS ⅛" LESS THAN THIS MEASUREMENT

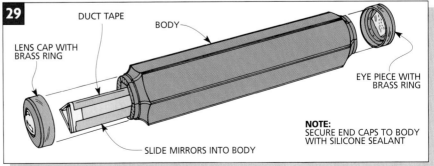

29 DUCT TAPE
BODY
LENS CAP WITH BRASS RING
EYE PIECE WITH BRASS RING
SLIDE MIRRORS INTO BODY
NOTE: SECURE END CAPS TO BODY WITH SILICONE SEALANT

When you think of a turning project, you usually think of a lathe. But the biggest problem with turning projects is that not every woodworker has a lathe. Fortunately, you can get the same results with a different tool and this jig.

A TURN FOR THE BETTER

To turn the ends on the Kaleidoscope, I reversed the lathe's cutting principle. Instead of spinning the workpiece and holding the cutting edge of a tool against it, I spun the cutting tool and moved the workpiece slowly against it. The spinning cutter is simply a router bit.

A BOX. The jig is essentially a router table — it's an open-sided box with the router mounted inside. The secret to its turning ability is an adjustable sliding center dovetailed into the top (see photo). This sliding center allows you to move the workpiece toward the bit in small increments as you "turn" a piece round.

CONSTRUCTION. First, cut the $3/4$" plywood sides of the box to size (*Fig. 1*). Two hardwood cleats join the sides. The cleat across the bottom lies flat so that the jig can be clamped to a benchtop.

The top for the jig starts out with a single piece of $1/4$" hardboard (*Fig. 1*). A $1\frac{3}{4}$"-dia. hole in the panel allows the router bit to extend through. The top is glued and screwed to the top of the box.

The work surface is a second layer of hardboard that consists of three pieces. The top side pieces are glued to the lower hardboard. The narrow sliding center between the sides has a row of pivot holes that control the diameter of the turned piece (*Fig. 2*). (I drilled several holes so I could use the jig for larger-diameter pieces in the future.)

CUTTING SEQUENCE. To make the dovetailed edges on these pieces, first tilt the saw blade to 45° and cut the sliding center to 2" wide (*Fig. 2*).

The two side pieces start off slightly oversize (they're trimmed after being glued in place). Then one edge of each side piece is beveled at 45°.

To mount these pieces, first align the center strip with the router hole and clamp it in place. Then glue the two top side pieces in position so the center slides without any side-to-side play (*Fig. 2*). After the glue dries, trim the edges of the sides flush with a flush trim router bit.

1

TOP BASE LAYER (1/4" HARDBOARD)

13½ 12

6¾ 8

1¾"-DIA. HOLE

#8 x 1" Fh WOODSCREW

T-NUT

12

1⅜ 6

12

#8 x 1½" Fh WOODSCREWS

CLEATS (¾"-THICK HARDWOOD)

SIDE (¾" PLYWOOD)

2½ 12

a. CROSS SECTION

1⅜

⅜" HOLE

⅜" T-NUT

NOTE: A SECOND LAYER OF HARDBOARD WILL BE ADDED TO THE TOP

ADJUSTMENT MECHANISM. The position of the sliding center is controlled by an adjustment mechanism. This mechanism consists of a threaded rod that holds the sliding center in position and allows for minute adjustments *(Fig. 3)*. There's also a machine screw that acts as a depth stop. This hardware is mounted in a hardwood block that's fastened to the end of the sliding center *(Figs. 2 and 3)*.

BLOCK. After cutting the block to size, two holes are drilled through it. One is a $3/16$"-dia. hole for the stop screw and the other is a $3/8$"-dia. hole for the adjustment rod *(Fig. 2a)*. Then screw and glue the block to the end of the sliding center.

THREADS. The adjustment rod threads into a T-nut that's mounted in the upper cleat *(Fig. 1)*. To locate the hole for the T-nut, push the sliding center into the jig so the block rests against the cleat. Next, drill a $3/8$" hole through the cleat using the hole in the block for alignment. Then mount a $3/8$" T-nut on the back of the brace with the threaded section projecting inside the box *(Fig. 1a)*.

ADJUSTMENT ROD. To make the adjustment rod, first cut a section of $3/8$" threaded rod $8^{1}/_{2}$" long. Next, secure a wing nut to one end by drilling a hole through the nut and rod. Then drive a 6d nail through the hole. Snip off the ends and file the ends flush *(Fig. 3)*.

SECURE ROD. The rod is secured in the block by jamming two nuts against each other. To keep the mechanism from spinning on its own, I slipped a rubber washer between two steel washers onto the rod on both sides of the block *(Fig. 3)*.

STOP ROD. To complete the adjustment mechanism, install the stop rod. This is a $1/4$" x $3^{1}/_{2}$" machine screw that threads through the top hole in the block.

USING THE JIG

The trick to using the jig is positioning the workpiece so it can rotate in one of the holes in the sliding piece while the edge turns against the bit. Then the threaded rod is adjusted inward to control the diameter of the cut. Obviously, the workpiece will need some kind of center to fit in the holes in the sliding piece.

To make a center, cut a rectangular block to fit inside the end and bore a hole through the center to hold the dowel. (Refer to *Figs. 7 and 8* on page 38.) Then insert the block into the workpiece and place the assembly in a hole in the sliding center. The details of the procedure are described on page 38.

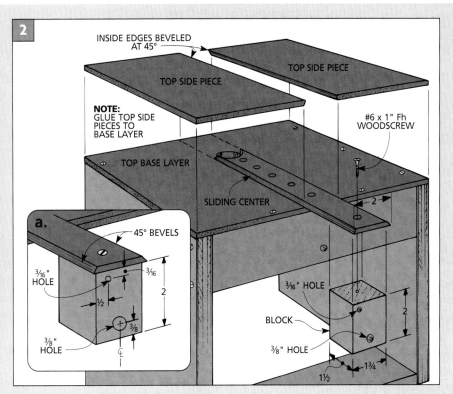

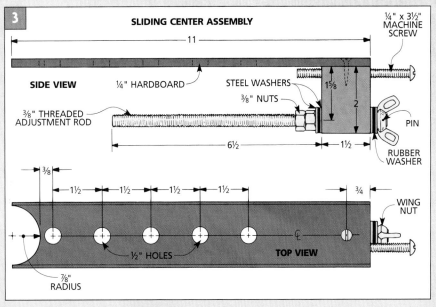

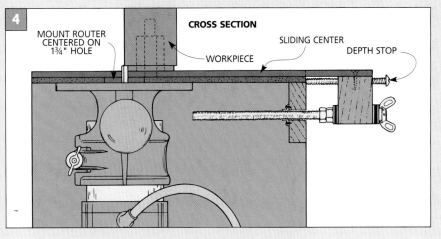

SCROLL SAWN

The care and craftsmanship in a scroll-sawn gift are immediately apparent. But like any skill, scrolling takes time to master. New scrollers can start with the simple patterns of the centerpiece or night light, then move up to fretwork like that of the jewelry box or bookends.

Holiday Lantern

All it takes is a scroll saw and a light bulb to create this Holiday Lantern. Plus, the removable panels make it easy to change the scenery. Building it is so much fun that you'll want to make a lot of extras.

Candlelight and the holiday season always seem to go together. And that's the inspiration behind this holiday project. I based my design on an old-fashioned lantern. But instead of glass sides, I used wood panels with scroll-sawn patterns. And instead of an oil lamp with a wick, I substituted a small light bulb. So when you turn on the switch, a warm holiday scene lights up.

I had a lot of fun coming up with the patterns for the panels of this lantern. In fact, I couldn't decide on just one. So I'm offering four different scenes so you can be the judge (see the patterns on the opposite page and on page 51).

And you don't have to choose just one pattern. Instead, I've designed the Holiday Lantern so the panels are removable (inset photo). The panels fit into grooves that are cut in the posts and top and bottom of the lantern. This way, you can make as many different designs as you wish (using my patterns or one of your own) and simply switch them whenever you feel like it. This is also a benefit when building several lanterns for each member of your family. A variety of panel designs comes in real handy.

REMOVABLE TOP. Making the panels interchangeable meant that the top of the lantern had to be removable. I tried

a couple of different ideas for fastening the top to the posts, but in the end the solution I came up with was a simple one.

I simply epoxied a small threaded stud into the top of each post. The top fits over the ends of the posts, and four nuts thread onto the studs to hold it in place. Then I covered the nuts with wood "hub caps."

SCROLL SAW. If you're new to scroll sawing, the techniques aren't really that difficult to master. All it takes is some patience and a steady hand. (See the Technique article on page 86.)

EXPLODED VIEW

OVERALL DIMENSIONS:
6⅞"W x 6⅞"D x 10H

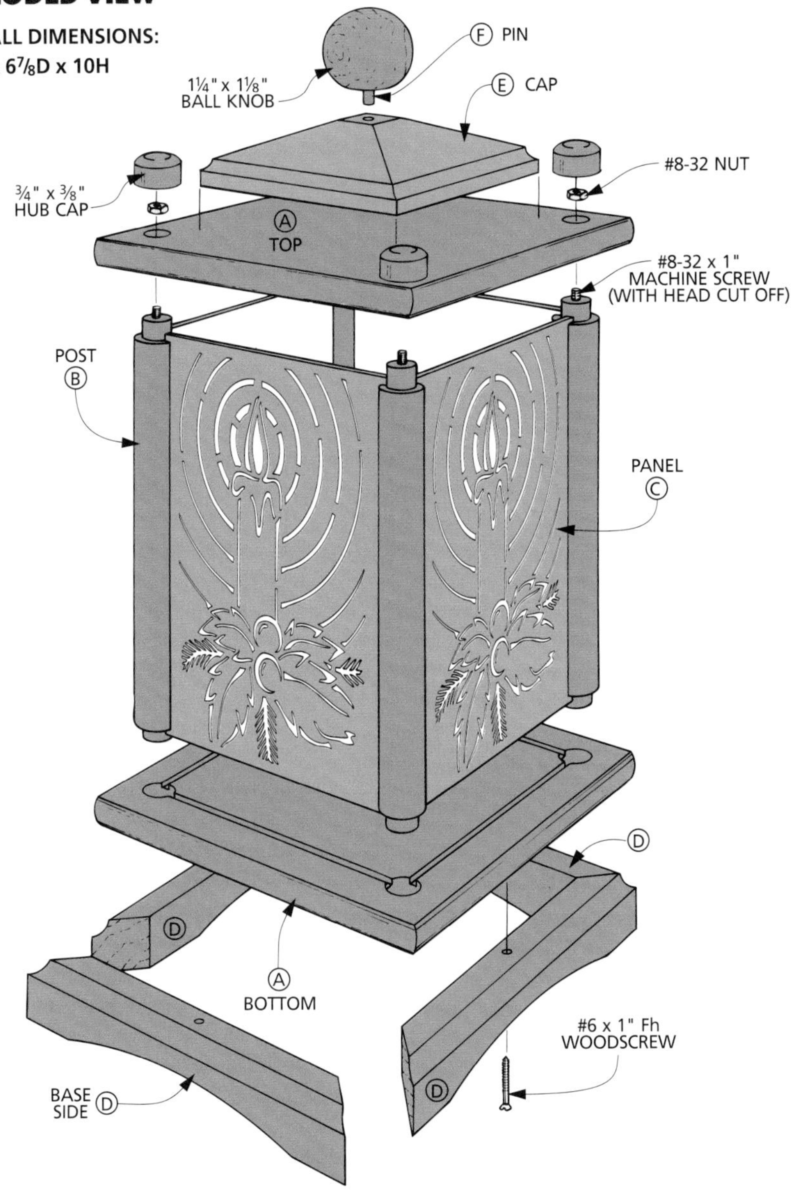

F PIN

1¼" x 1⅛"
BALL KNOB

E CAP

¾" x ⅜"
HUB CAP

#8-32 NUT

A
TOP

#8-32 x 1"
MACHINE SCREW
(WITH HEAD CUT OFF)

POST
B

PANEL
C

D

A
BOTTOM

#6 x 1" Fh
WOODSCREW

BASE
SIDE D

D

CANDLESTICK PATTERN (ENLARGE 200%)

MATERIALS LIST

WOOD
A	Top/Bottom (2)	½ x 6¾ - 6¾
B	Posts (4)	¾ dowel x 7
C	Panels (4)	⅛ ply - 4¾ x 6¼
D	Base Sides (4)	¾ x 1 - 6⅞
E	Cap (1)	1 x 4¼ - 4¼
F	Pin (1)	³⁄₁₆ dowel x ⅞

HARDWARE SUPPLIES
(4) No. 6 x 1" Fh woodscrews
(4) No. 8-32 x 1" machine screws
(4) No. 8-32 nuts
(4) ¾" x ⅜" birch hub caps
(1) 1¼" x 1⅛" ball knob
(1) Light socket
(4) Rice paper (5" rough x 7" rough)

CUTTING DIAGRAM

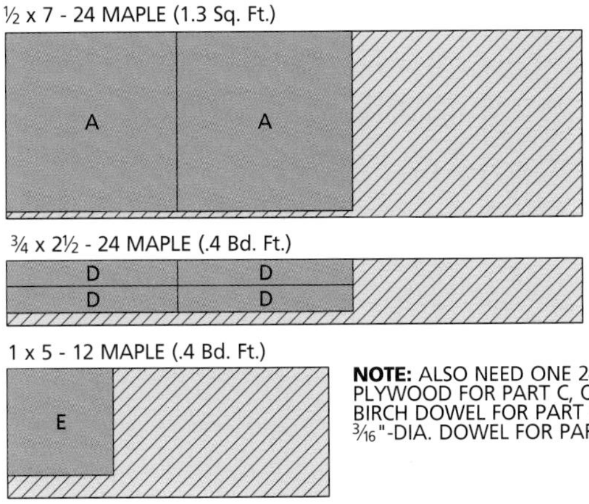

½ x 7 - 24 MAPLE (1.3 Sq. Ft.)

A   A

¾ x 2½ - 24 MAPLE (.4 Bd. Ft.)

| D | D |
| D | D |

1 x 5 - 12 MAPLE (.4 Bd. Ft.)

E

NOTE: ALSO NEED ONE 24" x 24" SHEET OF ⅛" BIRCH
PLYWOOD FOR PART C, ONE 36" PIECE OF ¾"-DIA.
BIRCH DOWEL FOR PART B, AND A SCRAP PIECE OF
³⁄₁₆"-DIA. DOWEL FOR PART F

1

TOP
(A)

GROOVES
FOR PANELS

POST
(3/4"-DIA.
DOWEL)
(B)

7

1"-DIA.
HOLE FOR
BULB
ASSEMBLY

NOTE:
POSTS ARE
GLUED INTO
BOTTOM
ONLY

BOTTOM
(A)

GROOVES
FOR PANELS

6¾

6¾

NOTE:
TOP AND
BOTTOM ARE
½"-THICK
STOCK

a.

(B)
POST

½

SIDE
VIEW

(A)

½

b.

TOP VIEW

TOP/
BOTTOM
(A)

½" DIA.

¾

¾

⅛"-WIDE
GROOVE

Before sitting down at the scroll saw, I built the framework of the lantern. This is nothing more than a ½"-thick maple top and bottom supported by four round posts. Then, after the main body of the lantern was complete, I cut the plywood side panels to fit.

TOP AND BOTTOM. The top and bottom (A) are both made out of solid ½"-thick maple stock. They're cut square, and then a ½"-dia. hole is drilled in each corner *(Figs. 1 and 1b)*. These holes will hold the posts that are added later.

The bottom also gets an additional hole for a bulb assembly that's added later. This 1"-dia. hole is drilled right in the center of the workpiece *(Fig. 1)*.

With all the holes drilled, rout the bull-nose profile on the edges of the pieces. All you'll need to do this is a router table and a ³/₈" roundover bit *(Figs. 2 and 2a)*.

Note: To avoid chipout, rout along the end grain edges first.

The last step to complete the top and bottom is to rout narrow grooves in between the holes to hold the side panels that are added later. The grooves are ⅛" deep and ⅛" wide *(Figs. 1b and 3a)*.

To make these grooves, I again used the router table. But because the router bit is completely covered by the workpiece, it's difficult to tell where to start the groove and where to stop it. So I clamped a couple of stop blocks to my router table fence *(Figs. 3 and 3a)*. This way, you won't push the workpiece too far and rout beyond the hole.

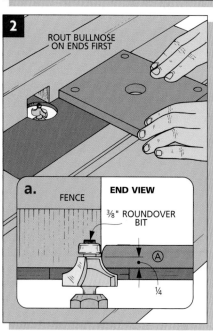

2

ROUT BULLNOSE
ON ENDS FIRST

a.

FENCE

END VIEW

³/₈" ROUNDOVER
BIT

(A)

¼

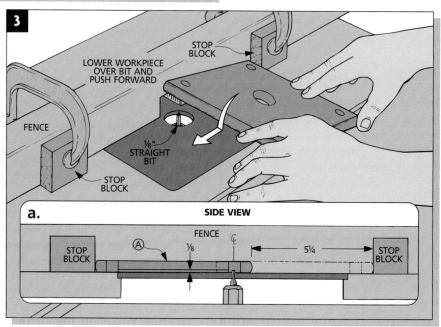

3

STOP
BLOCK

LOWER WORKPIECE
OVER BIT AND
PUSH FORWARD

FENCE

⅛"
STRAIGHT
BIT

STOP
BLOCK

a.

SIDE VIEW

FENCE

STOP
BLOCK

(A)

⅛

5¼

STOP
BLOCK

POSTS. The top and bottom are connected by four posts made from $3/4$"-dia. dowels. Tenons on the ends of the posts fit into the holes in the top and bottom.

I started by cutting the posts (B) to length *(Fig. 1)*. (I used a stop block on my miter gauge so they're the same length.)

To cut the $1/2$"-dia. tenons on the ends of the posts, I used a router table and a straight bit, simply rotating the workpiece into the bit to cut the tenon all the way around the dowel *(Figs. 4 and 4a)*. The trick is to set up the router table fence to establish the shoulder of the tenon first, then sneak up on the height of the bit until the tenon fits snug.

Note: I attached a zero-clearance auxiliary fence to my router table when cutting the tenons.

GROOVES. With the tenons cut on the ends of the posts, the next step is to cut a couple of grooves along the length of each post to hold the side panels *(Fig. 1)*.

I cut these grooves on a table saw, using a saw blade with a $1/8$"-wide kerf *(Figs. 5 and 5b)*. To keep the post from rotating as the grooves are cut, I made a couple of square blocks that fit tight over the tenoned ends of each post *(Fig. 5a)*.

The posts will get glued into the holes in the bottom piece. But to make the top removable (in order to change the side panels), I had to come up with another method for attaching it to the posts.

THREADED STUDS. The solution I came up with was to mount a threaded stud in the top end of each post. (I used a machine screw with the head cut off for the stud.) This way, the top can be fastened with four small nuts. The nuts are epoxied into wood "hub caps" to conceal them (see the photo below).

To mount the threaded studs, I first drilled a $3/16$" hole in the end of each post, using a simple jig to hold the post upright *(Figs. 6 and 6a)*. Then I epoxied the stud into the hole *(Fig. 7)*.

ASSEMBLY. Once the studs are in place, the posts can be glued into the bottom. When doing this, just make sure that the grooves in the posts are lined up with the grooves in the bottom. (I used a scrap piece of plywood to align them.)

Now, four $1/8$" plywood panels (C) can be cut to size to fit in the lantern *(Fig. 8)*. Then turn to page 47 and the Designer's Notebook on page 51 for pattern ideas.

Thread the nut onto the end of a screw to prevent epoxy from entering the threads while inserting it into the hub cap.

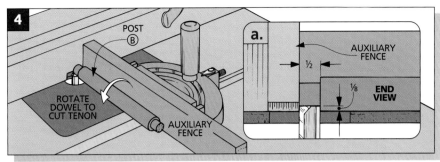

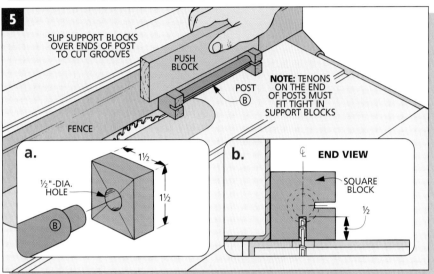

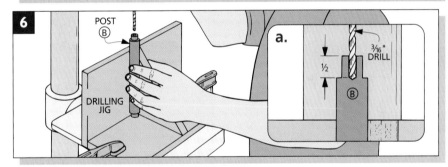

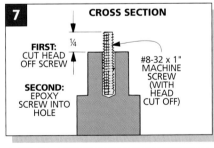

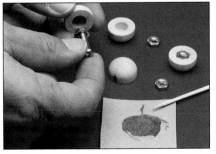

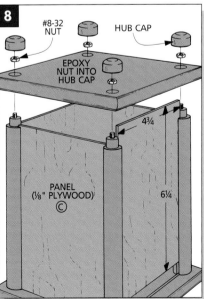

9

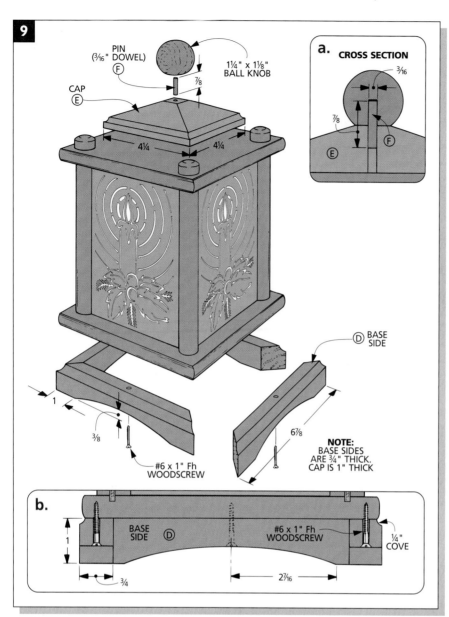

PIN
(3/16" DOWEL)
(F)

1 1/4" x 1 1/8"
BALL KNOB

7/8

CAP
(E)

4 1/4   4 1/4

a. CROSS SECTION

3/16

7/8

(E)   (F)

(D) BASE
SIDE

1

3/8

#6 x 1" Fh
WOODSCREW

6 7/8

NOTE:
BASE SIDES
ARE 3/4" THICK.
CAP IS 1" THICK

b.

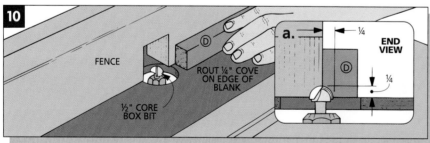

BASE
SIDE (D)

#6 x 1" Fh
WOODSCREW

1/4"
COVE

1

3/4

2 7/16

10

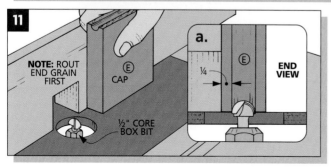

FENCE

(D)

ROUT 1/4" COVE
ON EDGE OF
BLANK

1/2" CORE
BOX BIT

a.   1/4

(D)

1/4

**END
VIEW**

11

NOTE: ROUT
END GRAIN
FIRST

(E)
CAP

1/2" CORE
BOX BIT

a.

(E)

1/4

(E)   **END
VIEW**

12

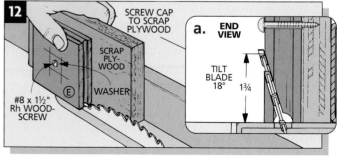

SCREW CAP
TO SCRAP
PLYWOOD

SCRAP
PLY-
WOOD

#8 x 1 1/2"
Rh WOOD-
SCREW

(E)   WASHER

**a. END
VIEW**

TILT
BLADE
18°   1 3/4

BASE & CAP

With the main body of the lantern complete, I began working on the base and the cap that fits on the top.

BASE. The base is just a mitered frame that's screwed to the bottom of the lantern. To make the four base sides (D), rip a couple of extra-long (18") blanks to width (1") and rout a 1/4" cove along one edge (*Figs. 10 and 10a*).

Next, the pieces can be mitered to length (6 7/8"). Before gluing them up, I laid out an arc along the bottom of each piece. After I cut the arcs out with a band saw, I sanded the edges smooth on the drill press, using a drum sander.

Once the frame is glued up, you can screw it to the bottom of the lantern using four small screws (*Fig. 9b*).

CAP. Now a cap (E) can be added to the top of the lantern (*Fig. 9*). It starts off as a square, 1"-thick blank. Then to create a cove around the edge, I used a 1/2"-dia. core box bit to rout a channel on all four edges of the blank that's centered on the thickness of the piece (*Figs. 11 and 11a*).

Next, a decorative bevel is ripped on all four edges of the blank to create a peaked "roof" *(Fig. 9)*. Cutting this bevel can be tricky, so to do this safely, I drilled a $3/16$"-dia. hole in the center of the blank and screwed it to a scrap board *(Figs. 12 and 12a)*. In addition to securing the blank, the screw also allows you to rotate the blank so you can bevel all four sides.

To complete the cap, I glued a round, hardwood knob to the top *(Fig. 9a)*. (I used a dowel pin to strengthen the joint.) Then the cap can be glued to the top.

Just make sure to orient the two pieces so the grain is running in the same direction.

Finally, I applied a couple of coats of oil finish to the lantern and added the light bulb assembly.

Note: To allow the panels to slide up and down freely, I tried to avoid getting any finish in the grooves of the posts. ■

Trim the rice paper backing to match the size of the panels (or slightly smaller). Then spray the back of the panel with adhesive and press the rice paper in place.

DESIGNER'S NOTEBOOK

With a variety of panels to choose from, you can swap them out when you feel like something different.

PATTERNS

■ Since this is a Holiday Lantern, you may want to build several. Rather than build each with the same motif, I made an assortment of patterns.

This way, you can take your pick from four completely different scroll-sawn scenes, all with a unique rice paper backing (photo above).

In addition to the candle, you have a choice of an outdoor scene (photo and pattern below left), tree ornaments (center), or Santa's stocking (right).

ENLARGE 200%

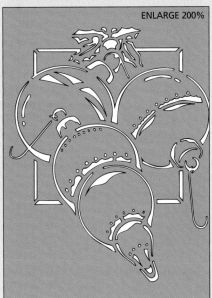

ENLARGE 200%

ENLARGE 200%

Jewelry Box

The elegant patterns on this box are not carved — they are first cut out of a hardwood panel with a scroll saw. Then the panel is glued to a second piece of hardwood for a unique, almost-carved look.

      ntricately carved boxes have always intrigued me. It's not what's inside that I find interesting. It's the attention paid to small details and the craftsmanship that make them irresistible. Show me a carved box, and I just have to pick it up and give it a closer look.

Because of this fascination, I've always wanted to build my own carved box, but there's always been a small hitch. I haven't done much carving and I never seem to have the time to learn. Recently though, when I was asked to design another jewelry box, I tried to get around this problem by giving it the "look" of a carved box — without the carving.

The solution wasn't too difficult. I created thin scroll-sawn panels for the sides of the box. These are backed up with solid panels. The end result doesn't look like a typical scroll saw project. It looks more like it's been carved.

SCROLL SAW DESIGNS. There are actually two different scroll saw designs you can choose for the box (see the Designer's Notebook on page 61). The Jewelry Box was initially designed with the dove patterns in the photo above.

Then someone mentioned that the box would make a great holiday project (to hold cards or candy). So there's also a poinsettia pattern with bells.

And if you really want to "brighten" the scroll saw pattern, you can back it up with brass instead of wood (see the Designer's Notebook on page 60). This requires only a minor modification, and I'll show you how to work with brass in the Technique article on page 68.

WOOD SOURCES. Each piece of the Jewelry Box is made from stock that is $1/2$" thick or less. An inexpensive way to end up with stock this thin is to resaw it yourself. (Refer to the Technique article on page 65 for more on this.) But there are other sources of thin stock, like hobby and craft stores, and woodworking mail-order catalogs. (See Sources, page 126.)

EXPLODED VIEW

OVERALL DIMENSIONS:
$10\frac{1}{2}$W x $7\frac{1}{2}$D x $5\frac{1}{2}$H

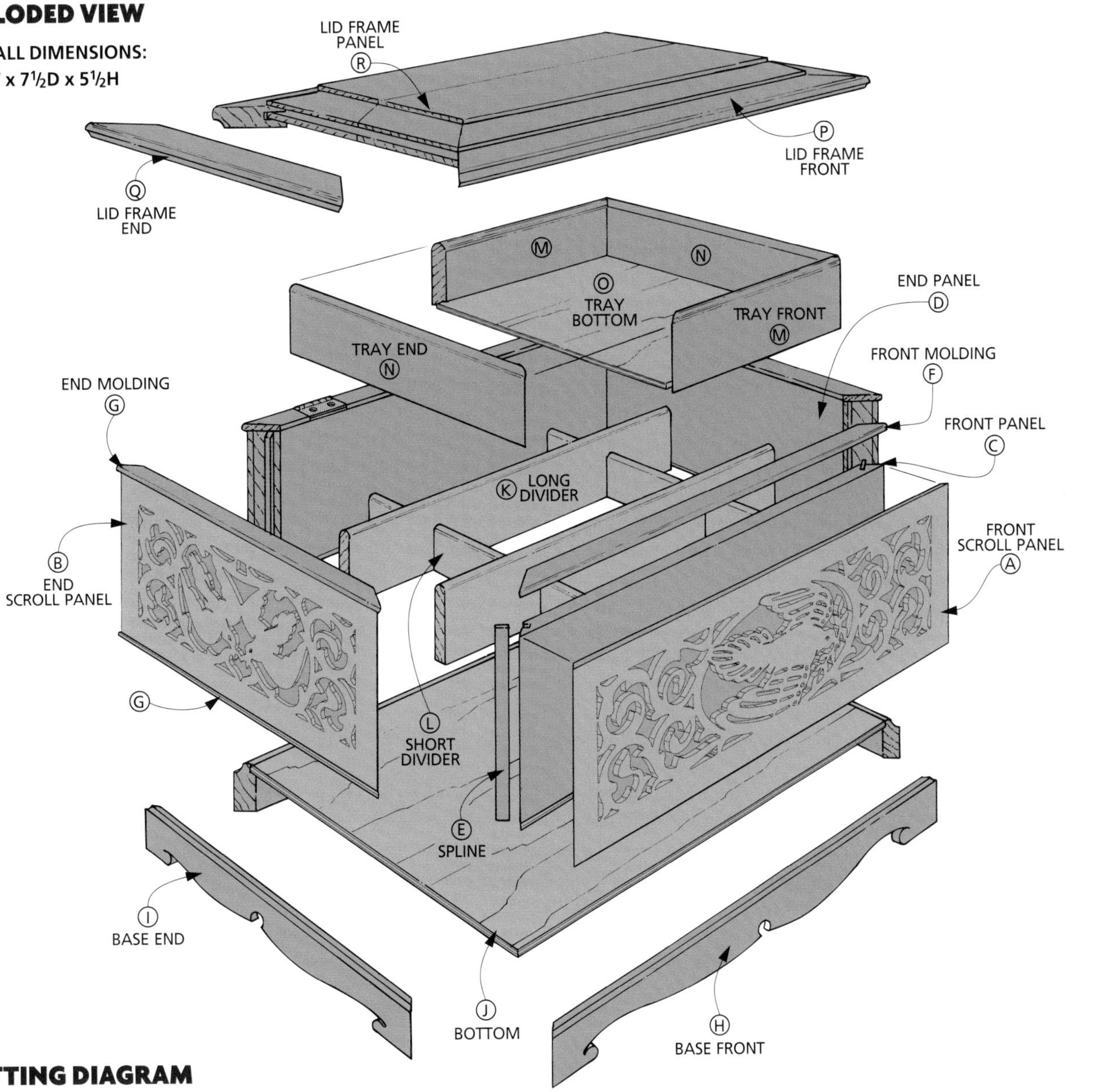

LID FRAME PANEL
R
P
LID FRAME FRONT
Q
LID FRAME END
M
N
O
TRAY BOTTOM
TRAY FRONT
M
TRAY END
N
END PANEL
D
FRONT MOLDING
F
END MOLDING
G
FRONT PANEL
C
K LONG DIVIDER
FRONT SCROLL PANEL
A
B
END SCROLL PANEL
G
L
SHORT DIVIDER
E
SPLINE
I
BASE END
J
BOTTOM
H
BASE FRONT

CUTTING DIAGRAM

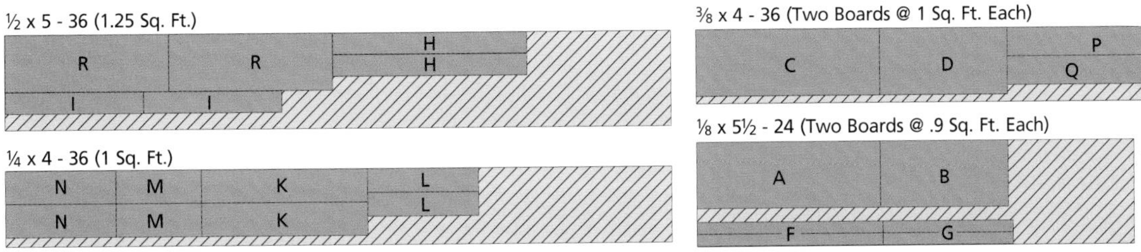

½ x 5 - 36 (1.25 Sq. Ft.)
R R H H I I
¼ x 4 - 36 (1 Sq. Ft.)
N M K L L N M K
⅜ x 4 - 36 (Two Boards @ 1 Sq. Ft. Each)
C D P Q
⅛ x 5½ - 24 (Two Boards @ .9 Sq. Ft. Each)
A B F G

ALSO NEEDED:
ONE 24" x 24" SHEET OF ¼" PLYWOOD FOR CASE AND TRAY BOTTOMS. SPLINES ARE CUT FROM WASTE

MATERIALS LIST

WOOD

A Front/Back Scroll Panels (2)	⅛ x 3½ - 10	
B End Scroll Panels (2)	⅛ x 3½ - 7	
C Front/Back Panels (2)	⅜ x 3½ - 10	
D End Panels (2)	⅜ x 3½ - 7	
E Splines (4)	⅛ x 5⁄16 - 3½	
F Front/Back Molding (4)	⅛ x 9⁄16 - 10⅛	
G End Molding (4)	⅛ x 9⁄16 - 7⅛	
H Base Front/Back (2)	½ x 1⅛ - 10½	
I Base Ends (2)	½ x 1⅛ - 7½	
J Bottom (1)	¼ ply - 6¾ x 9¾	
K Long Dividers (2)	¼ x 1¾ - 9	
L Short Dividers (2)	¼ x 1¼ - 6	
M Tray Front/Back (2)	¼ x 1¾ - 4½	
N Tray Ends (2)	¼ x 1¾ - 6	
O Tray Bottom (1)	¼ ply - 4¼ x 5¾	
P Lid Frame Front/Back (2)	⅜ x 1 - 10½	
Q Lid Frame Ends (2)	⅜ x 1 - 7½	
R Lid Frame Panel (1)	½ x 5⅞ - 8⅞	

HARDWARE SUPPLIES

(2) ¾" x 1" brass hinges w/ screws

For this box, I started with the pieces that attract the most attention: the scroll-sawn panels *(Fig. 1)*. I decided to use the dove patterns for my box. (Refer to the Designer's Notebook on page 61.)

There's also a holiday pattern featuring poinsettias, if you prefer.

SCROLL PANELS. To make the panels, you'll need to plane (or resaw) some stock down to ⅛" thick. (There's more on resawing stock in the Technique article on page 65.) Then the front (A), back (A), and end (B) scroll panels can be ripped 3½" wide and cut to rough length. (Mine were 12" and 9" long.)

Note: To create full-sized patterns for the panels, you'll need to enlarge the patterns shown in the Designer's Notebook on page 61 to 250%. If your copier won't enlarge this much, you can first enlarge them 200%, and then once more at 125%.

When attaching the patterns to the blanks, I used a spray mount adhesive because it's quick and clean, but rubber cement will also work *(Fig. 2)*. Also, to cut my scroll sawing time in half, I glued the two matching panels together (again, using spray mount adhesive) so each pattern only had to be cut once.

Before sitting down at the scroll saw, you'll first need to drill ¹/₁₆"-dia. starter holes in each inside section for blade access (see *Fig. 2a* and the photo). When cutting away the pattern, start with the small openings, leaving the largest ones for last. Then brush a little paint thinner along the joint line of the panels, let it soak in a bit, and gently pry them apart.

BACK-UP PANELS. With the scroll panels complete, I backed them up so the case sides would be thicker than ⅛". So I cut front (C), back (C), and end (D) panels from ⅜"-thick stock to the same rough size as the scroll saw panels *(Fig. 3)*. (To give the box a slightly different look, see the Designer's Notebook on page 60.)

But, before gluing the panels together, I applied a couple of coats of finish. (See the Finishing Tip on page 60.) This is a bit unusual, but with the panels glued together, it would be easy to let too much finish "puddle" into the tiny openings.

With the pre-finishing done, each scroll and backing panel can be glued together *(Fig. 3)*. Then they can be mitered to final length *(Fig. 4)*.

To strengthen the miters in these small pieces, I added hardwood splines. Cutting the kerfs that hold them isn't any trouble *(Fig. 5)*. But when cutting the splines (E), you need to make sure their grain direction is correct with the grain running across the width of the splines. (See the Technique on the next page.)

With the splines cut, the case can be glued together. As with any project, if it goes together square, the rest of the project will go that much easier. (In fact, you may want to cut a spacer to set inside as a kind of squaring form.)

MOLDING. At this point, the faces of the case look great, but the joint lines and splines on the edges are visible. So I

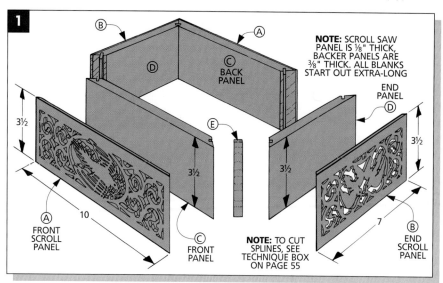

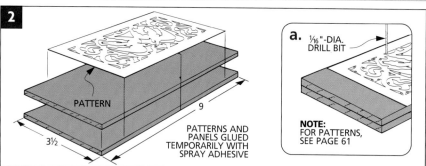

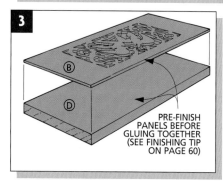

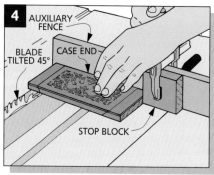

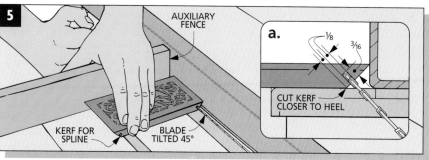

When it's time to cut splines to fit the miters, it's important to pay attention to the grain direction.

CROSS-GRAIN SPLINES. In order to get the strongest possible joint, the grain on the spline should run across the "width" rather than the "length" of the spline *(Fig. 1)*.

CUT KERFS. To cut the splines, I stood a board on end, raised the blade a little over 1" and cut two kerfs *(Figs. 1 and 1a)*. Flip the piece between passes to keep the thickness of the splines identical. (To support the blank, use a tall auxiliary fence or a slot cutting jig.)

CUT SPLINES FREE. Then lower the blade and place the board face down to cut each spline free *(Figs. 2 and 2a)*.

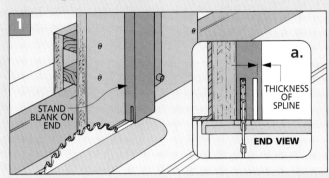

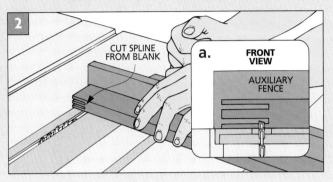

added ⅛"-thick front (F), back (F), and end (G) molding to the edges *(Fig. 6)*.

These pieces should end up the same thickness and width as the hinges used on the lid later. (Mine were ⅛" thick and ⁹⁄₁₆" wide.) But I found that the small roundover on the molding is easier (and safer) to make if the blanks start out extra wide (2") *(Fig. 7)*.

To round over the edge of the molding, I used a ¹⁄₁₆" roundover bit *(Fig. 7)*. But if you don't have this bit, don't worry. You can simply knock off the edges with a block plane and then sand the roundover by hand.

Now the molding pieces can be ripped to width (⁹⁄₁₆") *(Fig. 8)*. Then you can miter them to length and glue them to the box flush with the inside edges *(Figs. 6 and 6a)*. However, don't glue all the pieces in place at this point. The top back molding is mitered to length now, but it won't be glued in place until after the hinges (and lid) are attached later. (Refer to *Figs. 19 and 20* on page 59.)

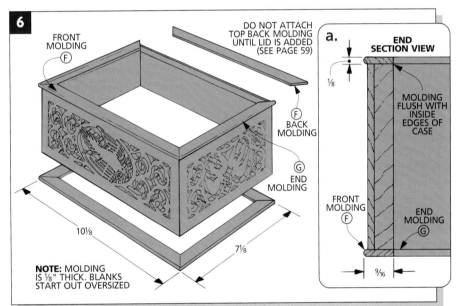

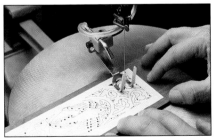

Before cutting the scroll saw designs, a pattern is temporarily glued to each piece and some access holes are drilled.

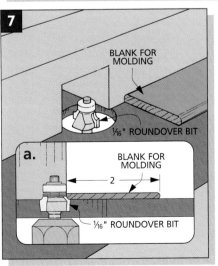

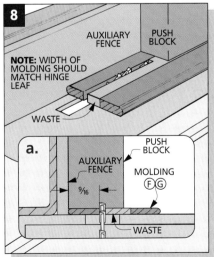

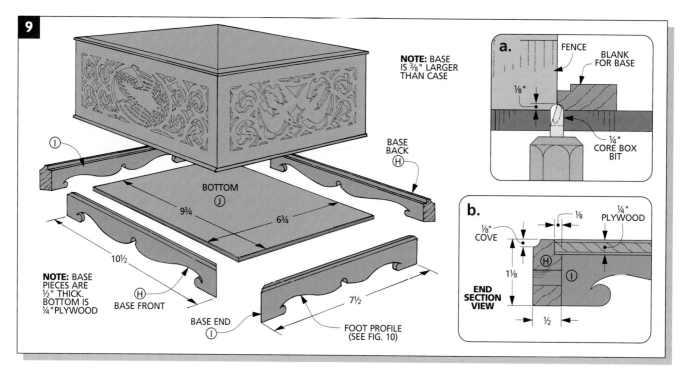

9

NOTE: BASE IS ³⁄₈" LARGER THAN CASE

BASE BACK (H)

BOTTOM (J)

9³⁄₄

6³⁄₄

10½

(I)

NOTE: BASE PIECES ARE ½" THICK. BOTTOM IS ¼" PLYWOOD

(H) BASE FRONT

BASE END (I)

7½

FOOT PROFILE (SEE FIG. 10)

a. FENCE — BLANK FOR BASE — ¹⁄₈" — ¼" CORE BOX BIT

b. ¹⁄₈" COVE — ¹⁄₈ — ¹⁄₈ — ¼" PLYWOOD — (H) — (I) — 1¹⁄₈ — ½ — END SECTION VIEW

BASE

The case sides are now complete. The next section to work on is the base and the bottom (*Fig. 9*). With all the scroll work on the sides of the case, it seemed like a good idea to leave the scroll saw out and give the base a few curves as well. So I built a base that featured a foot profile with a graceful curve.

BASE BLANKS. The four base pieces are cut from ¹⁄₂"-thick stock (*Fig. 9b*). I ripped the base front (H), back (H), and ends (I) to finished width (1¹⁄₈") but left them extra long while I did a little work at the router table.

When the base is assembled later, a small rabbet on the inside edges of the base pieces will hold a ¹⁄₄" plywood bottom (*Fig. 9*). So I routed a ¹⁄₄" wide,

¹⁄₈"-deep rabbet on each base piece to hold the plywood (*Fig. 9b*).

On the outside edges, I routed a ¹⁄₈"-radius cove. You may not have a cove bit this small, but a ¹⁄₄"-dia. core box bit will also do the trick (*Fig. 9a*).

Note: There's only one real difference between these two router bits. A cove bit has a bearing on top, while a core box bit doesn't.

After the cove detail has been routed on the top edge, the base pieces can be mitered to final length (*Fig. 9*). They should end up ³⁄₈" longer than the molding on the edges of the case.

When the base pieces are cut to final length, you can start on the profiles that create the "feet" on the bottom edges. As before, the first thing to do is create some full-size patterns. The ones shown

below need to be enlarged 200%. Then you can mount them to the base pieces the same way you mounted the scroll saw patterns earlier. (Again, I used spray mount adhesive to do this.)

Most of the decorative profile on the base pieces will be cut with the scroll saw. But I drilled a hole for the circular opening in the center first (*Fig. 10a*). (A ³⁄₈"-dia. Forstner or brad point bit will work best.) Drilling this hole ensures the opening will be perfectly round and will make the curves a little easier to cut.

After the profile has been cut and sanded smooth, the base is about ready to be assembled. All you need to do is cut a ¹⁄₄" plywood bottom panel (J) to fit the rabbets (*Fig. 9*). This will keep the base square and strong, so the miters don't need splines (unlike the case).

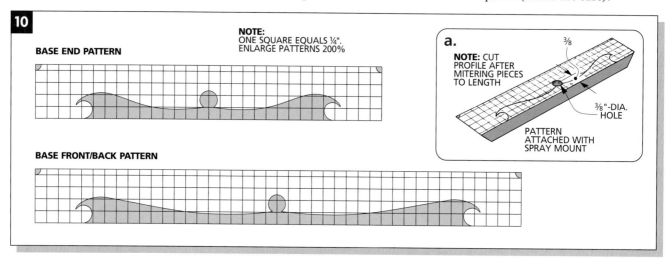

10

BASE END PATTERN

NOTE: ONE SQUARE EQUALS ¼". ENLARGE PATTERNS 200%

BASE FRONT/BACK PATTERN

a. NOTE: CUT PROFILE AFTER MITERING PIECES TO LENGTH — ³⁄₈ — ³⁄₈"-DIA. HOLE — PATTERN ATTACHED WITH SPRAY MOUNT

With the base glued together, it can be glued to the case. Just make sure the two are centered evenly.

DIVIDERS & TRAY

As I mentioned earlier, this box could be made into a holiday box for cards or candy. But for the Jewelry Box, I added a divider grid to keep the jewelry organized *(Fig. 11)*. And I also added a tray to slide along the top of the divider *(Fig. 14)*.

Note: If you're building a holiday version of the box, you can skip the procedure for making the dividers and tray and go on to building the lid.

GRID. The divider grid consists of four $1/4$"-thick workpieces that interlock with edge half laps *(Fig. 11)*.

What's a little unusual here is that the four divider pieces aren't the same height. The long dividers (K) are taller than the short dividers (L) *(Fig. 11a)*. This way, when the tray is set on top of the long dividers later, it will slide smoothly back and forth, because the short dividers won't get in the way.

After the dividers were cut to size, I cut two notches in each one *(Fig. 12)*. The width of the notches equals the thickness of the pieces ($1/4$") *(Fig. 12a)*. And the depth is half the height (width) of the short dividers.

Before the dividers are assembled, the last thing to do is round over their top edges *(Figs. 13 and 13a)*. Then, carefully apply some glue to the shoulders of the notches, and hold the divider grids together until the glue starts to set.

TRAY. In addition to the dividers, I also built a small tray to fit in the case *(Fig. 14)*. It slides back and forth along the two long dividers *(Fig. 14a)*.

I made my tray $1 3/4$"-tall, but the important thing is to size the pieces to allow a little clearance above the tray when it's set on the dividers *(Fig. 14a)*. (This will give you room to add an optional satin liner under the dividers later.) The tray front and back (M) are mitered $4 1/2$" long. The tray ends (N) can be mitered to fit between the front and back of the case. (Mine were 6" long.)

Like the dividers, the top edges of the small tray feature a simple roundover. And when that's routed, a $1/8$"-deep rabbet can be cut along the bottom inside edges to hold a $1/4$" plywood bottom. Then after the bottom panel (O) is cut to size, the tray can be glued together, and you can move on to the lid.

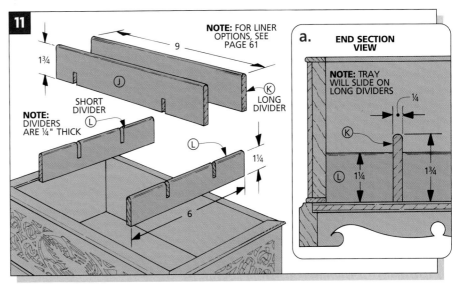

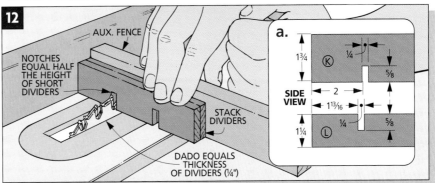

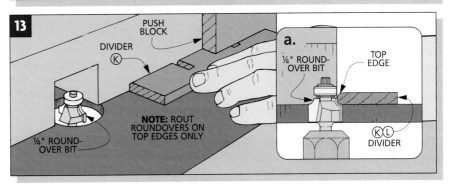

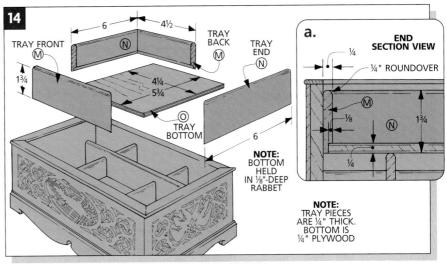

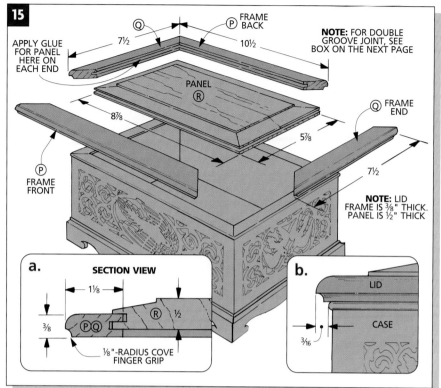

15

Q · P FRAME BACK

APPLY GLUE FOR PANEL HERE ON EACH END

7½ · 10½

NOTE: FOR DOUBLE GROOVE JOINT, SEE BOX ON THE NEXT PAGE

PANEL R

8⅞

Q FRAME END

5⅞

P FRAME FRONT

7½

NOTE: LID FRAME IS ⅜" THICK. PANEL IS ½" THICK.

a. SECTION VIEW

1⅛

⅜

P Q · R · ½

⅛"-RADIUS COVE FINGER GRIP

b.

LID

CASE

3/16

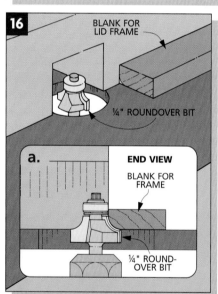

16

BLANK FOR LID FRAME

¼" ROUNDOVER BIT

a. END VIEW

BLANK FOR FRAME

¼" ROUND-OVER BIT

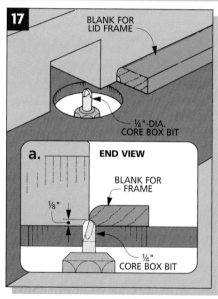

17

BLANK FOR LID FRAME

¼"-DIA. CORE BOX BIT

a. END VIEW

BLANK FOR FRAME

⅛"

¼" CORE BOX BIT

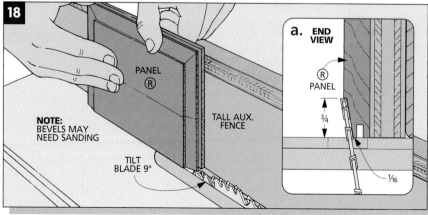

18

PANEL R

NOTE: BEVELS MAY NEED SANDING

TALL AUX. FENCE

TILT BLADE 9°

a. END VIEW

R PANEL

¾

1/16

LID

Other than a few finishing touches, the only thing left to build on this Jewelry Box is the lid *(Fig. 15)*. The lid is a frame and panel assembly, but what's a little unusual is that the raised panel stands proud of the frame, so it requires some slightly different joinery *(Fig. 15a)*. (More on that later.)

LID FRAME. I first ripped some ⅜"-thick stock 1" wide for the lid frame front (P), back (P), and ends (Q) *(Fig. 15a)*.

But before mitering the frame pieces to length, I routed the profiles on the outside edges. First, I routed a ¼" roundover on the top, outside edges *(Fig. 16)*. Then, to create a slight finger grip along the bottom edge, I routed a ⅛" cove *(Fig. 17)*.

After these profiles have been routed, the frame pieces can be mitered to finished length *(Fig. 15)*. And like the base, these pieces are cut ⅜" longer than the case molding *(Fig. 15b)*.

LID PANEL. Before you can complete the lid frame, you'll need to cut the lid panel (R) to finished size from ½"-thick stock *(Fig. 15)*. To do this, dry-assemble the frame and measure the opening. The panel should be cut ⅜" larger than this opening. (Mine was 5⅞" x 8⅞".)

DOUBLE GROOVE JOINT. With the panel cut to size, the next thing to do is cut the double groove joint that locks them together. This is a simple procedure and only requires one setup. (See the Joinery box on the next page.) But the setup has to be done carefully, so you'll need a couple of test pieces. (Make them ½" thick so you can also use them to set up the cut for the raised field.)

RAISED FIELD. The frame pieces are now complete. All that's left on the lid is to create the raised field *(Fig. 18)*. Here, the test pieces used earlier will come in handy. Tilt the saw blade 9°, raise it ¾", and add a tall auxiliary fence for support *(Fig. 18a)*. Sneak up on the position of the fence until the shoulder above the groove is 1/16". (The shoulder of the raised field should also be close to 1/16".)

When the tall auxiliary fence is set, you can cut the bevels on the lid panel *(Fig. 18)*. (You may also need to clean up the bevel with sandpaper if the saw blade leaves swirl marks.)

LID ASSEMBLY. Now you can glue the frame around the panel. Getting four mitered frame pieces glued up around a panel (without getting any glue in the grooves) can be a trick. So to make this procedure less hectic, I glued up the two corners of the frame first. Then I glued the two halves around the panel. And to hold the panel in place, put a drop of glue in the grooves at the center of each end piece only *(Fig. 15)*.

ATTACH TO CASE. At this point, both the lid and case are complete, so they can be put together. This lid is easier than most to attach because you don't have to cut any hinge mortises. The top back molding (F) that wasn't glued in place earlier will take care of this. I cut the mitered ends of this piece $1\frac{1}{2}$" long and glued them in place *(Fig. 19)*.

Now the $\frac{3}{4}$" x 1" brass hinges can be screwed to the case next to the molding *(Fig. 19)*. Then center the lid on top of the case so you can mark out the position of the hinges on the lid *(Fig. 19b)*.

After you've got the hinges screwed to both the lid and the case back, you still need to remove the lid one more time. This way, you can fill in the gap between the hinges with the leftover piece of molding *(Fig. 20)*. And before reattaching the lid, it's a good idea to go ahead and apply the finish to the case and lid first.

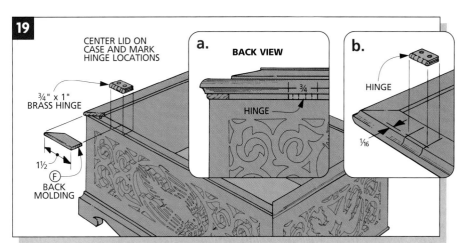

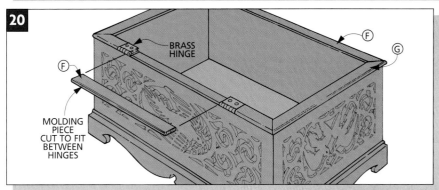

JOINERY .... *Double Groove Frame & Panel*

For the lid on this Jewelry Box, the panel is a solid wood piece that's raised above the face of the frame. This means the frame and panel have to be joined in a way that allows the panel to expand and contract with seasonal changes in humidity.

To do this, I used an interlocking double groove joint. It's made by cutting grooves in both the frame pieces and the panel. The grooves are positioned to leave tongues that fit in the opposing grooves.

By cutting this joint near the top of the frame, the panel will stand proud of the frame when it's assembled *(Fig. 1a)*.

This double groove joint only requires one setup on the table saw, but it has to be made carefully. I added an auxiliary fence to support the panel (when standing on end). Then I set the rip fence exactly one saw blade's width away from the blade *(Fig. 1)*. This allows the pieces to interlock properly. (For test pieces, I used $\frac{1}{2}$"-thick stock. I used these

same pieces for setting up the raised field cut later.)

When the fence and blade were set, I cut all the grooves on the frame pieces, making

sure their *top* faces were against the fence *(Fig. 2)*. Then I cut the grooves with the *bottom* face of the lid panel against the rip fence *(Fig. 3)*.

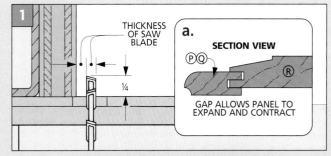

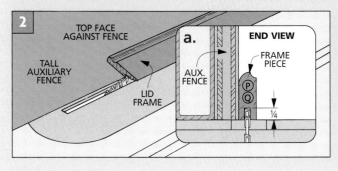

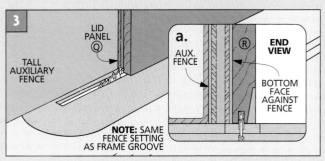

To keep too much finish from "puddling" in the cutouts, apply the finish to the panels before they are glued together. (I used a wipe-on finish to keep things simple.)

However, you don't want finish on the areas where you need to apply the glue. So first, tape the edges off on the inside face of the scroll-sawn panels and the outside face of the backer panels (see left photo). After the finish dries, carefully remove the masking tape and glue the panels together (right photo).

FINISHING & LINER

Since the scroll work was "finished" earlier, you've already gotten a head start on the last step in wrapping up the project. To complete the process, I applied a coat of the same finish used earlier to the insides of the case, the lid, and the base. Then a couple more coats can be applied to the entire box. However, I didn't try to get finish into the tiny scroll sawn openings. Here, I used a folded, lint-free rag, carefully wiping it so as not to catch the points of the scroll work.

OPTIONAL LINER. After the finish had dried, I added a padded liner to the inside of the case and the tray — kind of like pillows for the jewelry to rest on.

Note: The liner is optional. I thought it added a touch of class to the box.

The liner is a piece of cardboard and batting that's covered with fabric (all purchased at a fabric store). The cardboard is cut $1/16$" short of the case opening in length and width. Then it's set on a piece of batting that's about $1/16$" thick.

Note: I used the cardboard as a template to cut the batting.

For the fabric, I chose a piece of satin, cutting it 2" larger than the cardboard.

DESIGNER'S NOTEBOOK

Brass sheet brings out the "luster" in the Jewelry Box.

BRASS BACKING

■ As soon as the Jewelry Box was complete, it was suggested that I should have put a thin piece of sheet brass behind the scroll work. I agreed. The brass would really highlight the scroll saw design and make the box a great, one-of-a-kind "jewel" in itself. (I did the same thing with the Bookends shown on page 62.)

■ In order to slide a piece of brass sheet behind the scroll work, a shallow channel has to be cut in the front (C), back (C), and end (D) panels *(Fig. 1)*. This isn't difficult to do, but you need to do it before gluing the scroll saw panel and the backing panel together.

■ I used a $1/2$"-dia. straight bit in the router table to create a smooth channel. Set the bit a fraction of an inch higher than the thickness of the 30-gauge brass *(Fig. 1a)*. You should be able to easily slide the brass sheet in place.

■ After you've routed the channel, cut the brass sheet to fit inside. (See page 126 for sources of brass sheet stock.) I sandwiched the brass between two strips of wood and used a carbide tipped table saw blade to do this.

■ Then sand, buff, and polish the brass to bring out its luster. A coat of spray-on lacquer will prevent tarnishing. (See the Technique article on page 68 for more on this.) But don't slide the brass into place until you're ready to glue the case together *(Fig. 2)*.

MATERIALS LIST

HARDWARE SUPPLIES
(2) 30-gauge brass strips (3" x $6^3/4$" rough)
(2) 30-gauge brass strips (3" x $9^3/4$" rough)

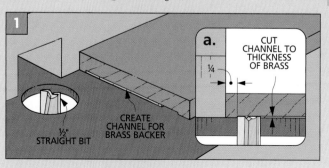

1

$1/2$" STRAIGHT BIT

CREATE CHANNEL FOR BRASS BACKER

a.

$1/4$

CUT CHANNEL TO THICKNESS OF BRASS

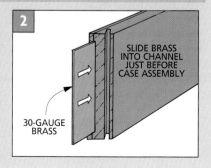

2

SLIDE BRASS INTO CHANNEL JUST BEFORE CASE ASSEMBLY

30-GAUGE BRASS

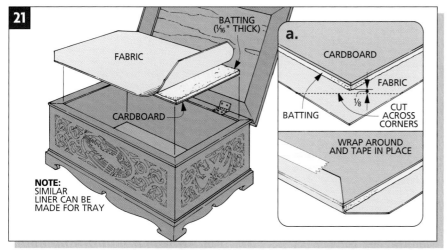

21

BATTING (1/16" THICK)

FABRIC

CARDBOARD

NOTE: SIMILAR LINER CAN BE MADE FOR TRAY

a.

CARDBOARD

FABRIC

BATTING

1/8

CUT ACROSS CORNERS

WRAP AROUND AND TAPE IN PLACE

Complete this elegant Jewelry Box with a stylish padded lining made from a piece of cardboard, some cotton batting, and your choice of fabric covering.

And to make it easier to wrap around the cardboard, I trimmed the corners of the fabric. Simply lay it good face down with the cardboard on top and cut across the corners, leaving about 1/8" (*Fig. 21a*).

Now you're ready to put the liner together. To do this, lay the fabric good face down and set the batting and cardboard on top. Then put strips of tape on the fabric and fold it over the cardboard. Try to pull the fabric evenly, or you may end up with ripples. And if there are little "ears" of fabric at the corners, you can either fold them under and tape or glue them in place, or set the liner in place and carefully tuck the ears down into the corners of the box. ■

DESIGNER'S NOTEBOOK

Choose between two patterns for the Jewelry Box: doves or a holiday poinsettia with bells.

PATTERNS

■ Cutting the dove scroll saw pattern for my Jewelry Box was a lot of fun. So I decided to build a second, holiday version of the box. For this one, I used the poinsettia pattern seen below.

■ Before you can do any scroll sawing for either project, though, you'll need to resize the patterns, enlarging each one by 250%. (If your copier won't handle 250%, start at 200%, then do it again at 125%.)

■ Now attach the pattern to the panel with spray adhesive (or you could use rubber cement), then drill the access holes, and cut out the waste with a fine-tooth (20-25 tpi) scroll saw blade.

SCROLL SAW PATTERNS (ENLARGE 250%)

Bookends

The scroll-sawn panels and brass plates make these Bookends both attractive and functional. A variety of customizing options are available, including three distinct scroll saw patterns and optional brass backing.

Many of us have good friends who are avid readers and a few that like to just collect books. So this year, I decided to make several sets of Bookends to give away as gifts.

Not your plain, purely functional type of bookend — I wanted something a bit more elegant. Something that would give you a sense of pride while displaying a few favorite hardbound volumes. And for a change of pace, I also wanted to do a little work at the scroll saw.

After a little thought, my solution was to capture a scroll-sawn panel in a mitered picture frame. This frame sits on a hardwood base with molding details and a rounded brass tongue on the bottom that sticks out and slides under the books.

SCROLL SAW PATTERNS. When it came to designing the patterns, I had a couple of ideas but needed some help putting them on paper. (I'm not much of an artist. But don't worry, you don't need to be either.) Instead, I had one of the *Woodsmith* illustrators take a shot at turning my ideas into scroll saw patterns.

My first idea was a pineapple pattern (a traditional symbol of hospitality). The other was less specific. I wanted a classic fretwork design. Our illustrator did a great job with both patterns and even came up with one of his own — a stag.

You'll find everything you need to get started with the patterns shown in the Designer's Notebook on the next page.

But if you have some artistic talent, don't limit yourself to these ideas; come up with some of your own. And experiment with different woods, too. I even backed up one of the scroll saw panels with a thin sheet of brass. (See the Designer's Notebook on page 67.)

BRASS. Working with brass is a lot like working with wood. It's a soft metal that cuts easily with carbide-tipped tools. And even though it might seem a little tricky at first, working with brass is fun. (See the Technique article on page 68 for more.)

EXPLODED VIEW

OVERALL DIMENSIONS:
7¼W x 5D x 8¼H

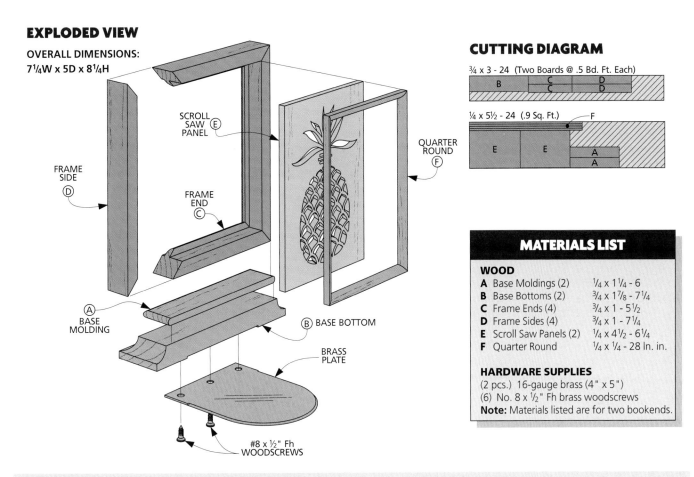

SCROLL SAW PANEL Ⓔ

QUARTER ROUND Ⓕ

FRAME SIDE Ⓓ

FRAME END Ⓒ

Ⓐ BASE MOLDING

Ⓑ BASE BOTTOM

BRASS PLATE

#8 x ½" Fh WOODSCREWS

CUTTING DIAGRAM

¾ x 3 - 24 (Two Boards @ .5 Bd. Ft. Each)

B | C | D
C | D

¼ x 5½ - 24 (.9 Sq. Ft.)   F

E | E | A
A

MATERIALS LIST

WOOD
A Base Moldings (2)   ¼ x 1¼ - 6
B Base Bottoms (2)   ¾ x 1⅞ - 7¼
C Frame Ends (4)   ¾ x 1 - 5½
D Frame Sides (4)   ¾ x 1 - 7¼
E Scroll Saw Panels (2)   ¼ x 4½ - 6¼
F Quarter Round   ¼ x ¼ - 28 ln. in.

HARDWARE SUPPLIES
(2 pcs.) 16-gauge brass (4" x 5")
(6) No. 8 x ½" Fh brass woodscrews
Note: Materials listed are for two bookends.

DESIGNER'S NOTEBOOK

Choose a pattern that features basic cuts, an outdoor scene, or hone your skills with intricate fretwork.

PATTERNS

■ The first pattern is of a pineapple. Popular in a country or traditional decor, it is a simple pattern to cut.

■ The next pattern, a stag, is a nice project for a den or family room. The detail makes this pattern a challenge.

■ The final pattern is a fretwork design with lots of cutouts that make it a perfect project for experienced scrollers.

ENLARGE 200%

ENLARGE 200%

ENLARGE 200%

As you will see, each Bookend is really just a small picture frame that sits on top of a base *(Fig. 1)*. I started with the base, which is two pieces of solid wood, plus a rounded brass plate. A scroll saw panel and the frame it sits in come later.

MOLDING. The first piece to work on is the base molding (A) *(Fig. 1)*. It's only $\frac{1}{4}$" thick so you'll have to plane down or resaw some stock first. If you're using a thickness planer, a lot of wood ends up on the shop floor as sawdust. A good alternative (especially if you don't have a planer) is to resaw some $\frac{3}{4}$"-thick stock using the table saw. (See the Technique article on the next page for more on this.) A hand plane will clean up the saw marks.

With $\frac{1}{4}$"-thick stock in hand, you can cut the molding to rough size. I cut mine to finished length (6"), but left it extra wide at this point ($3\frac{1}{2}$"). This not only made the piece safer to work with, it also allowed me to cut two molding pieces from each blank. (Though there's only one Bookend shown in *Fig. 1*, I actually made them in pairs.)

Next, I rounded over the edges of the oversized blank with a $\frac{1}{8}$" roundover bit *(Fig. 2)*. Since two pieces are being cut from this blank, all four edges need to be routed, not just three. And I started with the ends first so there's less chance of chipout. Finally, I added an auxiliary top to my router table. It's just a piece of $\frac{1}{4}$" hardboard with a smaller bit opening to give the base pieces extra support.

BOTTOM. After the molding pieces were ripped to width ($1\frac{1}{4}$"), the next piece to make is the base bottom (B) *(Fig. 1)*. This piece will end up a little bigger than the molding ($1\frac{7}{8}$" x $7\frac{1}{4}$"). But it also starts out oversized, and two pieces will be cut from a single blank.

The first thing to do to the bottom blank is rout a cove with a $\frac{1}{2}$" cove bit *(Fig. 3)*. Again, I routed the profile on all four edges of the blank and supported the workpiece with a square push block. Then the two bottom pieces can be ripped to finished width ($1\frac{7}{8}$").

RECESS FOR BRASS PLATE. To keep the bookend (and books) from falling over, a brass plate is set into the bottom. So the next thing to do is rout the recess that holds the plate *(Fig. 4)*. The recess is about $\frac{1}{16}$" deep, but the important thing is that it match the thickness of the brass.

To establish the size of the recess, I used an auxiliary fence with a couple of

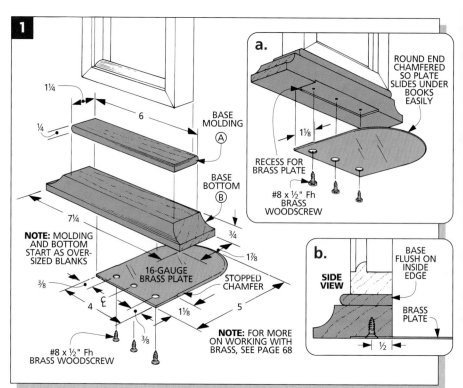

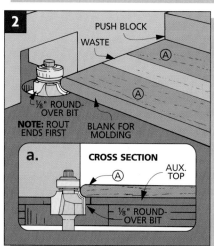

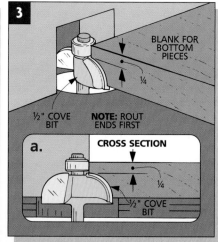

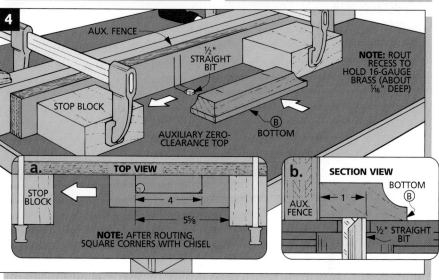

stop blocks clamped on either side of a straight bit *(Fig. 4)*. With a 1/2" straight bit, it will be necessary to make a few passes between the blocks. And after routing, the round corners will need to be squared up with a chisel.

Gluing the molding to the bottom piece is pretty simple. First, the molding is centered side-to-side *(Fig. 1)*. And second, the pieces should be flush along the back edge *(Fig. 1b)*.

BRASS PLATE. The brass plate is cut to size next, and the process isn't much different from the woodworking you've already done. (For more on working with brass, see the Technique on page 68.)

With the plate cut to size, I rounded the end with a hardboard template, a jig saw, and a flush trim bit. (This is covered in more detail on page 68.)

Finally, to make it easier to slide the plate under the books, I routed a stopped chamfer around the curve. Then the plate can be screwed to the base *(Fig. 1a)*.

TECHNIQUE . . . . *Resawing Thin Stock*

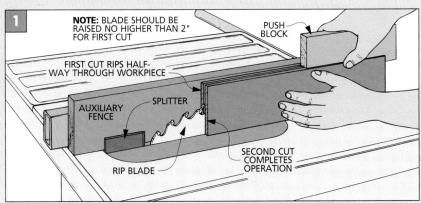

Several of the projects in this book call for thin stock (less than 3/4" thick). Sometimes you can buy thin stock at the lumberyard or through a mail-order catalog, but you'll often pay a premium price.

Another solution is to make thin stock yourself — by resawing a thick piece into two (or more) thinner pieces. This way, the wood costs less, and with just a little extra work, you get the stock the exact thickness you want.

TABLE SAW. Normally, I like to use a band saw for resawing. A sharp 1/2" resaw blade slices through a board like butter and with the thinner kerf on a band saw there is little waste. But if you don't own one, and the pieces you're resawing aren't too wide (up to 6 inches), you can resaw them on an ordinary table saw.

Resawing on the table saw is really just a ripping operation. But instead of the workpiece lying on its face, it's fed through the blade standing on edge.

SET-UP. The first thing I do when setting up my table saw to resaw is to install the proper blade. For the smoothest cut, I like to use a sharp, 24-tooth rip blade. A rip blade is thicker, so there's less tendency for it to flex while cutting.

SPLITTER. Whenever I resaw thin stock on the table saw, I also like to use a zero-clearance insert with a splitter *(Fig. 2)*. The insert prevents the workpiece from slipping down between the blade and the opening. And the splitter keeps the wood from "pinching" the back of the saw blade and kicking back.

There are plenty of nice manufactured inserts available, but I like to make my own out of hardwood. Medium-density fiberboard (MDF) can also be used. I use the insert that came with my saw as a template for laying out the new insert. And I glue in a splitter made out of a piece of 1/8"-thick hardboard *(Fig. 2)*.

Also, since I want as much control over the workpiece as possible, I like to attach a tall auxiliary fence to the saw's rip fence *(Fig. 1)*. This makes things safer because it helps keep the workpiece standing up straight during the resawing.

MAKE CUTS. To make the cut, I set the fence to resaw the board about 1/16" thicker than the final desired thickness. (After I finish resawing, I remove the marks left by the blade with a hand plane or thickness planer.)

Begin resawing by using a push block to feed the board past the blade. Also, be sure to hold the piece tight against the fence. (A featherboard clamped to the saw table can sometimes help.)

Note: Use a push block that hooks over the back of the workpiece *(Fig. 1)*.

I usually make the cut by gradually raising the blade to its full height.

After making the first pass, flip the piece end for end (keeping the same face against the fence) and make a second cut on the opposite edge *(Fig. 1)*.

On stock that's 3" wide or less, try to complete the cut with the second pass. (The fewer cuts the better.) But if the stock is wider than 3", raise the blade in 1/2" increments and run both edges through the saw a second time. Continue raising the blade in 1/2" increments until the cut is complete.

WIDE BOARDS. If the stock is wider than the capacity of your table saw (about 6" for most saws), you can use a hand saw to finish the cut and separate the two pieces. (A rip saw works best.)

There's one other thing to mention. When resawing on the table saw, you may experience small ramps (or gouges) at the start and end points of the resawn piece. To solve this problem, start with a blank that is about 6" longer than the desired length, then cut off the ends after you're done resawing.

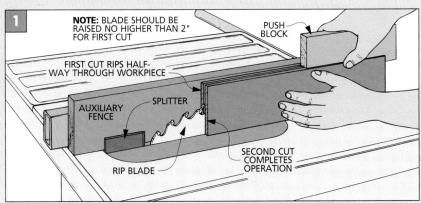

1 NOTE: BLADE SHOULD BE RAISED NO HIGHER THAN 2" FOR FIRST CUT

PUSH BLOCK

FIRST CUT RIPS HALF-WAY THROUGH WORKPIECE

AUXILIARY FENCE

SPLITTER

RIP BLADE

SECOND CUT COMPLETES OPERATION

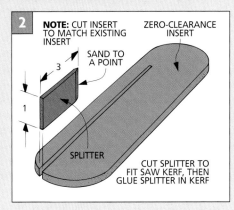

2 NOTE: CUT INSERT TO MATCH EXISTING INSERT

ZERO-CLEARANCE INSERT

SAND TO A POINT

3

1

SPLITTER

CUT SPLITTER TO FIT SAW KERF, THEN GLUE SPLITTER IN KERF

BOOKEND FRAME

Now that the bookend base is built, all that's left is to build a small picture frame and your choice of scroll saw panels to go inside it *(Figs. 5 and 9)*.

FRAME BLANKS. The frame holds the scroll saw panel in the front with built-in molding. Making the frame pieces is an easy three-step process: a roundover is routed, channels are cut to create the rabbets, and then the pieces are cut to width. However, as with the pieces for the base, it's better to start with oversized blanks. So for each frame, I cut one blank from 3/4"-thick stock (3" x 15").

ROUT ROUNDOVER. After the frame blanks were cut to size, I routed a 1/4" roundover along the top outside edges *(Fig. 6)*. This roundover has a shoulder, so the edge of the bit will need to be raised 1/8" above the table *(Fig. 6a)*.

RABBET. Behind the roundover, there will be a shallow rabbet the scroll saw panel fits into. But to safely create the rabbet, two 1/4"-deep channels need to be cut with a 3/4"-wide dado set *(Figs. 7 and 7a)*. Then the pieces can be ripped to width (1") *(Fig. 8)*. Just be sure to position the rip fence so you end up with a 5/8"-wide rabbet *(Fig. 8a)*.

MITER PIECES. Now you can begin mitering these pieces to create the frame. I started with the frame ends (C) *(Fig. 5)*. They should end up 1/2" shorter than the base. Then the frame sides (D) can be mitered to length.

A word of caution, though. These frame pieces (especially the ends) are short. So be careful to keep your hands well away from the saw blade.

ASSEMBLY. With the pieces mitered, the frame can be assembled. Gluing four mitered pieces together at the same time can be a little tricky. So I typically glue up two corners first and then, after the glue has had enough time to set up, glue the two halves together.

When gluing the frame to the base, the inside edges should be flush. To do this, I laid the base back-side down on the edge of my workbench with the brass plate hanging off the edge. Then I glued the frame to the base, using hand pressure. (I didn't want to put any clamping pressure on the miter joints at the top or the roundover profile at the bottom.)

SCROLL SAW PANELS. At this point, you're ready to make the scroll saw panels (E) *(Fig. 9)*. These are 1/4"-thick panels cut to fit in the rabbets.

The first thing to do is choose a pattern from the Designer's Notebook on page 63 and enlarge it 200% on a photocopier. (There are three scroll saw patterns to choose from: a pineapple for a country decor, a stag for the den, or a classic scroll pattern.) Then you can temporarily attach the photocopy to the panel with a spray mount adhesive.

Note: If you're making two panels with the same pattern, you can fasten them back-to-back with some carpet tape. This way, you'll only need to cut the pattern one time.

5

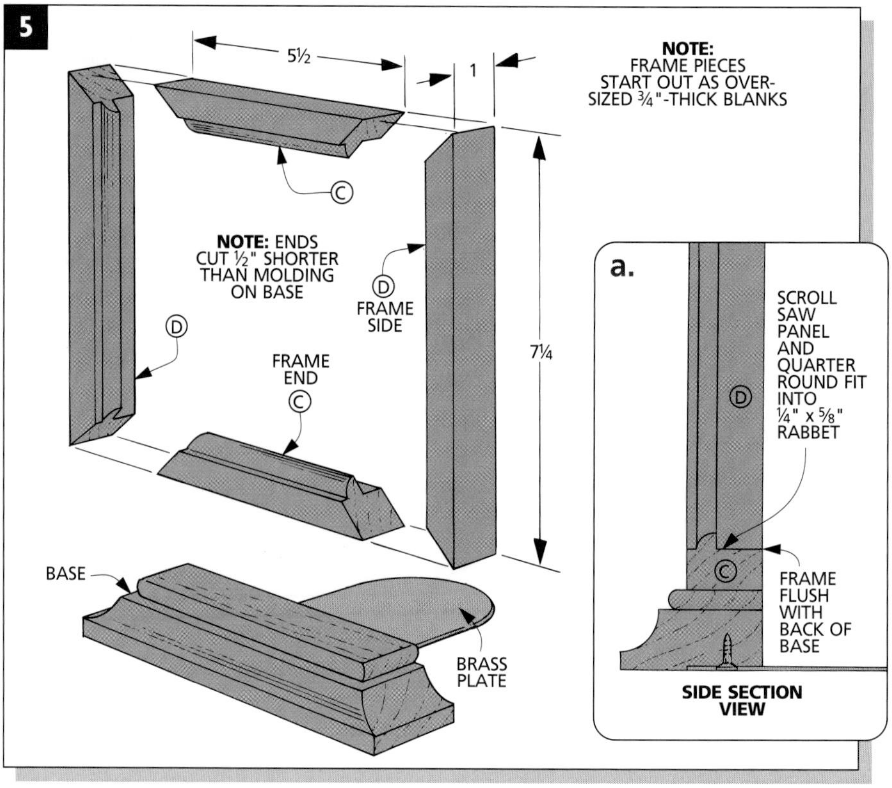
5½
1
NOTE: FRAME PIECES START OUT AS OVERSIZED ¾"-THICK BLANKS
C
NOTE: ENDS CUT ½" SHORTER THAN MOLDING ON BASE
D
FRAME SIDE
D
FRAME END
C
7¼
BASE
BRASS PLATE
a.
SCROLL SAW PANEL AND QUARTER ROUND FIT INTO ¼" x ⅝" RABBET
D
C
FRAME FLUSH WITH BACK OF BASE
SIDE SECTION VIEW

6

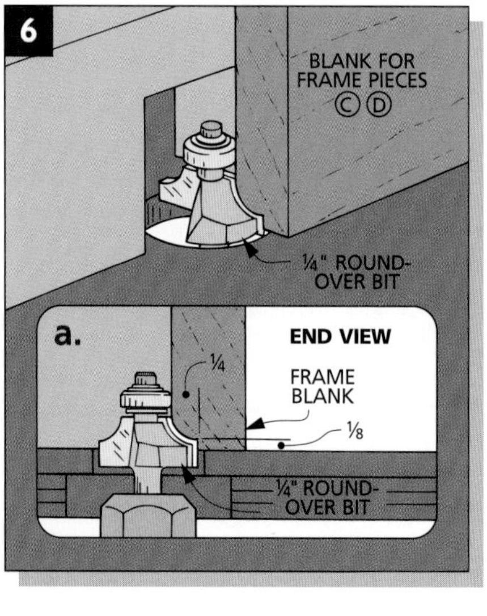
BLANK FOR FRAME PIECES C D
¼" ROUND-OVER BIT
a.
END VIEW
¼
FRAME BLANK
⅛
¼" ROUND-OVER BIT

7

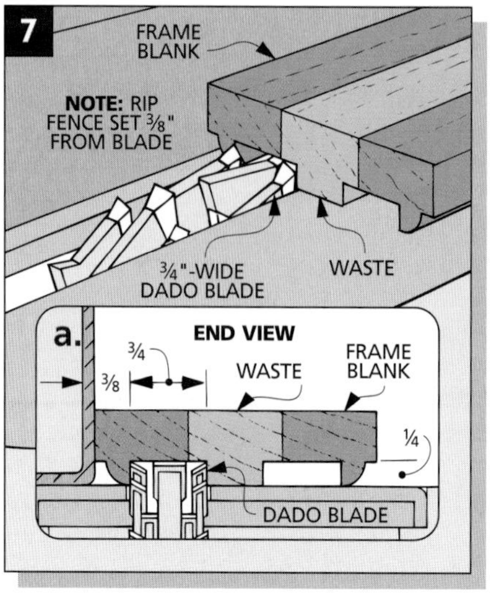
FRAME BLANK
NOTE: RIP FENCE SET ⅜" FROM BLADE
¾"-WIDE DADO BLADE
WASTE
a.
END VIEW
¾
⅜
WASTE
FRAME BLANK
¼
DADO BLADE

8

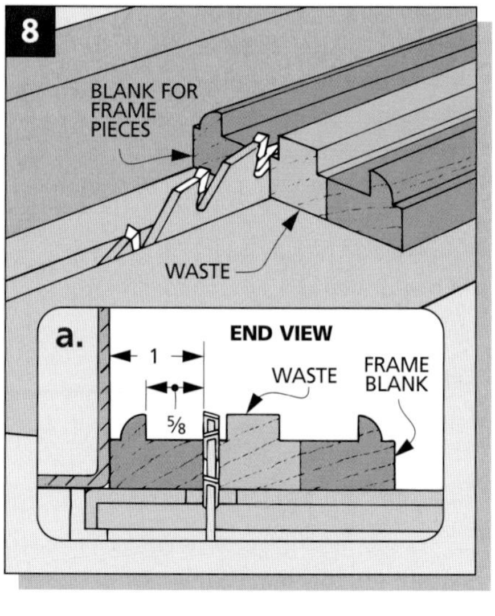
BLANK FOR FRAME PIECES
WASTE
a.
END VIEW
1
⅝
WASTE
FRAME BLANK

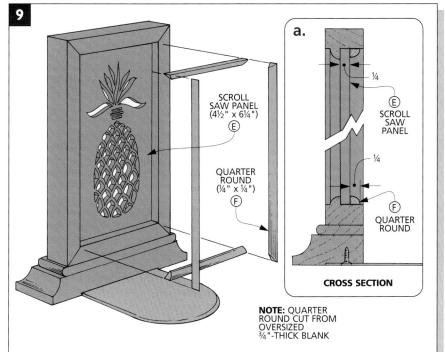

9

SCROLL
SAW PANEL
(4½" x 6¼")
(E)

QUARTER
ROUND
(¼" x ¼")
(F)

a.

¼

(E)
SCROLL
SAW
PANEL

¼

(F)
QUARTER
ROUND

CROSS SECTION

NOTE: QUARTER
ROUND CUT FROM
OVERSIZED
¾"-THICK BLANK

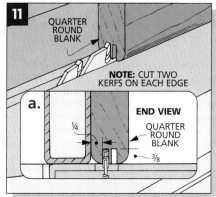

10

QUARTER ROUND
BLANK

¼" ROUNDOVER BIT

a. **END VIEW**

QUARTER
ROUND
BLANK

¾

¼" ROUND-
OVER BIT

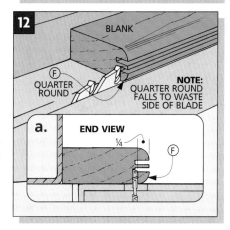

11

QUARTER
ROUND
BLANK

NOTE: CUT TWO
KERFS ON EACH EDGE

a. **END VIEW**

QUARTER
ROUND
BLANK

¼

⅜

12

BLANK

(F)
QUARTER
ROUND

NOTE:
QUARTER ROUND
FALLS TO WASTE
SIDE OF BLADE

a. **END VIEW**

¼

(F)

Now before the scroll saw pattern can be cut out, you'll need to drill holes for blade access. (I drilled ¹⁄₁₆"-dia. holes in all the openings.) Then the waste sections can be cut away on the scroll saw. To avoid weakening the panels, it's best to start with the smaller sections and save the larger ones for last.

QUARTER ROUND. To hold the scroll saw panel in the frame, I added small, mitered pieces of quarter round (F). To make these pieces safely, I start with an oversized blank, routing a ¼" roundover on each edge *(Fig. 10).*

Cutting the quarter round from the blank is a two-step process. First, I cut two kerfs on each edge with the fence set ¼" from the blade *(Fig. 11).* Second, the quarter round can be cut from the blank. However, you don't want to trap the small quarter round between the fence and the blade. So this time, reposition the fence so the quarter round falls to the waste side of the blade *(Fig. 12).*

Finally, the quarter round can be mitered to fit in the frame *(Fig. 12).* Then the pieces can be glued into the frame behind the scroll saw panel.

BRASS OPTION. For a slightly different look, you can place a small piece of sheet brass between the scroll saw panel and the quarter round. It gives the Bookends a distinctive look. See the Designer's Notebook below. ∎

TECHNIQUE ..... *Working with Brass*

There are times when I have to admit, some jobs can be a little scary. I remember cutting brass on the table saw for the first time. I was hesitant. It wasn't dangerous — my safety glasses were on, and a push block was in hand. But still, the thought of cutting metal was a bit scary. I half expected a shower of sparks or something equally dramatic.

SOFT METAL. But I needn't have worried. Unlike iron or steel, brass is a "soft" metal, so it can easily be cut with any carbide-tipped tool (like the combination blade at left). In fact, working with soft brass shapes is quite a bit like working with hardwood. (For sources of brass, see page 126.)

STRAIGHT CUTS. The projects that feature brass in this section require small sheets of thin brass (16 and 30 gauge). And the first thing to do is cut them to size on the table saw. (For this, I'd recommend wearing a long sleeve shirt to stop tiny pieces of brass from peppering your arms.)

As I mentioned earlier, any carbide-tipped combination table saw blade, jig saw blade, or router bit can be used to cut or shape brass. But when it comes to the table saw, I'd recommend you sandwich the brass between two pieces of 1/4" hardboard *(Figs. 1 and 1a)*.

I temporarily glued the brass to the bottom piece of hardboard with spray mount adhesive (though you can also use carpet tape). This makes the brass a bit easier to handle and prevents it from wedging under the fence. Plus, it will hold a real thin piece of brass flat, as it may want to "curl" up where the blade "pushes" up out of the table.

CURVED CUTS. Like straight cuts, you can also cut curves in brass. Either draw the curve freehand, or use a template to lay out the curve and then cut it with a jig saw *(Fig. 2)*. Here, you might want to buy a fine-toothed metal-cutting blade. It'll give you a smoother edge. But as with the table saw, you'll also need to fully support the piece. That's because the repeated up and down motion of the blade can bend the brass.

SMOOTHING CURVES. I'm not good enough with a jig saw to cut a perfectly smooth curve. So I always stay 1/16" from the line or template and then clean up the curve with a smooth mill file or drum sander. (Or a router, which I'll get to next.) A drum sander will remove the material quickly, but you'll have better control with a hand file.

MULTIPLES. I ended up making several identical rounded brass plates for

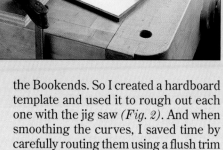

the Bookends. So I created a hardboard template and used it to rough out each one with the jig saw *(Fig. 2)*. And when smoothing the curves, I saved time by carefully routing them using a flush trim bit with a ball-bearing guide *(Fig. 3)*.

Routing brass seems even stranger than cutting it with a table saw. But again, it's a lot like routing wood. The brass should be moved from right-to-left across the router table, and you'll want to take light passes *(Fig. 3)*.

Also, to make the brass plates easier to slide under the books (16-gauge brass is about 1/16" thick), I routed a small, stopped chamfer around the curve of the tongue *(Figs. 4 and 4a)*.

CLEANING THE ROUTED EDGE. The edges of the brass matched the template perfectly, but they weren't perfectly smooth. In fact, the edge looked a little like the chipout you get routing against the grain on a piece of wood.

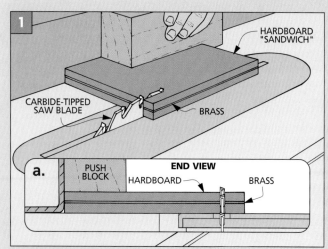

1

HARDBOARD "SANDWICH"

CARBIDE-TIPPED SAW BLADE

BRASS

a. PUSH BLOCK

END VIEW

HARDBOARD

BRASS

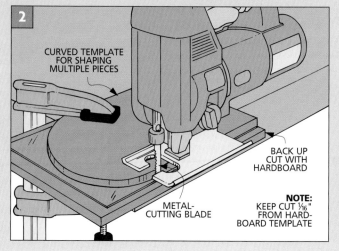

2

CURVED TEMPLATE FOR SHAPING MULTIPLE PIECES

BACK UP CUT WITH HARDBOARD

METAL-CUTTING BLADE

NOTE: KEEP CUT 1/16" FROM HARD-BOARD TEMPLATE

To smooth out these edges, all I did was backrout the brass — moving it in the opposite direction (from left to right) for the last pass *(Fig. 4)*. Typically, this is not a safe procedure, but I wasn't actually removing any material. It was more like burnishing the brass. (Just keep a good grip on the workpiece.)

ATTACHING BRASS. When it's time to attach brass to wood, I rely on brass woodscrews. I may use "instant" glue to hold the brass until the screws are added, but since wood expands and brass doesn't, I figure it's a safe bet that any glue bond is going to fail eventually.

DRILLING INTO BRASS. Before drilling pilot holes in brass, I usually take an extra step. Since brass is so smooth, I prevent the twist bit from slipping by first marking the center of the hole with an awl or a center punch *(Fig. 5)*.

To drill the hole, all you need is steady, even pressure. If you force the bit too much, on the back face of the brass you'll find a large "dimple" around the hole. (You may end up with a slight dimple anyway. But the larger the dimple, the more work you'll need to do with a file later when finishing up.)

COUNTERSINKING BRASS. Like drilling, countersinking in brass isn't much different either. However, I like to use a

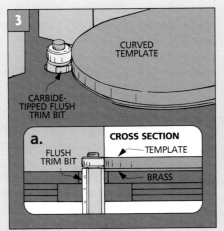

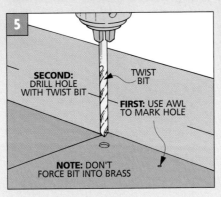

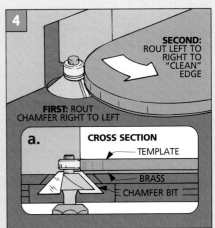

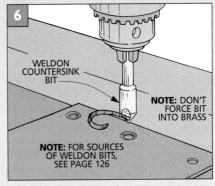

Weldon countersink bit. It works great to create clean, chatter-free cuts *(Fig. 6)*. (See Sources on page 126.)

But before you actually screw it in place, first polish the brass so it "reflects well" on all your work (see below).

BRINGING OUT THE LUSTER

Finishing brass requires sanding or polishing it finer and finer until it has the desired luster. But before you get started, take a second to mount the brass to a backer board with a spray mount adhesive. This will make it easier to secure to your bench and avoid fingerprints.

Typically, I sand brass starting at 320-grit (see left photo below). But if there are lots of deep scratches, you may need to start with a coarser grit like 180 or 220. For the projects in this section, I sanded everything to 600-grit and then followed up with 0000 steel wool.

If you want a mirror-like finish, you can buff the brass with a "charged" buffing wheel (center photo).

Finally, I'd recommend a polishing paste (right photo). Then you can spray on a coat or two of lacquer to keep it from tarnishing too quickly.

Sanding. *Sand up to 600-grit, sanding across the scratches left by the previous grit. Finish up with 0000 steel wool.*

Buffing. *For a mirror-like shine, use a soft buffing wheel that's been "charged" with a polishing compound.*

Polishing. *Whether or not you buff the brass, the last step is to polish it with a lint-free cloth and a polishing paste.*

Holiday Centerpiece

This cheerful centerpiece will be a favorite for years to come. And if you want to add to its appeal, build the optional base with a musical movement. It plays a holiday melody as the tree rotates.

There were a few chuckles from the guys in the shop when I started building the prototype for this centerpiece. I have to admit that as I sat down to work on the tree, I felt as if I was building a project for Santa's workshop.

But I had the last laugh when they saw the finished centerpiece. One person even promised me some of her home-made cookies if I would build one for her.

SCROLL SAW. At first glance, you might think this project requires a scroll saw. But actually, I designed the tree so there aren't any cuts in the middle of a work-piece. In other words, all the cuts you need to make for the tree begin and end on the edge of the workpiece. This means that you can use a scroll saw, a band saw, or even a coping saw to cut out the pieces of the tree. And since trees are random in shape and size, you don't have to worry about following a pattern exactly. Nevertheless, I've supplied a couple of patterns to serve as guidelines.

MUSIC BOX MOVEMENT. After building the prototype for this centerpiece, I decided it might be nice to add a musical movement to the base. So that's exactly what I did. (For more on this, see the Designer's Notebook on page 76.)

In order to create enough space for the musical movement, I had to come up with a way to make a thick, hollow base. I could have done this on a lathe, by turning a profile on a single, thick blank, and then hollowing out the middle. But instead, I used a router to create three "rings" of wood, each with a different profile routed on the edge. When glued together, these rings make a thick base, with a hole in the middle for the movement. (For more on this, see the Technique article on page 74.)

KIT. A kit with all the hardware (but not the plywood and hardwood needed to complete the project) can be ordered from *Woodsmith Project Supplies*. See page 126 for ordering information.

EXPLODED VIEW

OVERALL DIMENSIONS:
$9\frac{7}{8}$W x $9\frac{7}{8}$D x $14\frac{3}{8}$H

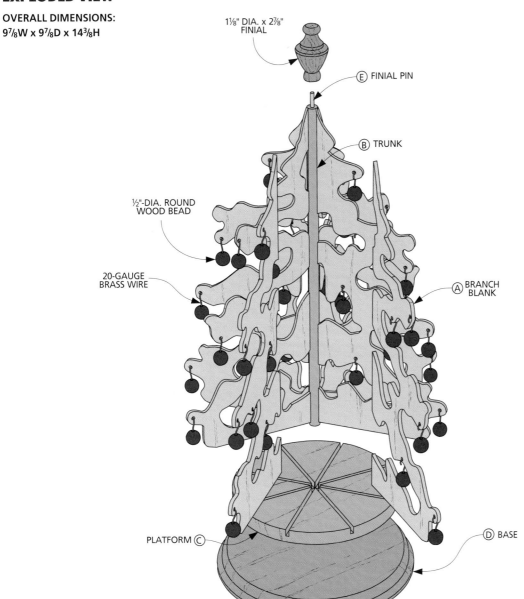

$1\frac{1}{8}$" DIA. x $2\frac{7}{8}$"
FINIAL

(E) FINIAL PIN

(B) TRUNK

$\frac{1}{2}$"-DIA. ROUND
WOOD BEAD

20-GAUGE
BRASS WIRE

(A) BRANCH
BLANK

PLATFORM (C)

(D) BASE

MATERIALS LIST

WOOD
A Branch Blanks (4) $\frac{1}{8}$ ply - $5\frac{7}{8}$ x $13\frac{5}{8}$
B Trunk (1) $\frac{3}{8}$ dia. x 12
C Platform (1) $\frac{1}{2}$ x 6 dia.
D Base (1) $\frac{3}{4}$ x $7\frac{1}{4}$ dia.
E Finial Pin (1) $\frac{1}{8}$ dia. x 1

HARDWARE SUPPLIES
(1) $1\frac{1}{16}$" dia. x $2\frac{7}{8}$" finial
(4) $\frac{3}{4}$"-dia. felt discs
(40) $\frac{1}{2}$"-dia. round wood beads
(8 ft.) 20 gauge brass wire

CUTTING DIAGRAM

$\frac{1}{8}$" BALTIC BIRCH PLYWOOD - 6 x $14\frac{1}{2}$

ALSO NEED: ONE 12" PIECE OF $\frac{3}{8}$"-DIA. DOWEL FOR PART B, AND A SHORT PIECE OF $\frac{1}{8}$"-DIA. HARD-WOOD DOWEL FOR PART E

$\frac{3}{4}$ x 12 - 24 CHERRY (2 Bd. Ft.)

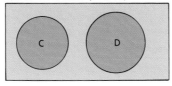

1

BRANCH PATTERN
(ENLARGE 200%)

NOTE: SEE PAGE 126
FOR A SOURCE OF ⅛"
BALTIC BIRCH PLYWOOD

NOTE: BRANCHES ARE NOT
IDENTICAL. CUT FOUR BRANCHES
OF EACH PATTERN

PATTERN #2

PATTERN #1

11⅞

4¾

Whether you plan to build the standard base or the musical version (see the Designer's Notebook on page 76), the tree is exactly the same. It's made up of eight "branches" and a "trunk" that fit in a round platform. I began with the branches.

Instead of making all the branch pieces identical, I used two patterns (four of each branch). The goal here is to give the tree a little variety. But there's another upside to doing it this way. By cutting all four branches of the same pattern at once, I also saved some time.

The branches are made out of ⅛"-thick Baltic birch plywood. (Baltic birch is available at some woodworking supply stores and through mail order catalogs. See page 126 for sources.) I cut four blanks for the branches, making them large enough so that two branches would fit on each blank. Then I taped all four blanks together with double-sided tape *(Fig. 2)*.

To lay out the branches, start by enlarging the patterns by 200% *(Fig. 1)*. Then after cutting each one out, affix them to the top blank using a spray adhesive or rubber cement. (You'll have to flip one pattern and place it face down in order to get them both on the same blank.)

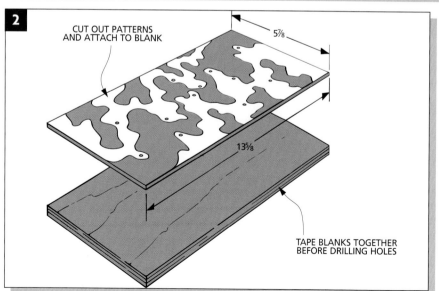

2

CUT OUT PATTERNS
AND ATTACH TO BLANK

5⅞

13⅝

TAPE BLANKS TOGETHER
BEFORE DRILLING HOLES

3

⅛"
DRILL
BIT

DRILL HOLES
FOR HANGING
ORNAMENTS

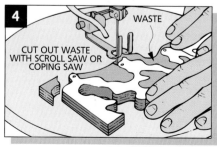

4

WASTE

CUT OUT WASTE
WITH SCROLL SAW OR
COPING SAW

DRILLING HOLES. Before beginning to cut the branches out, I drilled the 1/8" holes that will be used to hang the ornaments once the centerpiece is completed *(Fig. 3)*. Note that there are five holes on the first pattern and seven on the second.

CUTTING OUT THE BRANCHES. With the holes for the ornaments drilled, the branches can be cut out *(Fig. 4)*. Just follow the outlines of the pattern to remove the waste areas.

Once all the waste areas have been cut away, remove the double-sided tape and separate the branches. Now you're ready to start making the trunk and the platform that holds the branches.

Making the "trunk" of the tree is a snap. The trunk (B) is nothing more than a 3/8"-dia. dowel, cut 1/8" longer than the branches *(Fig. 3)*. (I made mine 12".) Then I drilled a 1/8"-dia. hole 1/2" deep on one end of the trunk for a finial that will be added later *(Fig. 5)*. But for now, just set the trunk and branches aside while you work on the platform.

PLATFORM

The branches and trunk are mounted in a round platform. This is simply a piece of cherry stock that's been planed to 1/2"-thick. In a sense, the platform serves as the "root system" of the tree. That's because there are four 1/4"-deep, intersecting kerfs to hold the branches and a hole to hold the trunk.

Although the finished platform (C) is round, I started out with a square blank. This makes it easier to cut the intersecting kerfs for the branches. Before beginning on the kerfs, however, I drilled a 3/8"-dia. hole 3/8" deep in the exact center of the blank for the trunk *(Fig. 6)*.

Next, I cut 1/4"-deep kerfs for the branches by making passes on the table saw *(Fig. 7a)*. It took me four passes. The first two passes were centered on the width and length of the blank. Then using a miter gauge and stop block, I cut diagonal kerfs from corner to corner across the blank *(Fig. 7)*.

CUTTING A CIRCLE. Usually, I use a band saw for cutting circles. But since I wanted the edge of the platform to be nice and smooth, I used a router table and a simple jig *(Figs. 8 and 8a)*. A pivot point on the jig and a matching pivot hole in the platform allow you to turn the blank in a perfect circle, trimming off each corner. (For more on this, see the Technique article on page 74.)

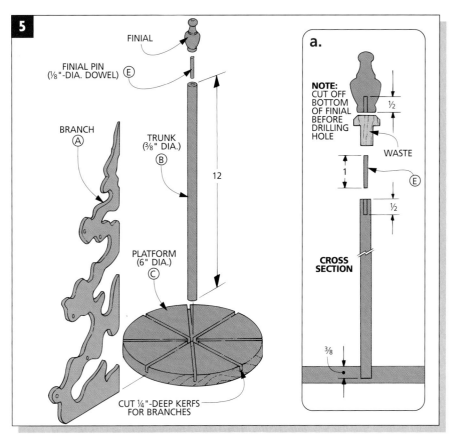

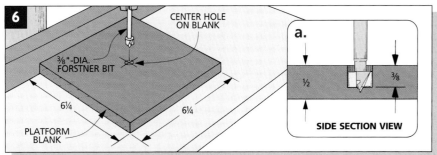

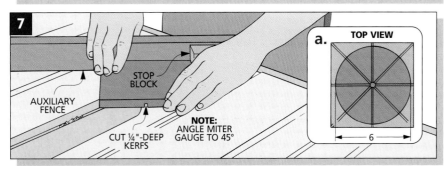

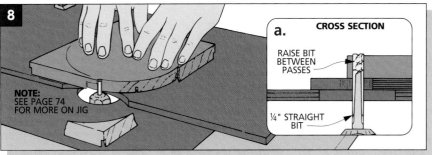

TECHNIQUE ... *Circles with a Router*

Usually, I use a band saw for cutting circles. But on the centerpiece I used a router table jig. That's because the jig gives me a clean, smooth edge. Plus, the optional music box base calls for cutting a circle on the inside of the workpiece.

The circle-cutting jig is just a piece of $1/4$"-thick hardboard with a small nail driven through one side *(Fig. 1)*. The nail serves as a pivot point to guide the ring blanks in a perfect circle (see photo).

OUTSIDE CIRCLES. Cutting outside circles is pretty simple. Start by making a small hole in the middle of the blank to allow it to slip over the pivot pin. You can use a nail the same size as the pivot pin to drill the hole. (The small dimple made when drilling the center hole can be used to locate the pilot hole.)

The next step is to set up the jig. This is just a matter of placing the hardboard base on the router table so the distance between the bit and the pivot pin equals the outside radius of the ring. Then clamp the jig to your router table.

Note: Since the outer diameter of each ring is different, you'll have to reposition the router jig for each one.

To cut the circle, start with the bit raised about $1/8$" above the router table. Now, carefully lower the blank over the pivot pin and the rotating bit. Then slowly turn the blank counterclockwise, making one complete revolution.

Now just repeat the process, raising the bit between passes until you've cut through the blank *(Figs. 2 and 2a)*.

INSIDE CIRCLES. When cutting the outside of a blank, the waste falls away from the bit. But when cutting the inside rings for the music box base, the waste is trapped. This could cause kickback.

To avoid this, I used double-sided tape to attach the blank to a backer board before routing the ring *(Fig. 1)*.

This $1/4$" hardboard backer board holds both the ring and the waste together securely even after you've made the final router pass *(Figs. 3 and 3a)*.

Note: Just make sure you don't rout all the way through the backer board when making the final router pass.

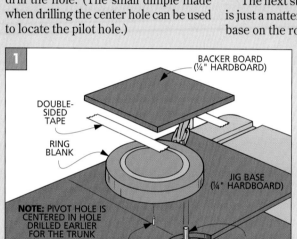

1

BACKER BOARD ($1/4$" HARDBOARD)

DOUBLE-SIDED TAPE

RING BLANK

JIG BASE ($1/4$" HARDBOARD)

NOTE: PIVOT HOLE IS CENTERED IN HOLE DRILLED EARLIER FOR THE TRUNK

PIVOT POINT

$1/4$" STRAIGHT BIT

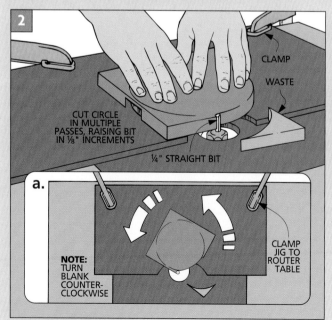

2

CLAMP

WASTE

CUT CIRCLE IN MULTIPLE PASSES, RAISING BIT IN $1/8$" INCREMENTS

$1/4$" STRAIGHT BIT

a.

NOTE: TURN BLANK COUNTER-CLOCKWISE

CLAMP JIG TO ROUTER TABLE

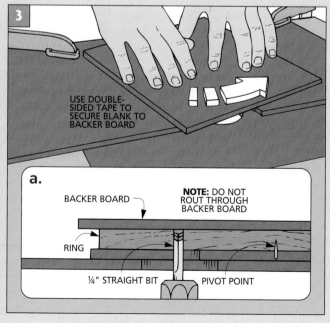

3

USE DOUBLE-SIDED TAPE TO SECURE BLANK TO BACKER BOARD

a.

BACKER BOARD

NOTE: DO NOT ROUT THROUGH BACKER BOARD

RING

$1/4$" STRAIGHT BIT

PIVOT POINT

ASSEMBLY

After the platform is finished, the tree portion of the centerpiece can be assembled. Start by gluing the trunk into the hole in the platform. Then the branches can be glued into the kerfs and to the trunk of the tree *(Fig. 9)*. Just make sure to alternate the two branch patterns as you go along *(Fig. 9a)*.

BASE. The platform serves its purpose by holding the branches and trunk of the tree. But to "spruce" up the tree (pun intended) I added a ³⁄₄"-thick base with an ogee profile under the platform *(Fig. 9)*.

Note: If you want to make the optional musical base instead, see the instructions on how to build it in the Designer's Notebook, starting on page 76.

Like the platform, the base (D) also starts off as a ³⁄₄"-thick, square cherry blank (7¹⁄₂" x 7¹⁄₂"). But after using the jig and the router table to cut it to its round shape, I decided to rout an ogee profile around the top edge *(Figs. 10 and 10a)*.

Once you've finished routing the ogee profile, the base can be glued to the platform. To help keep the two pieces aligned while gluing them up, I drove some small brads partially into the base and snipped their heads off so that about ¹⁄₁₆" of each brad remained *(Fig. 9)*. The cut-off brads prevent the tree and platform from sliding out of position as the large, flat faces of the pieces are being glued up.

FINIAL. No tree is complete without a decoration of some kind at the top. In this case, I used a store-bought finial.

Note: I couldn't find a finial in the exact size I wanted, so I bought a longer one and cut it down to 1⁷⁄₈" long.

To attach the finial, I marked the bottom (where it was cut off) with a scratch awl *(Fig. 11)*. Then I drilled a ¹⁄₈"-dia. hole ¹⁄₂" deep in the bottom of the finial. Now the finial can be glued to the

top of the trunk, using a finial pin (E) (refer to *Fig. 5* on page 73).

FINISH. It's hard to get even coverage when finishing the branches. So I decided to use a spray lacquer. When it was dry, I added some felt pads to the bottom of the base and made some ornaments to hang on the branches using wood beads and wire (see photos below). ■

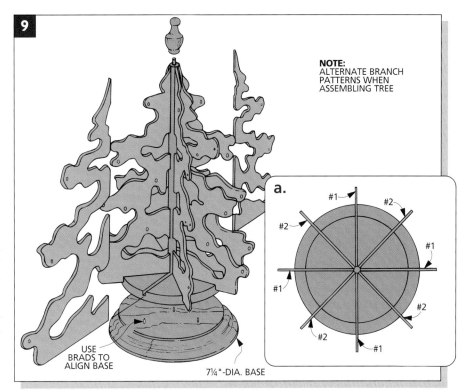

NOTE: ALTERNATE BRANCH PATTERNS WHEN ASSEMBLING TREE

USE BRADS TO ALIGN BASE

7¼"-DIA. BASE

a. #1 #2 #2 #1 #1 #2 #2 #1

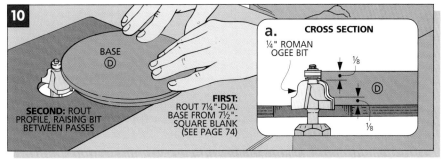

BASE (D)

SECOND: ROUT PROFILE, RAISING BIT BETWEEN PASSES

FIRST: ROUT 7¼"-DIA. BASE FROM 7½"-SQUARE BLANK (SEE PAGE 74)

a. CROSS SECTION

¼" ROMAN OGEE BIT

⅛

⅛

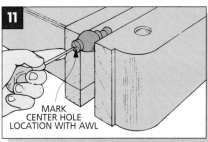

MARK CENTER HOLE LOCATION WITH AWL

Paint the ¹⁄₂"-dia. beads with a spray enamel. Stringing the beads on a dowel first makes it easier to paint them.

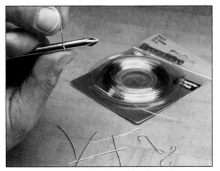

Then, to make the hooks for the ornaments, simply cut 20-gauge wire in 2"-long pieces and bend them into shape.

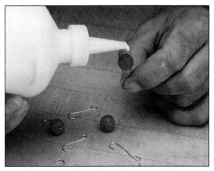

Finally, a small bend at the end of the wire wedges into the hole in the bead. And a drop of glue holds the wire in place.

With a special music box movement, your centerpiece will revolve slowly as it plays a holiday favorite. To build the hollow base that holds the movement all you need is a couple of router bits.

CONSTRUCTION NOTES:

■ Although it might look difficult to build, the base for the music box movement is really straightforward. It's just three wood rings (including the original base), each with a different, decorative profile routed on the edge. When they're glued together one on top of the other, the base rings create a built-up molding in the shape of a large "donut." Then a plywood bottom is added to conceal the "hole" of the donut. The extra depth allows for the rotating musical movement.

■ To make the base rings, I started by cutting a square blank for each one. The blanks for the base (D) and base middle (F) are cut from 3/4"-thick stock, while the blank for the base bottom (G) is made from 1/2"-thick material. Each blank is 1/4" larger than the finished diameter of the ring *(Fig. 1)*.

Note: It's important that the blanks are flat. If you can't find any flat, wide boards, it's better to glue up the blanks from narrow stock.

■ Cutting the base rings out of the blanks requires making a smooth, circular cut on both the inside and the outside of the ring. To do this, I used the same jig as when making the platform. (For more on this technique, see page 74.)

■ After cutting the three base rings to size, the outside edge of each gets routed with a different profile. This way, when the rings are glued together, they will create a series of built-up moldings.

The same ogee profile is routed on the base (D). (Refer to *Fig. 10a* on page 75.) Then rout a 1/2" roundover with a shoulder on the edge of the base middle *(Fig. 1a)*. Finally, a 1/4" cove is routed underneath the base bottom *(Fig. 1b)*.

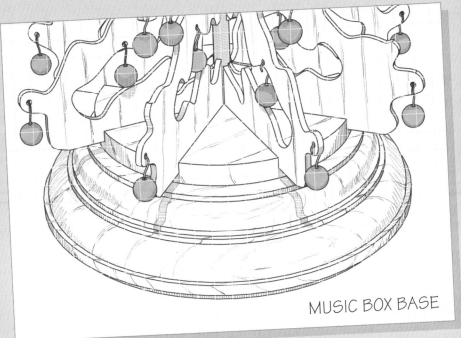

MUSIC BOX BASE

■ At this point, you're ready to rout the inside ring. The problem is, there's no way to hold on to this ring as it's cut away.

To solve this, I fastened a backer board to the ring blank with double-sided tape before I routed it out *(Fig. 2)*. Position the

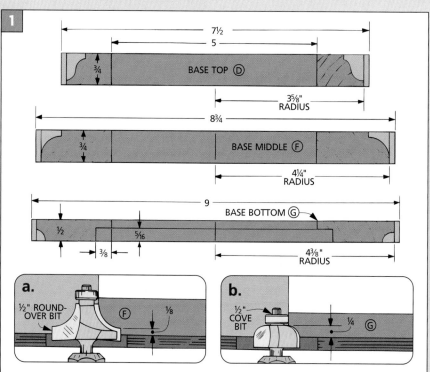

1

7½
5
¾ BASE TOP ⒟
3⅝" RADIUS

8¾
¾ BASE MIDDLE ⒡
4¼" RADIUS

9
BASE BOTTOM ⒢
½   5/16
⅜
4⅜" RADIUS

a.
½" ROUND-OVER BIT
⒡   ⅛

b.
½" COVE BIT
¼   ⒢

MATERIALS LIST

NEW PARTS
F Base Middle (1)   3/4 x 8½ dia.
G Base Bottom (1)   ½ x 8¾ dia.
H Bottom (1)   ¼ ply x 5¾ dia.

HARDWARE SUPPLIES
(1) Musical movement w/ turntable

blank on the pivot pin and slowly lower it over the spinning router bit. Raise the bit $1/16''$ between passes until the ring is cut from the blank.

■ There's one last detail to take care of before gluing the three rings together. A rabbet needs to be routed in the base bottom (G) to accept a bottom made from $1/4''$-thick plywood. I did this on the router table, using a rabbet bit *(Figs. 3 and 3a)*.

The rabbet is cut slightly deeper than the thickness of the bottom so that the base will rest flat on the bottom ring instead of the plywood bottom *(Fig. 4a)*.

Safety Note: This operation puts your fingers close to the bit. Use a guard over the bit to keep your fingers away from it.

■ After cutting the rabbet, I cut the $1/4''$-thick plywood bottom (H) to fit in the recessed opening *(Figs. 4 and 4a)*. Use the same method as for making the rings.

■ Keeping the base pieces aligned while gluing them up can be tricky. To make things easier, I assembled the base in stages, starting with the base bottom and middle. Next, I added the base top, and then finally the plywood bottom.

Note: For a better appearance, I assembled the three base pieces so the grain runs in one direction.

■ The musical movement I used for this centerpiece comes with a plastic turntable *(Fig. 5a)*. (For sources of musical movements with a turntable, see page 126.) The centerpiece is attached to the turntable so the movement is wound by turning the tree. Then as the music plays, the whole centerpiece revolves slowly.

■ Attaching the turntable to the bottom of the tree is easy. It's just a matter of applying a bead of silicone sealant to the bottom of the platform and centering the turntable on the platform *(Fig. 5)*.

■ Positioning and gluing the musical movement to the bottom is a little more involved. If the movement isn't positioned correctly when it's glued down to the base, the tree and the base won't align while the tree is turning.

■ To solve this problem, I threaded the music box onto the turntable before gluing it down to the base *(Fig. 6)*. Then I added a thick layer of silicone to the bottom of the movement and glued it down to the bottom of the base, making sure to center the tree over the base.

■ And to create a clearance gap so the tree won't rub on the top of the base as it turns (as well as to make sure the tree sits level), slip four thin washers between the platform and the top ring of the base while the silicone sets up *(Fig. 6a)*.

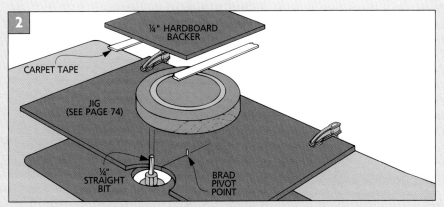

2
¼" HARDBOARD BACKER
CARPET TAPE
JIG (SEE PAGE 74)
¼" STRAIGHT BIT
BRAD PIVOT POINT

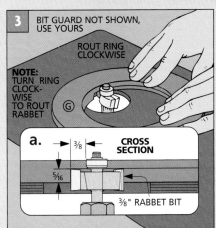

3 BIT GUARD NOT SHOWN, USE YOURS
ROUT RING CLOCKWISE
NOTE: TURN RING CLOCKWISE TO ROUT RABBET
G
a. 3/8 CROSS SECTION
5/16
3/8" RABBET BIT

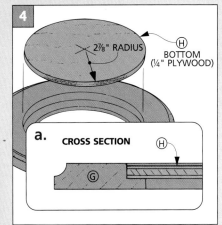

4
2⅞" RADIUS
H BOTTOM (¼" PLYWOOD)
a. CROSS SECTION H
G

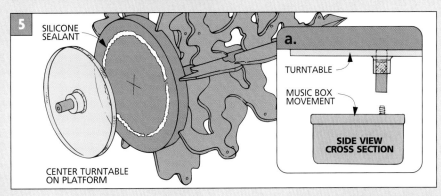

5 SILICONE SEALANT
a.
TURNTABLE
MUSIC BOX MOVEMENT
SIDE VIEW CROSS SECTION
CENTER TURNTABLE ON PLATFORM

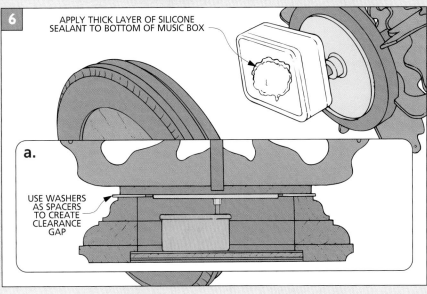

6 APPLY THICK LAYER OF SILICONE SEALANT TO BOTTOM OF MUSIC BOX
a.
USE WASHERS AS SPACERS TO CREATE CLEARANCE GAP

Night Light

Light up the night with four interchangeable patterns featuring enchanting scenes that are sure to please your child. All it takes to build it is a scroll saw, a small light bulb, and a weekend in the shop.

Some projects get their charm from the wood that's missing. This Night Light is one of those projects. It's just a box with the sides, top, and bottom made from solid wood. What makes it interesting is the interchangeable front panel that screens the light shining from a small bulb inside.

I designed this Night Light with four of these scroll-sawn hardwood panels. Then, depending on your mood or the season, you can slide one in front of the light, and store the others in a compartment in the back of the box.

PANEL DESIGNS. If you're artistic (or have clip art on your computer), it would

be easy to come up with hundreds of different ideas for your own panels. I've included four examples for the panels in my Night Light. Each has a magical quality that will look nice in a child's bedroom or sitting on a hallway table or stand. (You can find the patterns in the Designer's Notebook on page 82.)

WOOD. I used cherry for all the parts of the Night Light. The color and warmth of cherry enhance the glow cast by the light. And because cherry is close-grained, it cuts well on a scroll saw.

SUPPLIES. The light fixture is a Christmas-tree-size (4-watt) bulb that clips tightly into the base of the box. This

light bulb fixture, along with a full-size drawing of each of the four patterns (and a piece of felt cloth for the bottom) is available from *Woodsmith Project Supplies.* (See Sources on page 126.)

THIN STOCK. Except for the sides, each piece in this project is made from wood that's 1/2" thick or less. Finished stock this thin can be found, but it may cost a bit more. A good alternative is to resaw the stock from thicker boards. (For more on this, go to the Technique on page 65.)

SCROLL SAWING. And to learn the secret to making the most of your scroll saw projects, I suggest you check out the Technique article on page 86.

EXPLODED VIEW

OVERALL DIMENSIONS:
6W x 5¼D x 9H

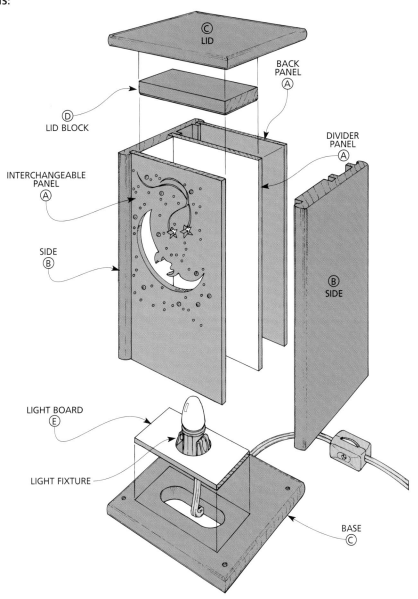

LID
C

BACK
PANEL
A

LID BLOCK
D

DIVIDER
PANEL
A

INTERCHANGEABLE
PANEL
A

SIDE
B

B
SIDE

LIGHT BOARD
E

LIGHT FIXTURE

BASE
C

MATERIALS LIST

WOOD

A	Panels (6)	¼ x 4¾ - 8
B	Sides (2)	¾ x 4¾ - 8
C	Base/Lid (2)	½ x 5¼ - 6
D	Lid Block (1)	½ x 2 - 4
E	Light Board (1)	⅛ x 2 - 4

HARDWARE SUPPLIES

(4) No. 6 x 1" Fh woodscrews
(1) Felt cloth (6" x 6")
(1) Night light socket switch w/ cord
(1) 4-watt frosted bulb

CUTTING DIAGRAM

¾ x 5½ - 36 (Two Boards @ 1.2 Bd. Ft. Each)

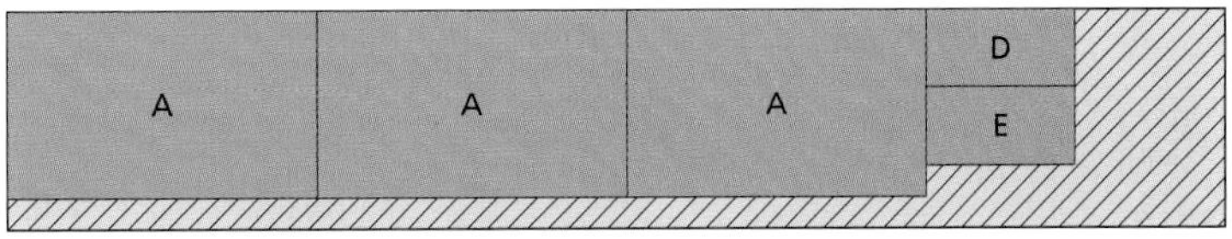

A	A	A	D
			E

¾ x 5½ - 36 (1.2 Bd. Ft.)

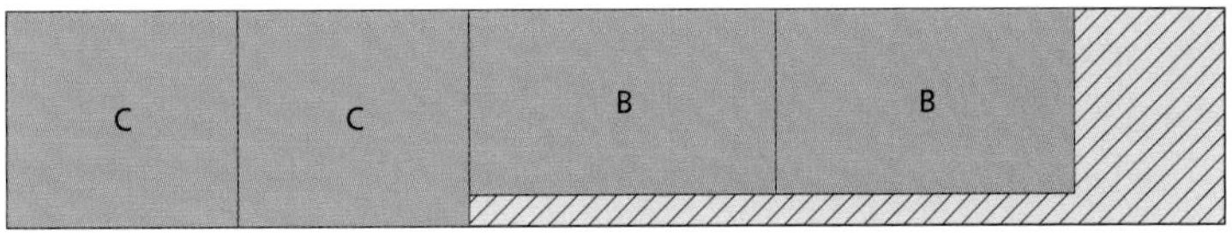

C	C	B	B

Start building the Night Light by cutting the six panel blanks — four for the interchangeable panels (A), plus one divider panel (A), and one back panel (A). The Night Light box is built around these.

PANEL BLANK. To make these six $1/4$"-thick panels, first cut a piece of $3/4$"-thick stock to final width ($4^3/4$") and rough length (26") *(Fig. 1)*.

RESAW PANELS. Then resaw this into two panels that are each slightly thicker than $1/4$". I used the table saw and made two passes with a sharp blade *(Fig. 1)*. (For more on this procedure, see the Technique article on page 65.) You could also use a band saw or thickness planer to reduce the stock to $1/4$".

Now, sand or plane the saw marks from all the panels so they're all $1/4$" thick. Then cross-cut both blanks to produce six 8"-long panels *(Fig. 2)*.

Note: You could use plywood, but the plies will show on the finished panels.

PATTERNS. Now use the patterns in the Designer's Notebook on page 82 to lay out the designs and cut them out.

SIDES

After resawing and cutting the six panels to size, the next step is to make the grooved sides of the box.

SIDE BLANK. The two sides (B) start out as one blank of $3/4$"-thick stock. Cut the blank to finished width ($4^3/4$") and rough length ($16^1/2$") *(Fig. 3)*.

PANEL GROOVES. Next, cut three $1/4$"-wide grooves for the panels to slide into.

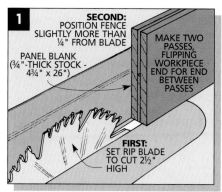

I used the table saw with a rip blade to form all the grooves. But before cutting the grooves in the blank, cut a test piece the same size as the blank to check the width and position of each groove.

The first grooves to cut are the two outside ones *(Fig. 3)*. To do this, I set the fence $1/4$" from the inside edge of the blade, and raise it $3/8$" above the table.

Now you can make one pass to cut a kerf in the test piece to form the outside edge of the groove. Then turn the piece end for end and cut a kerf near the other edge. When you're satisfied with the kerf depth and its distance from the edge, cut kerfs on both edges of the actual workpiece, following the same procedure.

Next you can reposition the fence and make a second pass on the test piece, so that the $1/4$" panels fit snugly in the grooves in the test piece. Then make the cuts on the actual workpiece to complete the two outside grooves.

You'll form the groove for the divider panel in the same way. This groove should be located 2" from the back edge of the box sides *(Fig. 3)*.

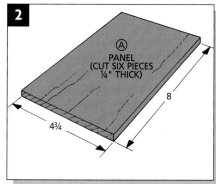

STORAGE CHAMBER. Next, I cut a 1"-wide storage chamber by making a series of passes through the rip blade *(Fig. 3)*.

To make the sides appear thinner than they actually are, trim the front and back edges down to $1/2$" thick *(Fig. 4)*. To do this, set the table saw blade $1/2$" from the fence and $3/8$" high *(Fig. 5)*.

BULLNOSE PROFILE. After trimming the outside edges of the sides, rout a bullnose profile on them with a $3/8$" roundover bit in a router table. To do this, first raise the bit $1/4$" high and round over the outside edges (grooved face *up*) *(Fig. 6)*. Then raise the roundover bit $1/2$" high, flip the workpiece over, and round over the inside edges (grooves *down*) *(Fig. 7)*.

PRE-ASSEMBLY. Now cut the side piece into two 8"-long sections *(Fig. 3)*. Then glue the back and divider panels in place between the two sides.

BASE & LID

Begin making the base and lid of the Night Light by cutting an over-size blank to final width ($5^1/4$") and rough length

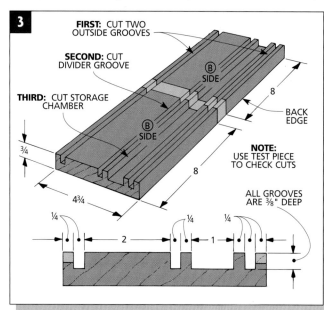

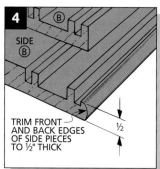

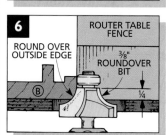

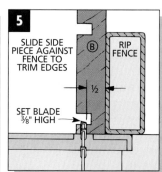

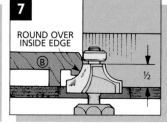

($12\frac{1}{2}$"). Then you'll want to resaw and sand the blank to a final thickness of $\frac{1}{2}$".

At this point, you can cut the blank into two pieces (each 6" long) to form a base (C) and a lid (C) *(Fig. 8)*.

ELECTRICAL FIXTURE. A "finger slot" in the base allows access to the electrical fixture. To make this, bore two holes in the base, then cut out the waste between them with a jig saw *(Fig. 8a)*.

Next, form a $\frac{1}{4}$"-deep groove for the electrical cord in the bottom of the base using the router table *(Fig. 9)*.

After cutting this groove, soften all the edges of the top and bottom with a $\frac{3}{8}$" roundover bit. To do this, raise the bit $\frac{1}{4}$" above the table *(Fig. 10)*.

ASSEMBLING THE BOX

When the base and lid are complete, finish assembling the box. Do this by first drilling countersunk shank holes on the bottom side of the base *(Fig. 11a)*.

Then center the base on the side assembly and temporarily clamp them together. The sides should be inset equally all around the base *(Fig. 11)*. (In my case, this was $\frac{1}{4}$".)

Now drill pilot holes through the shank holes into the bottom ends of each side piece *(Fig. 11a)*. Then glue and screw the base in place.

LID BLOCK. The lid fits snugly onto the top by means of a lid block that's glued to the underside of the lid *(Fig. 12)*.

To make the lid block (D), start by cutting a $\frac{3}{4}$" piece of stock to fit the

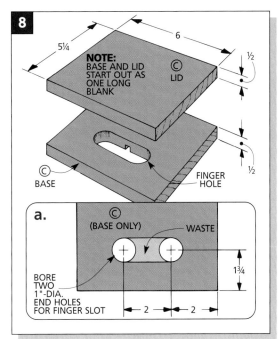

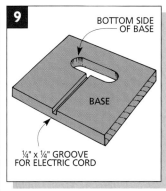

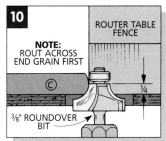

opening of the light chamber (with an interchangeable panel in place).

With the lid block cut to size, you can rout a narrow chamfer along all four edges of one side of the block. (The chamfered edges let you remove and replace the lid more easily.)

Now, lay out the position of the lid block on the bottom of the lid *(Fig. 12a)* and glue the block in place.

LIGHT BOARD. The light has a spring retainer that's designed to seat into a $\frac{1}{8}$"-thick board with a 1" hole *(Fig. 13)*.

To make the light board (E), first measure the opening at the bottom of

the light chamber. Then cut a piece of $\frac{1}{8}$" stock to fit this opening *(Fig. 13a)*. Bore a 1" hole through the center of this piece, then glue the light board in place in the bottom of the base.

FINISH. Finally, to complete the project, I applied a tung oil finish to the box.

Note: I found the box reflected more light through the panels after I painted the inside surfaces of the light chamber (not including the interchangeable panel) with a white enamel paint *(Fig. 13)*.

Now you can glue a piece of felt on the bottom of the box. This will hold the electrical cord in place. ■

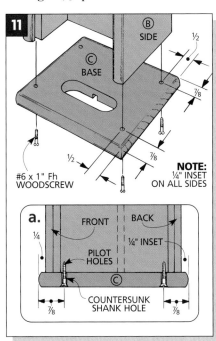

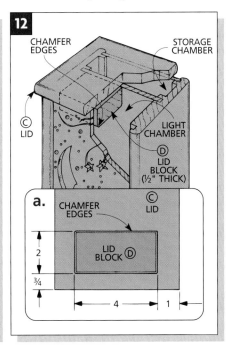

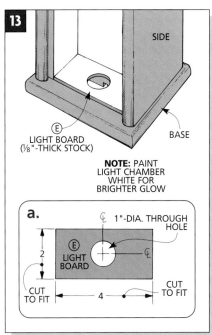

DESIGNER'S NOTEBOOK

Perfect for a child's bedroom, these Night Light patterns provide a soothing glow when it's needed most. A hidden compartment inside the light holds the three extra panels when they're not being used.

PATTERNS

■ The magic of the Night Light is in the scroll-sawn panels. Here are some suggestions for making four interchangeable panels. The patterns shown here are half size, so enlarge them 200%. (Or you can receive all four of the full-size patterns from *Woodsmith Project Supplies*. See Sources, page 126.)

Note: The lighter areas of the drawings are those that should be cut away. (I used a No. 5 skip tooth blade to cut each of the patterns.)

■ First, finish sand each of the panel blanks. Then glue a pattern to the blank using spray adhesive or a light coat of rubber cement.

■ Before you begin to saw, drill starting holes for the pierce (or inside) cuts, and for the other holes.

■ On the Falling Stars panel, drill the holes for the background stars first (using $\frac{1}{16}$" and $\frac{1}{8}$" drill bits).

Note: The points on the moon and the falling stars will be sharpest if you form them with two intersecting cuts, rather than by trying to pivot around them.

■ For the Jack O'Lantern, drill out the stars ($\frac{1}{16}$" and $\frac{3}{32}$" bits) and the moon ($\frac{3}{4}$" bit) first. Then cut out the details of the pumpkin. Pivot around the blade only when cutting out the eyes and the mouth.

■ Next, cut around the fence parts. And finally, cut around the cat.

■ Cat Fishin' requires the most starting holes. Drill them first, then cut out the smaller areas.

■ Cut around the cat last so you'll have plenty of support when you're scrolling between the leaves.

■ For Snowy Pine, drill holes for the snowflakes ($\frac{1}{16}$" bit) and the tree ornaments ($\frac{3}{32}$"). Then drill starting holes for the snow on the branches. Next cut the tree outline, and finally the snow on the ground.

■ Finish the panels by dipping them in a shallow pan of tung oil. Then poke out the excess finish from the drill holes with a wire brad.

FALLING STARS
ENLARGE 200%

JACK O'LANTERN
ENLARGE 200%

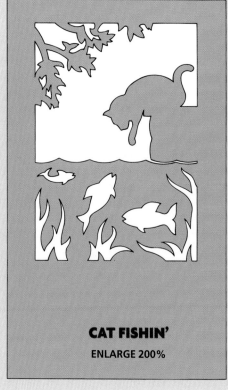

CAT FISHIN'
ENLARGE 200%

SNOWY PINE
ENLARGE 200%

Fretwork Picture Frame

This hinged, hardwood frame with a fretwork panel looks good from either side, making it perfect for a desk or parlor table. All it takes is a scroll saw and a few hours to turn a plain frame into this elegant one.

O ccasionally, I enjoy sitting down and cutting fretwork patterns with my scroll saw. The change in pace is a nice break from my typical woodworking routine.

But like any time I spend in the shop, I want to end up with something I can be proud of. Something that belongs out in plain sight on a mantel, a night stand, or in a grandchild's bedroom.

This Fretwork Picture Frame is just the kind of project I enjoy. It doesn't take much time. It keeps me from getting rusty on a tool that doesn't get a lot of use in my shop. Plus, it turns a plain frame into an attractive heirloom project.

WOOD. I've used thin stock for the fretwork panel. It's got to be thin to fit into the frame, and it's a lot easier to cut thin material on a scroll saw. Plus, I think it looks nicer than a thick panel. Any species of wood will do, but I used cherry because of its tight grain.

STRAIGHT LINES. You might notice that most scroll saw patterns have lots of curved lines in their design. That's partly because curved lines are easier to cut than a straight line. But I always like a challenge, so I've included a design with a lattice pattern that includes lots of straight lines. (Check out the Designer's Notebook on page 85 for more on this.)

PREP WORK. A small fretwork project should be relaxing. And a little preparation goes a long way to making scroll sawing a lot easier. See the Technique article on page 86 for some tips.

MATERIALS LIST

WOOD
A	Panels (2)	$1/8$ x $3^1/2$ - $4^3/4$
B	Frame Sides (4)	$1/2$ x $1/2$ - $5^1/2$
C	Frame Tops/Btms. (4)	$1/2$ x $1/2$ - $4^1/4$

HARDWARE SUPPLIES
(2) No. 4 x $1/2$" Fh woodscrews
(2) $3/4$" x $1^1/16$" brass hinges w/ screws

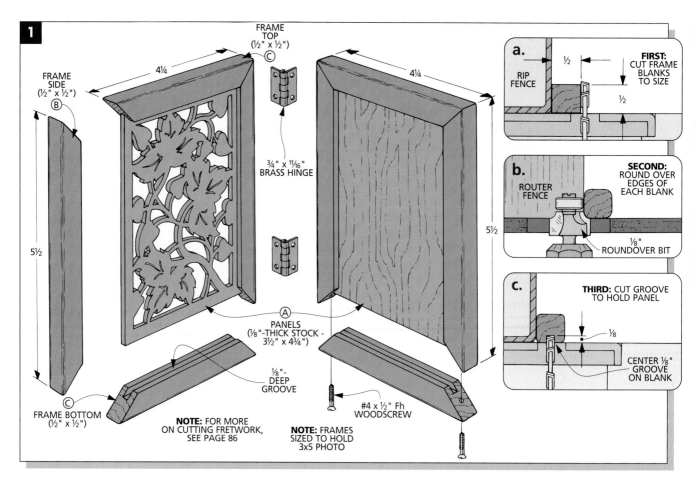

1

FRAME
TOP
(½" x ½")
Ⓒ

FRAME
SIDE
(½" x ½")
Ⓑ

4¼

4¼

5½

5½

¾" x ¹¹⁄₁₆"
BRASS HINGE

Ⓐ

PANELS
(⅛"-THICK STOCK -
3½" x 4¾")

⅛"-
DEEP
GROOVE

Ⓒ

FRAME BOTTOM
(½" x ½")

NOTE: FOR MORE
ON CUTTING FRETWORK,
SEE PAGE 86

#4 x ½" Fh
WOODSCREW

NOTE: FRAMES
SIZED TO HOLD
3x5 PHOTO

a.
RIP
FENCE
½
FIRST:
CUT FRAME
BLANKS
TO SIZE
½

b.
ROUTER
FENCE
SECOND:
ROUND OVER
EDGES OF
EACH BLANK
⅛"
ROUNDOVER BIT

c.
THIRD: CUT GROOVE
TO HOLD PANEL
⅛
CENTER ⅛"
GROOVE
ON BLANK

PANELS

The best way to begin is to cut two identical panels: one for the fretwork and another to back the photo *(Fig. 1)*. I designed them to hold 3x5 photos. But after taking a few measurements, I realized that 3x5 photos aren't exactly 3" by 5". So if you have a particular picture you want to put in this frame, cut the panels to match the size of your photo. (My panels were 3½" x 4¾".)

Once the panels are cut to size, it's time to cut the fretwork pattern in one of the panels. So set the other panel aside, and photocopy the pattern shown at left or in the Designer's Notebook on the opposite page. For some tips on cutting fretwork patterns, see the Technique article on page 86.

FRAMES. When the fretwork is complete, you can move on to making the frame pieces. I started with extra-long blanks that were ½" square *(Fig. 1a)*. Just be sure to make a few extra. You'll need them when setting up the cuts.

I wanted the frames to be simple so the attention would be on the photo and the fretwork. So for decoration, all I did was rout ⅛" roundovers on all the edges of the blanks *(Fig. 1b)*.

Next, to hold the panels, a centered groove is cut in each piece *(Fig. 1c)*. This groove should be just wide enough to hold the panels. With my ⅛"-thick panels, a single pass on the table saw with a combination blade was all that was needed. (Use a test piece to set up the saw.)

ASSEMBLY. Now the frame pieces are ready to be mitered to finished length and then assembled around the panels. With the frame for the fretwork, this is

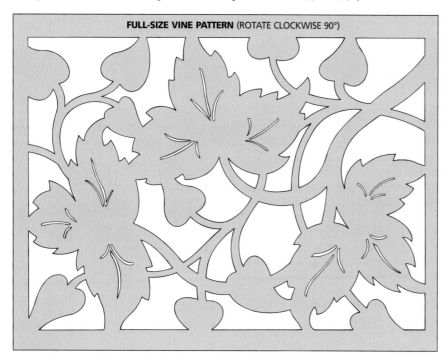

FULL-SIZE VINE PATTERN (ROTATE CLOCKWISE 90°)

Cutting curved fretwork is relatively simple, but throw in some straight lines and it becomes a challenge.

LATTICE PATTERN

■ When designing the lattice fretwork pattern, my main objective was to add some straight lines. I wanted to try completing a project that was just a little more challenging. You see, it's easier to cut a curved line with a scroll saw than it is to cut straight lines.

■ This pattern has a lattice design with a geometric grid in the middle. One way to make straight cuts a little easier is to use an auxiliary fence clamped to the scroll saw table. Position the fence so the blade is perpendicular to the cut line, then just run the straight edge of the workpiece against the fence.

Note: Some scroll saws let you adjust the blade holder to counteract the tendency of the blade to drift. Rotating the blade so it aligns with the drift angle helps keep cuts straight.

■ A file makes quick work of cleaning up (see the Finishing Tip below).

FULL-SIZE LATTICE PATTERN (ROTATE 90°)

simply a matter of gluing and clamping the frame around the panel.

But the frame for the photo has to be assembled a little differently. Here, I glued up one corner at a time until three of the pieces were together, making a U-shaped assembly. Then the bottom piece is simply screwed in place *(Fig. 2)*.

At this point, the panel backing the photo fits too snug in the grooves to include the photo and an acetate cover. You could widen the groove, but I sanded the panel just enough to reduce its thickness until everything fit into the grooves.

FINISH. Finally, I finished the frames with an oil finish. Then I stacked them together and joined them with a pair of brass hinges *(Fig. 3)*.   ■

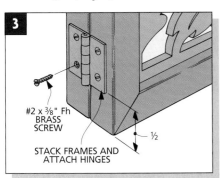

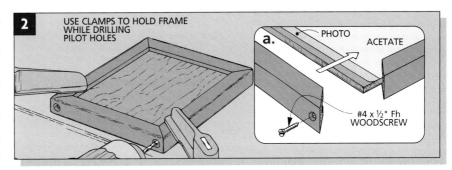

2 USE CLAMPS TO HOLD FRAME WHILE DRILLING PILOT HOLES

a. PHOTO
ACETATE
#4 x ½" Fh WOODSCREW

3
#2 x ³⁄₈" Fh BRASS SCREW
STACK FRAMES AND ATTACH HINGES
½

FINISHING TIP........ Fretwork

For final touch-ups use a half-round diamond file (photo above). It works great because it has a round side for curved edges and a flat side for flat edges.

Then, to get finish into all the crevices, shape a large piece of aluminum foil into a reservoir deep enough to submerge the panel (photo above).

TECHNIQUE .... *Scroll Sawing*

For me, time in the shop is all about relaxing, even though most of the woodworking I do requires me to be on my feet for long periods at a time. But occasionally, I'll get to sit in front of my scroll saw and work on a small fretwork project for a little change of pace.

Note: Every project in the second section of this book has at least one panel that has to be cut on a scroll saw.

Using a scroll saw really isn't that difficult, it just takes a little patience and the right setup.

GETTING READY

Just like any project, there's always a little preparation to be done before you can actually get started cutting on a small project like the picture frame.

CHOOSING A PATTERN. The first thing to do is pick out a pattern — and some are easier than others. I find a floral design with curved, flowing lines, like the vine pattern on page 84, is easier than a geometric design, like the latticed pattern. It's harder to cut straight lines and repeated shapes because mistakes stand out. (See the Designer's Notebook on page 85 for tips on solving this problem.)

MOUNTING A PATTERN. With the pattern selected, cut a solid-wood panel to size and mount the pattern. (You could also use plywood for scroll saw panels, that is if you don't mind seeing the plies after it's cut out.) To mount the pattern, I first make a photocopy and use a temporary spray adhesive. It goes on quickly and comes off without a mess. (Just make sure you use a temporary adhesive.)

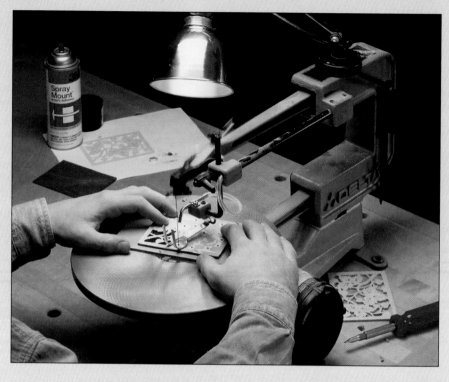

BACKING UP THE PATTERN. With the pattern in place, I often take one extra precaution — especially on panels that will be seen from the back as well as the front (like those on the Fretwork Picture Frames, and the projects on pages 62 and 70). I use a backing board to reduce the chance of having chipout on the back side of the panel *(Fig. 2)*.

PREPARING THE SCROLL SAW

Now that the scroll saw panel is ready, make sure your scroll saw is too. First, it's important that you have the right blade.

For cutting intricate fretwork patterns, I generally use a No. 5 reverse tooth blade, as you can see in the Shop Tip box on the next page. (For scroll saw supplies, see Sources on page 126.)

With the blade installed, I tension it so it will only flex 1/8" from front to back under finger pressure. Then I cut a kerf in a piece of scrap stock to use as a guide to square up the table *(Fig. 1)*.

Adjust the hold-down so it applies enough pressure to keep the wood on the table, but not so much that you can't feed the stock through. Finally, make a test cut to see that it cuts properly.

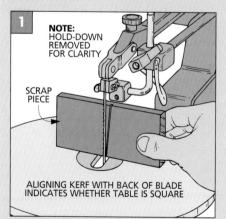

Squaring the Table. *To square a scroll saw table, cut a kerf in a scrap. Then line up the kerf with the back of the blade.*

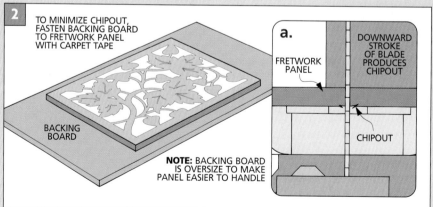

Backing Board. *The downward stroke of a scroll saw blade tends to chip out the bottom face of a panel. To minimize this, I like to use a reverse tooth blade and attach the panel with carpet tape to a backing board made from 1/8" hardboard.*

Picture Frame. *Here's a fretwork panel that looks just as good from the back as it does from the front. The reason for this is the choice of blade — for panels that will be seen from both sides, use a reverse tooth blade (see Shop Tip below).*

GETTING STARTED

Now you're ready to start the fretwork. But actually, the place to begin is at the drill press, not the scroll saw.

STARTER HOLES. Because fretwork is mostly inside cuts, the first step is to drill starter holes so you can feed the scroll saw blade through the panel *(Fig. 3)*. And make sure the starter holes are away from the lines to avoid chipout *(Fig. 4)*.

MAKING THE CUTS. When the holes are drilled, you can begin cutting. With patterns like those on pages 84 and 85, there's no particular progression. But some patterns have one or two very large openings. A large opening will usually leave the panel fragile in some areas, so I cut them last.

I tend to remove the waste from an opening in small pieces, instead of trying to get it all in one shot. For example, some sharp corners I'll cut in two or three steps *(Fig. 5)*. For other corners, the trick when rotating the panel is to push

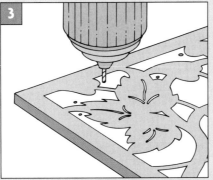

Starter Holes. *Drill ⅛" holes wherever you can. The small veining in parts of this pattern require 1/16" starter holes.*

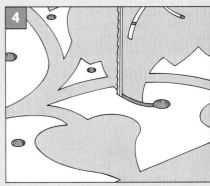

Hole Locations. *Locate starter holes at easy "entry points." But keep them away from the lines to avoid chipout.*

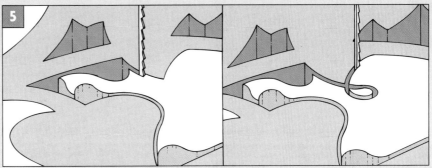

Cutting Outside Corners. *Clean, sharp corners aren't difficult — just take your time. To cut an outside corner, you don't need to make a quick, sharp turn. Instead, loop your way around in the opposite direction.*

the piece against the sides and back of the blade (the edges that don't cut).

With fretwork, the thing that takes some getting used to is rotating the panel as you work. Fortunately, all this takes is a little practice.

FEED RATE. Finally, your feed rate is very important. Don't push the wood through too fast. I like to work slowly using gentle pressure. If your blade is bowing under the pressure, you're moving too fast. For cutting straight lines, you can clamp a guide fence onto your saw's table and feed your stock by it.

SHOP TIP

Choosing Blades

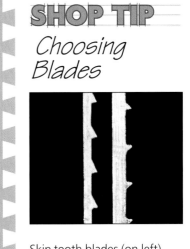

Skip tooth blades (on left) work fine for scroll work that will only be seen from one side. But for panels that are seen from both sides, I prefer a "reverse tooth" blade.

Unlike a skip tooth blade, the teeth at the bottom of a reverse tooth blade (on right) face up. This way, the bottom teeth cut on the upstroke to reduce chipout.

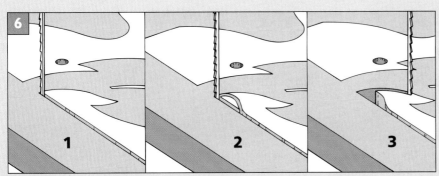

Inside Corners. *Instead of cutting an inside corner in a single pass, I often try to do it in three steps. First, cut straight into the corner (Step 1). Then back the blade out and loop around from the other side to get a crisp corner (Step 2). Now spin the piece around and continue cutting out from the corner (Step 3).*

Keepsakes

Each of the handsome projects in this section will carry with it memories of the person who built it. Whenever the recipient checks the time or their look, puts away their favorite jewelry, or lingers over a treasured photo, they'll be reminded of the time and thought you put into making a special gift just for them.

Hand Mirror

The trick to cutting the top of this mirror to a perfect circle "revolves" around a simple pivot pin. Once you know the secret, the Hand Mirror is an easy weekend project that makes a great gift.

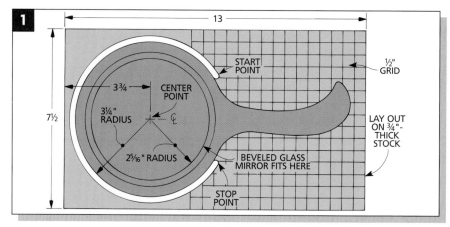

There were a few challenges in making this mirror. First, I had to figure a way to cut the outside top edge to a perfect circle. And then how to rout a circular recess for a round mirror.

The solution to both of these problems is to use a pivot pin and a router. By rotating the router around the pin, you can rout perfect circles. Then, by varying the distance between the bit and the pin, you can rout two concentric circles.

OPTIONS. To "carve" an initial on the back of the mirror, I used a router and straight bit, and then I hand-textured the background. I've included step-by-step instructions for this in the Designer's Notebook on page 93.

PATTERN. This mirror is for a right-handed person *(Fig. 1)*. For a left-handed person, you must cut out the pattern so the handle turns the other way. (*Woodsmith Project Supplies* offers a full-size pattern and all twenty-six

alphabet letters, as well as the beveled glass mirror, see Sources on page 126.)

ROUTING STEPS

The first step in making the mirror is to replace your router base plate with a shop-made plate. To make this base plate,

see the Shop Jig box on the next page. After the new base plate is complete, you can use this set-up to cut out the top of the Hand Mirror and rout the recesses.

MIRROR BLANK. To make the mirror, start by cutting a $3/4$"-thick blank to size ($7^1/2$" x 13) *(Fig. 1)*. Then lay out the pattern on the blank.

1

13

START POINT

$1/2$" GRID

3¾

CENTER POINT

$3^1/4$" RADIUS

℄

$7^1/2$

$2^5/16$" RADIUS

BEVELED GLASS MIRROR FITS HERE

LAY OUT ON $3/4$"-THICK STOCK

STOP POINT

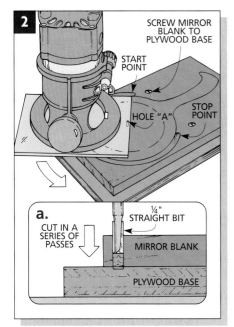

2 SCREW MIRROR BLANK TO PLYWOOD BASE

START POINT

HOLE "A"

STOP POINT

a. CUT IN A SERIES OF PASSES

¼" STRAIGHT BIT

MIRROR BLANK

PLYWOOD BASE

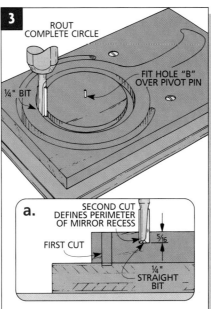

3 ROUT COMPLETE CIRCLE

¼" BIT

FIT HOLE "B" OVER PIVOT PIN

a. SECOND CUT DEFINES PERIMETER OF MIRROR RECESS

FIRST CUT

5/16

¼" STRAIGHT BIT

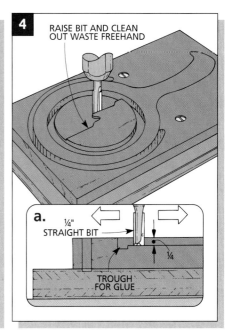

4 RAISE BIT AND CLEAN OUT WASTE FREEHAND

a. ¼" STRAIGHT BIT

¼

TROUGH FOR GLUE

To keep the router bit from cutting into my bench when routing all the way through the blank, I screwed the blank to a piece of plywood and then clamped the plywood to the bench *(Fig. 2)*.

PIVOT PIN. Next, drill a ¹⁄₁₆"-dia. hole halfway through the blank for the pivot pin at the centerpoint of the circle. Now drive a 17-gauge brad into the hole. Then snip off the brad ¼" above the surface.

OUTSIDE EDGE. With the pivot pin in place, you're ready to begin routing. You'll cut out the outside edge of the mirror by making repeat passes with the router and a ¼" straight bit *(Fig. 2)*. Since you

don't want to rout a complete circle and cut off the handle, mark start and stop points short of where the handle will be.

Next, set the bit ¼" deep and drop the base plate hole that's farthest from the bit (hole "A") over the pivot pin. Then, tip the router at a slight angle so the bit is directly over the start point and turn on the router (see *Fig. 2* in the box below).

Note: If you're using a plunge router, you won't have to tip the router.

Now, slowly plunge the straight bit into the blank. Then pivot the router around the circle until you reach the stop point. Repeat this process, lowering the

bit ¼" (or less) between passes until the bit cuts through the blank *(Fig. 2a)*.

ROUT MIRROR RECESS. Next, to rout the recess for the mirror, reset the bit ⁵⁄₁₆" deep, and position the other pivot hole ("B") over the brad. Now rout a complete circle *(Fig. 3)*. (This will rout a groove slightly larger in diameter than the mirror to allow for wood movement.)

CLEAN OUT WASTE. Finally, I reset the router to ¼" deep and removed the pivot pin. Then I cleaned out the waste freehand *(Fig. 4)*. This creates the recess for the mirror and a ¹⁄₁₆"-deep trough for glue squeeze-out *(Fig. 4a)*.

SHOP JIG .... *Small Circle Trammel*

The new router base plate needs to be larger than the original plate so it can be set over a pivot pin. Then it's used for routing the circular shape around the top of the Hand Mirror, the recesses for the glass mirror, and optional carving.

BASE PLATE. I cut the new base plate to size (6" x 7½") from a piece of ¼" acrylic plastic (or use hardboard) *(Fig. 1)*.

Now, center your router's original base plate over the new plate and use it as a template to locate the mounting holes and bit hole. Then drill these holes and mount the plate to your router.

PIVOT HOLES. Next, drill two ¹⁄₁₆"-dia. holes ("A" and "B") in the new base plate *(Fig. 1)*. These holes will fit over a pivot pin that's driven into the workpiece. (I used a 17-gauge brad for a pin.)

To locate the pivot holes, first mount a ¼" straight bit in the router. Drill one hole ("A") 3¼" from the outside edge of the bit *(Fig. 1)*. This hole will be used to guide the router when routing the outside edge of the mirror blank.

Now drill a second hole ("B") 2⁵⁄₁₆" from the edge of the bit *(Fig. 1)*. This hole is used when routing the recess for the beveled glass mirror. (And on the back to form a border for the initial, see the Designer's Notebook on page 93.)

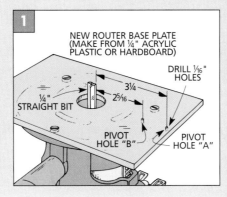

1 NEW ROUTER BASE PLATE (MAKE FROM ¼" ACRYLIC PLASTIC OR HARDBOARD)

DRILL ¹⁄₁₆" HOLES

3¼

¼" STRAIGHT BIT

2⁵⁄₁₆

PIVOT HOLE "B"

PIVOT HOLE "A"

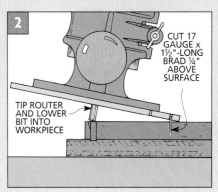

2 CUT 17 GAUGE x 1½"-LONG BRAD ¼" ABOVE SURFACE

TIP ROUTER AND LOWER BIT INTO WORKPIECE

After the recess for the beveled glass mirror is cleaned out, you can cut the blank to final shape using a band saw (or jig saw). But before you do that, you'll need to rout a decorative chamfer around the edge of the recess.

CHAMFER. To rout the chamfer, I used the same technique as before (routing with a pivot pin) *(Fig. 5)*. To do this, you'll have to drive the pivot pin (17-gauge brad) back into the small hole in the center of the mirror recess.

Then mount a 45° V-groove bit in the router and set the router bit $1/4$" below the base plate *(Fig. 5a)*.

Note: You can't use a chamfering bit with a bearing here since the bearing won't clear the bottom of the recess.

Next, position the router base so the pivot hole closest to the bit (pivot hole "B") sits over the pivot pin. Now turn on the router and plunge the bit into the workpiece. Then move the router in a counterclockwise direction. This will rout a chamfer around the recess with a face that's $1/8$" wide.

After the chamfer is routed, the blank can be removed from the plywood.

Note: If you plan on carving the initial on the back side, turn the blank over and rout the perimeter of the carving at this time. (See *Step 1* in the Designer's Notebook on the next page.)

CUT TO SHAPE. Once all of the routing is complete, the handle can be cut to shape on the band saw *(Fig. 6)*. I started by rough cutting the handle about $1/16$" outside the layout line.

SAND TO SHAPE. Next, mount a $1\frac{1}{2}$"-dia. sanding drum in the drill press and sand up to the outline around the handle *(Fig. 7)*. Don't sand the circular (top) part of the mirror or you may gouge it out of round. Just sand so there's a smooth transition between the mirror circle and the handle *(Fig. 7a)*.

BULLNOSE EDGE. Now, you can rout a soft bullnose profile all the way around the entire piece *(Fig. 8)*. To do this, mount a $1/2$" roundover bit in the router table and set it $5/16$" above the table.

Then rout both the top and bottom edges of the mirror. After routing, lightly hand sand the edge to remove the flat spot at the center, but don't round over the edges. Here, you want a crisp line.

FINISH. Before mounting the beveled glass mirror, I finished the wood with three coats of tung oil. Do not apply finish to the recessed area where the beveled glass mirror will be mounted.

GLUE MIRROR IN PLACE. Now the beveled glass mirror can be glued in place. I used a moisture-resistant silicone sealant and applied a thin bead onto the recess *(Fig. 9)*. (Silicone sealant is elastic and will allow the wood to expand and contract with changes in humidity.)

Finally, position the beveled glass mirror into the center of the recessed area and press it down firmly into the silicone sealant *(Fig. 9a)*.

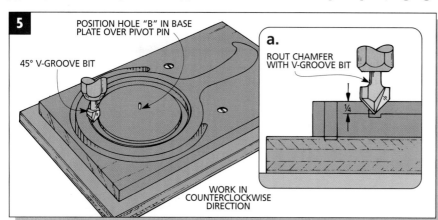

5 POSITION HOLE "B" IN BASE PLATE OVER PIVOT PIN
45° V-GROOVE BIT
WORK IN COUNTERCLOCKWISE DIRECTION
a. ROUT CHAMFER WITH V-GROOVE BIT
$1/4$

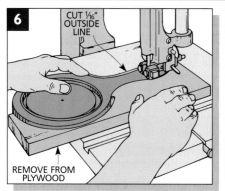

6 CUT $1/16$" OUTSIDE LINE
REMOVE FROM PLYWOOD

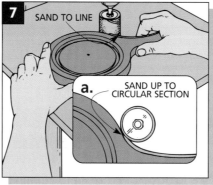

7 SAND TO LINE
a. SAND UP TO CIRCULAR SECTION

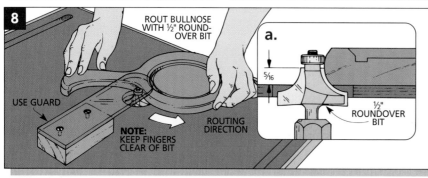

8 ROUT BULLNOSE WITH $1/2$" ROUND-OVER BIT
USE GUARD
NOTE: KEEP FINGERS CLEAR OF BIT
ROUTING DIRECTION
a. $5/16$
$1/2$" ROUNDOVER BIT

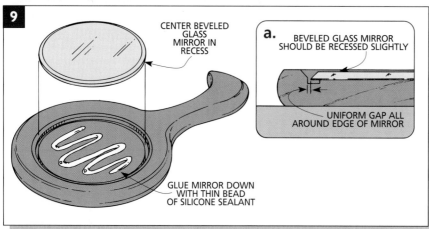

9 CENTER BEVELED GLASS MIRROR IN RECESS
GLUE MIRROR DOWN WITH THIN BEAD OF SILICONE SEALANT
a. BEVELED GLASS MIRROR SHOULD BE RECESSED SLIGHTLY
UNIFORM GAP ALL AROUND EDGE OF MIRROR

DESIGNER'S NOTEBOOK

Carving an initial on the back of the Hand Mirror makes it a more personal gift. And carving it isn't all that difficult. You can do most of the job with a router. Then give an old tool — a nail set — a new use.

RAISED INITIAL

■ Full-size patterns of the letters below are available from *Woodsmith Project Supplies* (see page 126). They're printed with a centerline and a centerpoint, so they're easy to align.

■ To align the letter, first draw a centerline down the back of the mirror and through the pivot pin *(Step 1)*. Next, press the centerpoint of the letter pattern down over the pivot pin. Align the centerlines on the pattern and the mirror back and glue the pattern down.

■ Now cut around the pattern with a razor knife and discard the background *(Step 2)*. Then mount a ¹/₈" straight bit in a router and remove the waste areas *(Step 3)*.

■ Next, remove the letter pattern and sand the recessed area and soften the edges of the letter *(Steps 4 and 5)*.

■ Finally, I stippled (or dotted) the background with a nail set (see photo). I found that by firmly tapping a ³/₃₂" nail set, I created a very different look than I got from lightly tapping a ¹/₁₆" nail set *(Step 6)*.

$$A\ B\ C\ D\ E\ F\ G\ H\ I\ J\ K\ L\ M$$
$$N\ O\ P\ Q\ R\ S\ T\ U\ V\ W\ X\ Y\ Z$$

ENLARGE LETTER BY 800% (3 X 200%)

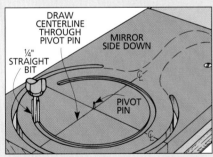

1 To rout perimeter of the recess for an initial, screw blank to plywood with mirror side down. Rout a ¹/₁₆"-deep circle by setting pivot hole "B" on the pivot point.

DRAW CENTERLINE THROUGH PIVOT PIN — MIRROR SIDE DOWN — ¹/₄" STRAIGHT BIT — PIVOT PIN

2 Align letter pattern in circle and glue with rubber cement or spray adhesive. Cut around outside edge of the letter with a sharp knife. Discard background.

REMOVE PIVOT PIN AFTER ALIGNING LETTER

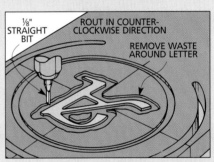

3 Mount a ¹/₈" straight bit in router and set ¹/₁₆" deep. Make a freehand pass around the outside edge of the letter. Get as close as possible without touching the letter.

¹/₈" STRAIGHT BIT — ROUT IN COUNTER-CLOCKWISE DIRECTION — REMOVE WASTE AROUND LETTER

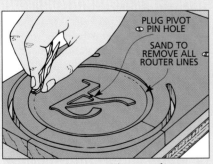

4 Remove waste with same ¹/₈" router bit, and then peel off letter pattern. Plug pivot pin hole with sliver from edge of blank. And sand recessed area level.

PLUG PIVOT PIN HOLE — SAND TO REMOVE ALL ROUTER LINES

5 Next, soften the edges of the letter. To do this, hold the side of the nail set at a slight angle and rub the sharp edges of the letter until they're rounded.

SOFTEN EDGES OF LETTER

6 Finally, stipple or dot the background using a ³/₃₂" or smaller nail set. Hold the nail set upright and tap firmly with a hammer, following the pattern above.

STIPPLING PATTERN — USE EVEN PRESSURE

Decorative Boxes

A small box doesn't have to be complicated to build to look great. These Decorative Boxes may be diminutive in size, but they get their extravagant appearance from exotic hardwoods and burl veneers.

For the record, I really enjoy making little boxes. They allow me to be extravagant with exotic woods and veneers that I couldn't afford on larger projects. And, unless I'm trying to be tricky, boxes don't require complicated joinery — just careful fitting.

For example, I made the square box in the photo above with solid walnut sides. The sides are simply mitered to fit around a plywood lid panel covered with Carpathian elm burl veneer.

The hexagonal box in the photo also has mitered sides, made from an exotic hardwood named zebrawood. The lid panel is veneered with maple burl.

Note: Despite their different shapes, there are only a couple of things done differently if you decide to build a hexagonal box instead of a square one. I've noted those things in the text.

VENEER. Burl veneer can be tricky to work with. The Technique on page 108 has some tips to make it easier. (See Sources on page 126 for information on how to find hardwood burl veneers.)

THIN STOCK. The $1/4$"-thick sides of the Decorative Box can be resawn from a $3/4$"-thick piece of stock. Ripping it in half and planing it to exact thickness is easy to do using a simple jig and a hand plane. I'll tell you more about how to build the

jig, and then how to use it in the Technique article on page 96.

INLAY. For the inlay strips that set off the burl veneer on top from the sides of the box, hand planing is not an option. That's because the strips are only $1/32$" thick. Instead you'll have to use a technique that's similar to the one used to make splines. (See the Technique article on page 98.) By using a zero-clearance fence and a fine-tooth blade, you can shave off really thin strips that fall away from the blade, safe and sound.

Note: Use a contrasting wood (or lighter color stain) for the inlay strip. It helps to set off the burl veneer even more.

EXPLODED VIEW

OVERALL DIMENSIONS:
$4\frac{1}{2}$W x $4\frac{1}{2}$D x $2\frac{1}{2}$H

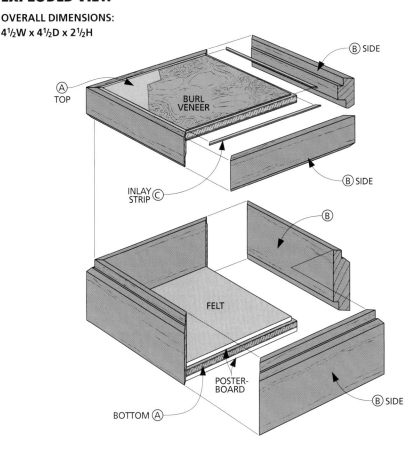

A TOP

B SIDE

BURL VENEER

B SIDE

INLAY STRIP C

B

FELT

POSTER-BOARD

BOTTOM A

B SIDE

VENEERED PANELS

This box is made up of just a few parts: top and bottom panels, the sides and some inlay strips. The only difference between the top and bottom is the covering. That's because the top panel gets a burl veneer, while the bottom is covered with felt.

Note: I'm showing how to build the square box in the drawings. If you choose to build a hexagonal box, the procedure is the same, except where noted.

THE PANELS. I started by making the veneered top panel and the felt-lined bottom panel. You need to make these panels first in order to size the rabbets that are used to mount the panels in the side pieces (refer to *Fig. 3* on page 96).

Start by cutting the $\frac{1}{4}$" plywood panels to a rough size of $4\frac{1}{2}$" square *(Fig. 1)*.

Note: I used Baltic birch plywood. It works well as a sub-base for veneer, but any thin plywood will work.

Then I laminated Carpathian elm burl veneer to both sides of the top panel.

The plywood bottom panel is also cut to a rough size of $4\frac{1}{2}$" square, but the felt

isn't added until later (so it won't get filled with sawdust). The bottom will be cut to size later, after the rabbets have been added to the sides (*Fig. 7* on page 97).

SIDES

After the top and bottom panels are made, the stock for the sides is cut to size. Because these are small pieces I started

with extra long pieces and then cut them to length after routing the rabbets and groove. Begin with two pieces of $\frac{3}{4}$"-thick stock at least 3" wide by 15" long. This length also allows a little extra for some test pieces. Now, resaw these pieces to get two pieces $\frac{3}{8}$" thick and plane the surfaces smooth *(Fig. 2)*. (See the Technique on page 96 for more on this.) Then rip the two pieces to a final width of $2\frac{7}{8}$".

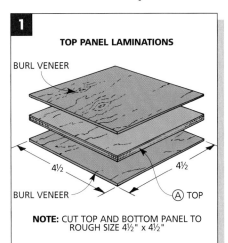

1

TOP PANEL LAMINATIONS

BURL VENEER

$4\frac{1}{2}$ $4\frac{1}{2}$

BURL VENEER

A TOP

NOTE: CUT TOP AND BOTTOM PANEL TO ROUGH SIZE $4\frac{1}{2}$" x $4\frac{1}{2}$"

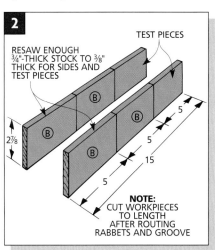

2

TEST PIECES

RESAW ENOUGH $\frac{3}{4}$"-THICK STOCK TO $\frac{3}{8}$" THICK FOR SIDES AND TEST PIECES

$2\frac{7}{8}$

B   B   B

B   B   B

5   5   5   15   5

NOTE: CUT WORKPIECES TO LENGTH AFTER ROUTING RABBETS AND GROOVE

ROUT RABBETS. A couple of rabbets hold the top and bottom panels in place. The best way I've found to shape these small pieces is with a straight bit mounted in a router table. To rout the rabbets for the top panel, first set the bit to cut 1/8" deep. Then adjust the fence so the width of the rabbet equals the thickness of the veneered top panel *(Fig. 3)*.

When routing the rabbet, I like to feed the workpiece from left to right (instead of the normal direction of right to left) *(Fig. 4)*. This "backrouting" lessens chipout on the shoulder that will be the top edge of the side piece.

Safety Note: When backrouting, the bit will try to pull the workpiece. Hold

onto the workpiece tightly and, most importantly, take light cuts.

To rout the bottom rabbet, adjust the fence so the rabbet is just a bit deeper than the combined thickness of the base plywood and one piece of posterboard *(Fig. 3a)*. (The felt for the bottom panel is mounted to a piece of posterboard.)

OVERLAPPING RABBETS. The next step involves using a little ingenuity to get a snug fit between the lid and the base. The best way to get a good fit is to assemble the box, then cut the top off to form the lid. There's a nifty technique that makes an overlapping rabbet joint where the lid and base meet *(Fig. 11)*.

To make these rabbets, two grooves are cut — one is on the inside of the side pieces before the box is assembled, and

the second is on the outside of the box after it's assembled *(Fig. 3)*.

ROUT GROOVES. Begin by routing a 3/8"-wide groove, 5/8" down from the top edge of each workpiece *(Fig. 5)*.

Note: The depth of the groove is important — it should be as close to half the thickness of the stock as possible.

CUT SIDES TO LENGTH. After the grooves are routed, the sides can be cut to length. Start by cutting the two workpieces into six pieces approximately 5" long. (Save two of the pieces to use as test pieces later.) Now set the blade to a 45° angle and miter both ends of each piece. (On a hexagonal box set the blade to 30° and cut eight workpieces into 3" lengths.)

When mitering these pieces to length, clamp a stop block to the auxiliary fence on the miter gauge so the point-to-point measurement on the sides is 4 1/2" (2 3/4" for a hexagonal box) *(Fig. 6)*.

CUT PANELS TO SIZE. After the sides have been cut to length, dry-assemble the box with band clamps. Then cut the top and bottom panels to size, sneaking up on the cuts until the panels fit snugly in the rabbets *(Fig. 7)*.

GLUE THE SIDES. When the top and bottom panels fit, the sides can be glued together. Use the panels to keep the sides square, but don't glue them in place yet.

SEPARATE BASE & LID

Before cutting the base from the lid, I used a test piece to set the bit height and fence position on the router table.

POSITION THE FENCE. The fence is set to rout a groove on the outside of the box

3 CROSS SECTION

2 7/8

1/8 → Ⓐ TOP PANEL

GROOVE PLACEMENT (SEE FIGS. 5 AND 8)

a. 1/8

CUT BOTTOM RABBET SO FELT IS SLIGHTLY RECESSED

Ⓑ

BOTTOM PANEL

3/8

POSTER-BOARD 1/8

Ⓐ

FELT

FEED IN OPPOSITE DIRECTION TO LESSEN CHIPOUT

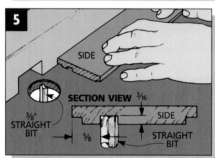

5 SIDE

SECTION VIEW 3/16

3/8" STRAIGHT BIT

SIDE

5/8

STRAIGHT BIT

TECHNIQUE . . . . *Working with Thin Wood*

Most of the projects in this book use thin stock — 1/2", 3/8", and even 1/4" thick. Although 1/2"-thick stock is sometimes available at hardwood lumberyards and a few mail order woodworking suppliers (see page 126), anything thinner than that is difficult to find.

HAND PLANE. The solution is to purchase 3/4"-thick stock and plane it down yourself. Of course, if you have a portable thickness planer, that's an easy task. The alternative is to resaw the rough stock to a thickness that's 1/32" to 1/16" over the final thickness. Then use a hand plane to smooth it the rest of the way.

The problem I find when doing this is the hassle of constantly checking the thickness of the piece while at the same time making sure it's an even thickness all the way across the piece.

JIG. On small pieces it's worth making a simple jig to guide the plane to the proper thickness. Just cut a piece of plywood as a base and place the resawn piece on the plywood. Then rip two strips to the final thickness you want for the workpiece. Tack these two strips beside the workpiece, countersinking the brads.

Now just plane the workpiece down, angling the plane slightly so the heel and

toe are over the guide strips. They will stop the plane when the workpiece is planed down to their thickness.

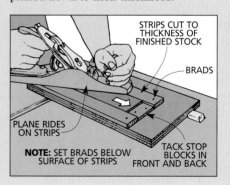

STRIPS CUT TO THICKNESS OF FINISHED STOCK

BRADS

PLANE RIDES ON STRIPS

NOTE: SET BRADS BELOW SURFACE OF STRIPS

TACK STOP BLOCKS IN FRONT AND BACK

that overlaps the groove already cut on the inside of the box. The overlap should be about $1/16$", which means setting the fence $15/16$" from the bit *(Fig. 8)*.

Since these two grooves overlap, they will form the two overlapping rabbets on the lid and base *(Fig. 3)*.

ADJUST BIT HEIGHT. The critical part of this cut is adjusting the height of the bit. You want the groove on the outside of the box to be slightly deeper than the groove that's already cut on the inside. (This sets the clearance between the two rabbets. If the groove is too deep the lid will be loose. If the groove is too shallow, the lid will be tight.)

Use one of the pieces left over after cutting the sides as a test piece. Set the depth of cut until the second groove is just a hair deeper than the first groove *(Fig. 8)*.

CUT GROOVES. When the set up works on the test piece, cut grooves on two opposite sides of the box *(Fig. 9)*.

Note: To give myself something to hold onto, I pressed the top and bottom panels in place in the box.

MAKE FILLER STRIPS. Then, to keep the box from collapsing when the next two grooves are routed, cut two filler strips to fit in the grooves and tape them in place *(Fig. 10)*. Then, cut the two grooves on the remaining two sides of the box.

Remove the strips, and the overlapping rabbets on the lid and base should slide together *(Fig. 11)*.

APPLY INLAY STRIP

After the sides are assembled, the box is ready for the finishing touches. I began by applying an inlay strip to the top panel. (See the Technique on page 98 to make your own inlay strips.) This strip is rabbeted into the edge of the top panel.

RABBET. To rout the rabbet, adjust the bit to cut a hair shallower than the thickness of the strip *(Fig. 13)*. (The strip is sanded flush with the top later.)

Next, adjust the fence to cut a rabbet equal to the width of the strip. To prevent this thin piece from sliding into the opening in the fence, I clamped a plywood facing to the fence *(Fig. 12)*.

MITER THE STRIPS. After the rabbets are cut, glue the panel into the box's lid. Then the ends of the inlay strips (C) are mitered with a sharp chisel to fit in the rabbets. To guide the chisel, I made a mitering block from a scrap of 2x4 cut off at a 45° angle *(Fig. 14)*. (A 30° angle for the hexagonal box.)

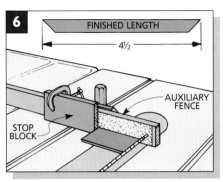

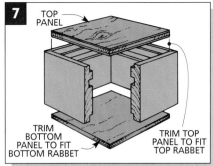

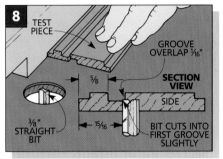

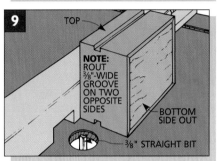

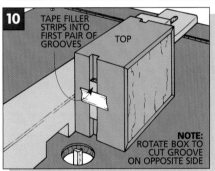

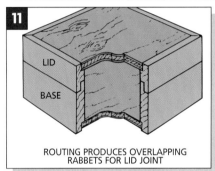

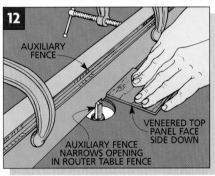

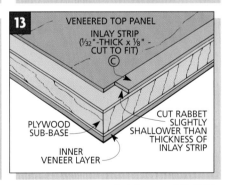

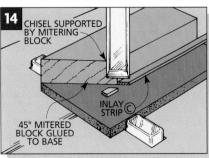

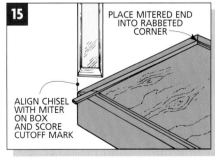

First, miter one end of the strip. Then, place the strip with the point in one corner of the rabbet and mark the position of the opposite point *(Fig. 15)*. Now cut this corner on the block. With all the strips mitered, glue them into the rabbets.

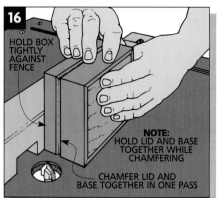

16

HOLD BOX TIGHTLY AGAINST FENCE

NOTE: HOLD LID AND BASE TOGETHER WHILE CHAMFERING

CHAMFER LID AND BASE TOGETHER IN ONE PASS

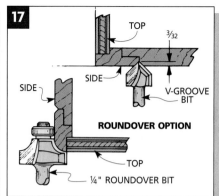

17

TOP

3/32

SIDE

SIDE

V-GROOVE BIT

ROUNDOVER OPTION

TOP

1/4" ROUNDOVER BIT

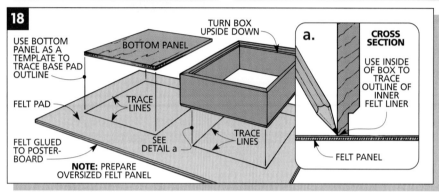

18

USE BOTTOM PANEL AS A TEMPLATE TO TRACE BASE PAD OUTLINE

TURN BOX UPSIDE DOWN

BOTTOM PANEL

FELT PAD

TRACE LINES

FELT GLUED TO POSTER-BOARD

SEE DETAIL a

TRACE LINES

NOTE: PREPARE OVERSIZED FELT PANEL

a.

CROSS SECTION

USE INSIDE OF BOX TO TRACE OUTLINE OF INNER FELT LINER

FELT PANEL

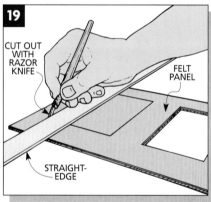

19

CUT OUT WITH RAZOR KNIFE

FELT PANEL

STRAIGHT-EDGE

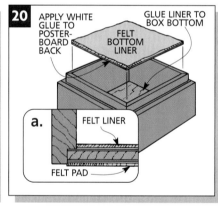

20

APPLY WHITE GLUE TO POSTER-BOARD BACK

GLUE LINER TO BOX BOTTOM

FELT BOTTOM LINER

a.

FELT LINER

FELT PAD

CHAMFER LID EDGES. Next, I chamfered the edges where the lid and base meet. This can be done by holding the box together and against the fence while making a single pass over a V-groove bit on the router table *(Figs. 16 and 17)*.

Note: The top edges on my box are square. For a softer profile, the top edge could be eased with a 1/4" roundover bit on the router table *(Fig. 17)*.

FELT PADS

The box has a felt liner inside and a felt pad on the bottom. The trick to making the felt fit properly is applying it to a posterboard backing first *(Fig. 18)*.

GLUE FELT TO POSTERBOARD. To glue the felt in place, I used an aerosol spray adhesive. Spray the adhesive on a piece of felt large enough to make both the bottom pad and the liner. Then mount it to the posterboard *(Fig. 18)*.

TRACE PATTERNS. Now go ahead and trace the bottom panel on the posterboard for the bottom pad *(Fig. 18)*. Then turn the box upside down to trace a second outline for the liner *(Fig. 18a)*.

Once the patterns are traced on the posterboard, cut out the pad and the liner with a razor knife *(Fig. 19)*.

FINAL ASSEMBLY

After sanding the box, I applied three coats of spray polyurethane finish. Then, when the finish was dry, I glued the bottom panel into the box. Finally, I glued the felt bottom liner and felt pad to the bottom panel *(Fig. 20)*. ∎

TECHNIQUE .... *Cutting Inlay Strips*

The procedure I use for making thin inlay strips is similar to the method I use to cut splines. But there is one difference — these inlay strips are *very* narrow and thin. They're so small that they slip down into the slot in the saw's insert plate. The best way to solve this problem is to use a zero-clearance insert.

CUTTING THE STRIPS. Once the insert is in place the inlays can be cut from a piece of scrap with a fine-toothed blade.

To cut the inlays, start by setting the distance between the fence and the blade to equal the desired *width* of the inlay *(Step 1* in drawing). In my case, I set it to

cut a 1/8"-wide strip. Then set the blade height to about 1/2".

TWO PASSES. Now make a pass and then flip the piece around so the opposite face is against the fence and make another pass *(Step 2* in drawing).

Reset the fence so the piece falls on the "waste" side of the blade *(Step 2)*. It should be cut a little more than the thickness of the veneer you're using so it can be sanded down flush after it's glued in.

When the third cut is made, the strips fall away from the blade where they can't kick back. And the insert prevents the strips from slipping down below the saw.

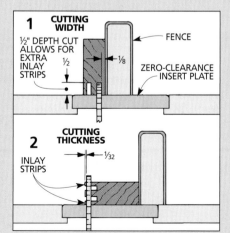

1 CUTTING WIDTH

1/2" DEPTH CUT ALLOWS FOR EXTRA INLAY STRIPS

1/2

1/8

FENCE

ZERO-CLEARANCE INSERT PLATE

2 CUTTING THICKNESS

INLAY STRIPS

1/32

Picture Frame

There are several ways to dress up this simple frame with decorative strips of wood. And instead of using miters, the corners are joined by stub tenons that fit into the same grooves as the picture.

nitially, it appears that making this Picture Frame would be a rather involved process. It looks as if there's a lot of fitting thin little squares of veneer in perfect position on the front of the frames. But that's not the case. And you'll find that it's not that difficult to build the frame (or any one of the variations I've designed) in just a few hours.

The "veneer" is actually a thick piece of wood that's glued to the front of the frame and then trimmed off to leave only a $^3/_{32}$" thickness. And the design is routed through the veneer just deep enough so the contrasting wood (the base frame itself) shows through.

If you want to build a frame that has a slightly different corner detail, see the Designer's Notebook on page 103.

CORNER JOINTS. There's something else different about this frame. It's not joined with difficult-to-cut miter joints. Instead I used a much simpler joint — a stub tenon and groove — to bring all four corners together.

The groove serves a double purpose. In addition to holding the tenon at the corners, it also holds the picture, glass, and backing. And the bottom is left open, so the picture can be easily changed out.

FRAME PIECES. As with other projects in this book, you'll be working with thin

stock here. The pieces that make up the frame sides, top, and bottom are all only $^5/_8$" thick. It can be difficult to find stock this thickness. (And expensive.) To solve this problem, I simply used a band saw and hand plane to mill my own thin stock. You can read more about how to resaw and work with thin stock in the Technique articles on pages 65 and 96.

WOOD. The wood you use for your Picture Frames is not that important, but it is a good idea to use contrasting woods for the base and veneer layers. Then when the accent details are added (refer to page 103), the contrast will really show off your craftsmanship.

EXPLODED VIEW

OVERALL DIMENSIONS:
7W x $^{23}/_{32}$D x 8$^1/_2$H

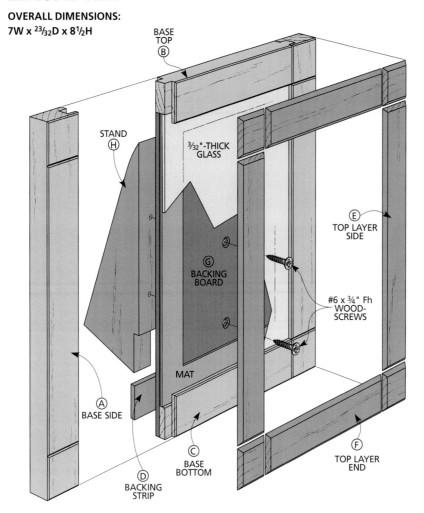

STAND
(H)

BASE
TOP
(B)

$^3/_{32}$"-THICK
GLASS

(E)
TOP LAYER
SIDE

(G)
BACKING
BOARD

#6 x $^3/_4$" Fh
WOOD-
SCREWS

MAT

(A)
BASE SIDE

(C)
BASE
BOTTOM

(D)
BACKING
STRIP

(F)
TOP LAYER
END

MATERIALS LIST

WOOD

A	Base Sides (2)	$^5/_8$ x 1 - 8$^1/_2$
B	Base Top (1)	$^5/_8$ x 1 - 5
C	Base Bottom (1)	$^5/_8$ x 1 - 5
D	Backing Strip (1)*	$^3/_{16}$ x 1 - 4$^1/_2$
E	Top Layer Sides (2)	$^5/_8$ x 1 - 8$^1/_2$
F	Top Layer Ends (2)	$^5/_8$ x 1 - 4$^1/_2$
G	Backing Board	$^1/_8$ ply - 5 x 7$^3/_4$
H	Stand	$^5/_8$ x 2$^1/_4$ - 6

*Note: Backing Strip (D) is resawn from Base Bottom (C).

HARDWARE SUPPLIES
(2) No. 6 x $^3/_4$" Fh woodscrews
(1 pc.) $^3/_{32}$" glass, 5" x 7"

BASE FRAME

The Picture Frame consists of a base frame with a thin layer of a contrasting wood glued on top of it. Then, when the pieces are thicknessed and cut to size, a series of V-groove patterns are routed into the face of the frame to highlight these contrasts. (See the Designer's Notebook on page 103 for a few alternate designs for your frames.)

Before building anything, the first thing you'll want to decide is the size of the photo you're going to be framing. All the measurements shown here are for a 5x7 photo *(Fig. 1)*.

Begin work on the base frame by resawing a 32"-long piece of stock to $^5/_8$" thick. Then rip it 1" wide.

GROOVE. Once the workpiece is cut to size, the next step is to cut the groove for the stub tenon and groove joint. To allow for the correct setback on the front of the frame after the top layer of wood is added, the groove is cut off-center on the thickness of the workpiece ($^1/_8$" back from the front face) *(Fig. 2)*.

I cut the groove $^5/_{16}$" wide. This accommodates the glass ($^3/_{32}$"), an optional mat, the photo, and a $^1/_8$"-thick backing.

To cut the groove on the table saw, adjust the height of the dado blade to cut $^1/_4$" deep *(Fig. 2)*. Now place the front face of the workpiece against the rip fence and cut the groove.

FRAME PIECES. Once the groove is cut in the workpiece, the four pieces of the frame can be cut to length *(Fig. 1)*. Cut two sides (A) 8$^1/_2$" long, and the top (B) and bottom (C) pieces each 5" long.

STUB TENONS. The next step is to cut the stub tenons on the ends of the top and

---

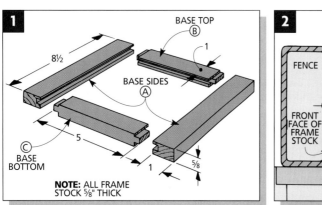

1

BASE TOP
(B)

8$^1/_2$

BASE SIDES
(A)

1

5

BASE
BOTTOM
(C)

1

$^5/_8$

NOTE: ALL FRAME STOCK $^5/_8$ THICK

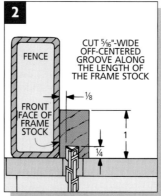

2

FENCE

CUT $^5/_{16}$"-WIDE OFF-CENTERED GROOVE ALONG THE LENGTH OF THE FRAME STOCK

$^1/_8$

FRONT FACE OF FRAME STOCK

1

$^1/_4$

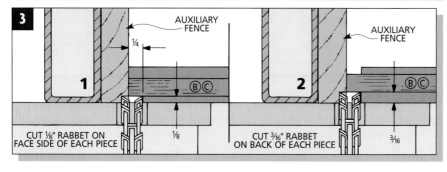

3

AUXILIARY FENCE

$^1/_4$

1

(B)(C)

CUT $^1/_8$" RABBET ON FACE SIDE OF EACH PIECE

$^1/_8$

AUXILIARY FENCE

2

(B)(C)

CUT $^3/_{16}$" RABBET ON BACK OF EACH PIECE

$^3/_{16}$

bottom pieces to fit the groove. Since the groove is off-center, the tenons are cut off-center on the thickness to match *(Fig. 3)*.

To cut the tenon shoulders on the face of each piece, you'll need to cut a $1/8$"-deep rabbet *(Step 1 in Fig. 3)*. And then to complete the tenons, cut a $3/16$"-deep rabbet on the back side *(Step 2)*.

BOTTOM PIECE. The glass, photo, and backing slide out through an opening in the frame bottom. To create the opening, resaw the frame bottom piece in two.

To do this, set the rip fence $5/16$" from the inside edge of the blade *(Fig. 4)*. Place the front face of the piece against the fence and run the piece through. The $5/16$"-thick piece is the finished frame bottom (C). But save the waste piece and resaw it, if necessary, to $3/16$" thick *(Fig. 4a)*. It will be glued to the backing board as a backing strip (D) later.

FRAME ASSEMBLY. Once all the pieces are cut, glue and clamp the frame together *(Fig. 5)*. To hold the bottom piece flush with the frame face until the glue is completely dry, I cut temporary spaces and slipped them into the grooves with the tenons *(Fig. 5a)*.

TOP LAYER

After the base frame is assembled, you can glue on the top layer of contrasting wood. You could glue on a $3/32$"-thick layer, but there's an easier way. I glued on a thicker layer ($5/8$") and then, when the glue was dry, resawed most of it leaving a $3/32$"-thick layer.

Start by gluing on the top layer in four pieces: the two sides (E) are each $8 1/2$" long. And the end (F) pieces are each $4 1/2$" long *(Fig. 6)*. (There's a variation of this that has a different wood glued to the corners. Refer to the Designer's Notebook on page 103.)

FINAL THICKNESS. When the glue is dry, trim the extra thickness off the top layer in two passes. First, set the rip fence $3/4$" from the blade, and hold the back of the frame against the fence to make a pass on all four frame pieces *(Fig. 7)*. Next, move the fence slightly to leave the top layer $3/32$" thick and skim the remaining stock off all pieces. Finish up the pieces by scraping and sanding off the blade marks for a smooth surface.

ROUT THE PATTERN. Next, rout the pattern into the frame face with a V-groove bit mounted in a router table *(Fig. 8)*. Begin by routing the outside edge of the frame. Just set the fence so the point of

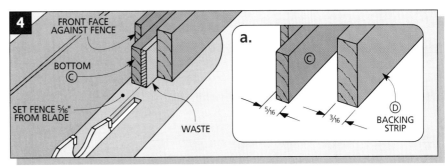

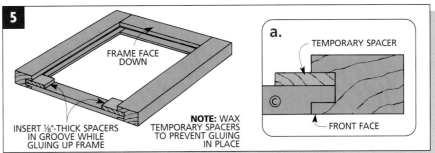

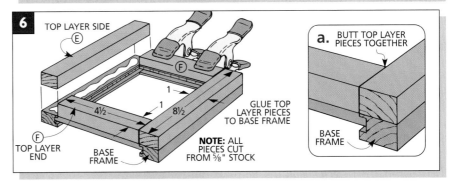

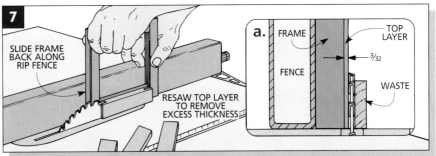

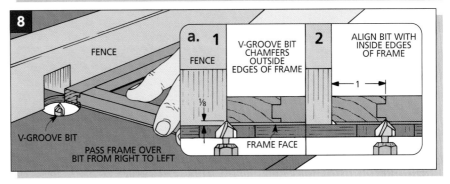

the V-groove bit is aligned flush with the face of the fence *(Step 1 in Fig. 8a)*.

Next, reposition the router table fence (leave the bit at the same height), so the point of the V-groove bit aligns with the inside edge of the frame *(Step 2)*. Now rout these grooves so they intersect at all four inside corners of the frame opening.

The last step in constructing the Picture Frame is to make the backing board and stand. The backing board holds the photo and glass in the frame. And the stand is a wedge-shaped block screwed to the back of the backing board *(Fig. 9)*.

BACKING BOARD. The backing board (G) can be made of any stiff $1/8$"-thick material, such as hardboard, but I decided to use $1/8$" plywood. Cut the plywood to width to fit the groove in the frame. (Mine measured 5".) As for length, cut the board to fit from the top of the groove to the bottom of the frame ($7^3/4$").

STAND. Next, cut the wedge-shaped block for the stand (H) from a $5/8$"-thick piece of stock (to match the frame) on the band saw *(Fig. 10)*. Then slightly round the top end with a sander *(Fig. 9a)*.

BACKING STRIP. Now cut a notch in the bottom of the long edge of the stand to accommodate the backing strip (D) that was cut off the bottom frame piece earlier *(Fig. 9)*. I ended up using one end of the strip as a template to mark the location of the notch *(Fig. 11)*.

The next step is to glue the backing strip in place *(Fig. 9)*. It fills in the area between the two sides of the frame.

Finally, you can now screw the stand to the backing board *(Fig. 9)*.

Note: I didn't glue the stand to the backing board. This way, if I ever want to hang the frame on the wall, it's simply a matter of unscrewing the stand.

FINISH AND ASSEMBLY. Once the backing board and stand are assembled, you can apply a clear finish to all the frame parts. I decided to spray on two coats of clear satin polyurethane. Once the finish is dry, the contents can be inserted in the frame.

GLASS. Several things go in the frame along with the photo. The first is the glass. I used a standard thickness ($3/32$") piece of glass that measured 5" x 7". But you could use a piece of $1/8$" acrylic plastic. Slide the glass through the bottom of the frame so it drops into place behind the frame face *(Fig. 12)*.

MAT AND PHOTO. If you're using a pre-cut mat, it goes into the frame next. These mats are often available at frame shops and art supply stores in a variety of colors. With the mat lying in place over the glass, slide the photo into the frame face down on the mat *(Fig. 12)*.

BACKING BOARD. Finally, slide the backing board (G) into the grooves in

the frame side pieces *(Fig. 13)*. Be sure to push it all the way in.

FILLERS. Depending on the thickness of the glass and the mat you use, the contents of the frame might be too loose. If

this is the case, remove the backing board and insert one or more piece of cardboard or heavy paper to act as filler on top of the photo. Then slide the backing board back in place. ∎

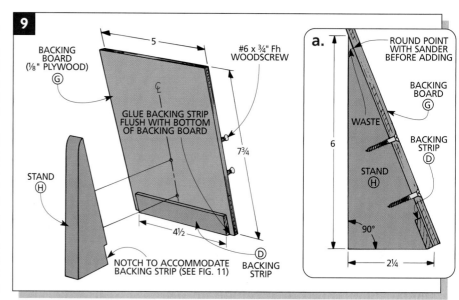

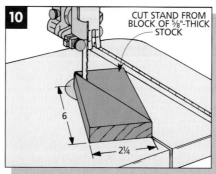

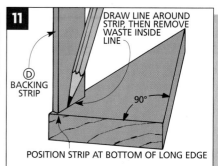

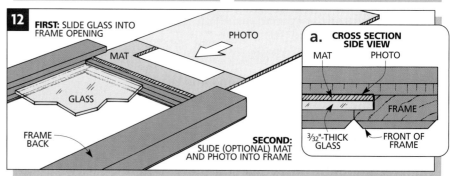

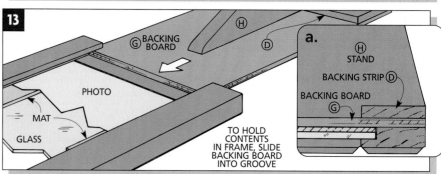

DESIGNER'S NOTEBOOK

Here are three alternate designs for your frames, with details that show off your favorite photograph. Each one is easy to make — just like the original — but the possibilities for different looks are endless.

CORNER PATTERNS

■ The first frame is a slight variation of the original design (see the left photo). The difference is that an additional groove is routed in each face of the frame to create four small squares at each corner.

■ To make this design, first complete the basic frame as before. Then re-position the V-groove bit so the point is centered on the frame side *(Fig. 1)*.

■ The most important thing about this design is to get the bit exactly centered on the width of the frame *(Fig. 1a)*. To do this, start with a very shallow cut, and then check the position of the bit to be sure it's centered. Now, re-adjust the height of the bit to cut a 1/8"-deep groove (to match the other grooves in the frame).

■ Finally, rout the center groove across all four frame side and top faces.

■ In the next variation (refer to the middle photo above), two contrasting woods are glued to the base frame, rather than one. The routed design, however, is the same as the original frame.

■ To make this design, first cut four 1"-square pieces from a third contrasting wood for the corners of the top layer. Then cut the other pieces of the top layer from a different wood. For the basic frame that holds a 5" x 7" photo, make the top

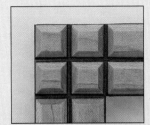

Extra Groove. *This simple variation of the basic frame is made by routing an additional groove centered on each frame piece.*

Accent. *To add an extra accent to your frame, glue 1"-square blocks of a contrasting wood onto the corners of the base frame.*

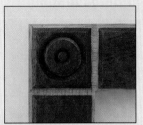

Circles. *The circles in this corner square are made with two bits you might not expect — a plug cutter and a countersink.*

and the bottom pieces 4 1/2" long and the side pieces 6 1/2" long.

■ Now glue the pieces to the base frame with the square pieces in the corners. All of these pieces should butt against each other tightly *(Fig. 2)*.

■ Once the glue is completely dry, resaw the frame to final thickness. Then on the router table, rout the same pattern as on the original frame.

■ To make the circles in the corner squares (right photo above), I used a plug cutter and a countersink. The countersink I used is the type that fits around a drill bit. With the bit removed, it leaves a portion of the circle uncut.

■ Start work on the completed original frame. To get the circles centered in the

corner squares, I used an auxiliary fence and stop block on the drill press to help align the frame *(Fig. 3)*.

■ To do this, first mount a 1/16" drill bit in the chuck and align the point of the bit with the center of one of the squares. Next, move the fence and stop block against the frame and clamp them to the drill press table *(Fig. 3)*.

■ Now, to make the large circle, plunge a 1/2" plug cutter into the veneer just deep enough for the wood of the base frame to show through *(Fig. 3a)*.

■ Next, replace the plug cutter with the countersink *(Fig. 3b)*. Retract the drill bit into the countersink so the bit will not enter the wood. Now make a cut the same depth as the plug cutter circle.

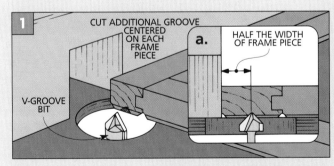

1 CUT ADDITIONAL GROOVE CENTERED ON EACH FRAME PIECE
a. HALF THE WIDTH OF FRAME PIECE
V-GROOVE BIT

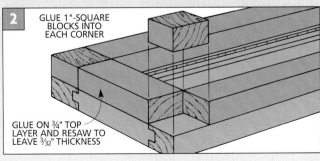

2 GLUE 1"-SQUARE BLOCKS INTO EACH CORNER
GLUE ON 3/4" TOP LAYER AND RESAW TO LEAVE 3/32" THICKNESS

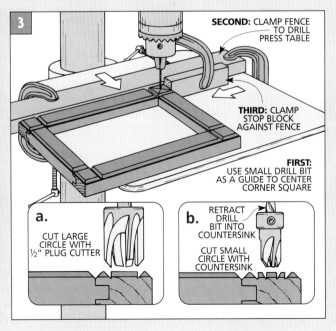

3 SECOND: CLAMP FENCE TO DRILL PRESS TABLE
THIRD: CLAMP STOP BLOCK AGAINST FENCE
FIRST: USE SMALL DRILL BIT AS A GUIDE TO CENTER CORNER SQUARE
a. CUT LARGE CIRCLE WITH 1/2" PLUG CUTTER
b. RETRACT DRILL BIT INTO COUNTERSINK
CUT SMALL CIRCLE WITH COUNTERSINK

Music Box

Building this small Music Box presents an unexpected challenge — how to rout details on such small workpieces. The solution is to work with an oversize blank first. Then cut the pieces from it.

Our family owned a simple wooden music box that I enjoyed listening to when I was a child. Many years later, I decided to build one for my own growing family.

When I planned the design for the box, I wasn't thinking about what a challenge it would be to build. After all, it only has five parts and none of them are that complicated. But then I realized that routing such small workpieces can be a little tricky. So I solved the problem by starting with an oversized blank. Then I routed all the details *before* I cut the pieces to size. But that wasn't the only thing I had to carefully plan around.

I also used a technique on the lid that takes a little practice — working with veneer. It was great trying this on the small lid, and I didn't have to worry about a major effort. (For more on this, see the Technique article on page 108.)

CHIP CARVING. As an alternative, you may want to try a chip carving on the lid. (Shown in the background of the photo.) To be successful at chip carving, you want to work into it gradually. That's why I decided to stick to a simple project for my first attempt. You'll be surprised how easy it is to get good results with just a little practice. To learn more, see the Designer's Notebook on page 109.

MUSIC WORKS. Another challenge was trying to figure out a way to get the music works to start when I opened the lid and to stop when I closed it. The secret is a small pin connected to the wire shut-off arm of the music movement. (A kit that includes the music works is available from *Woodsmith Project Supplies*. See Sources on page 126.)

I've found the best way to make sure this goes smoothly is to have it all working properly *before* the box is fully assembled. I wound up dry-assembling it several times before actually gluing it up.

FINISH. After the box was glued up, I used a spray-on lacquer finish.

EXPLODED VIEW

OVERALL DIMENSIONS:
6W x 5D x 2⅝H

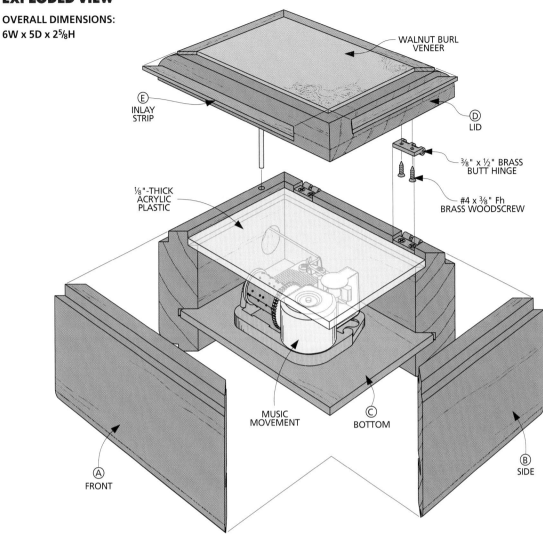

WALNUT BURL
VENEER

E
INLAY
STRIP

D
LID

⅜" x ½" BRASS
BUTT HINGE

#4 x ⅜" Fh
BRASS WOODSCREW

⅛"-THICK
ACRYLIC
PLASTIC

MUSIC
MOVEMENT

C
BOTTOM

A
FRONT

B
SIDE

MATERIALS LIST

WOOD

A	Front/Back (2)	½ x 2⅛ - 6
B	Sides (2)	½ x 2⅛ - 5
C	Bottom (1)	⅛ x 2¹¹⁄₁₆ - 3¹¹⁄₁₆
D	Lid (1)	½ x 3¼ - 4¼
E	Inlay Strip	¹⁄₁₆ x ¼ - 20 ln. in.

HARDWARE SUPPLIES

(1) Music movement w/ keywind system
(1 pc.) Walnut burl veneer, 3¼" x 4¼"
(2) ⅜" x ½" brass butt hinges
(4) No. 4 x ⅜" Fh brass woodscrews
(1 pc.) ⅛"-thick acrylic plastic, 3⅜" x 4⅜"

CUTTING DIAGRAM

½ x 3½ - 24 (.6 Sq. Ft.)

ALSO NEED: SMALL PIECE OF CONTRASTING HARDWOOD
OR COMMERCIAL INLAY BANDING FOR PART E

BLANK

The Music Box is made up of small-sized front, back, and side pieces. To make it safe to work on them, instead of routing four individual pieces, I routed a single long blank, then cut the pieces to length.

To make the blank, start with a 1/2"-thick piece of stock. Rip it to finished width and rough length (2 1/8" x 24").

ADD DETAILS. After the blank is cut to size, rout a 1/4" roundover with a 1/8" shoulder along one edge *(Fig. 1a)*. Adjust the bit so the shoulder is on the bottom edge of the blank to form the base.

Next, add a "shadow line" around the top outside edge of the blank *(Fig. 1b)*. I used a 1/2" straight bit, setting it to make a 1/8"-deep cut. Then I moved the fence to rout a 3/16"-wide rabbet on the blank.

At this point, you'll need to rout a lip the same depth as the shadow line on the top inside edge for an acrylic plastic dust cover *(Fig. 1c)*. Simply move the fence over to make a 1/4"-wide rabbet.

Finally, cut a 1/8"-wide groove for the bottom to fit into *(Fig. 1d)*. To cut this groove, raise the table saw blade 1/4" above the table. Then position the fence 3/4" from the *outside* of the blade. With the inside of the blank face down, place the base edge of the blank against the fence and cut the groove.

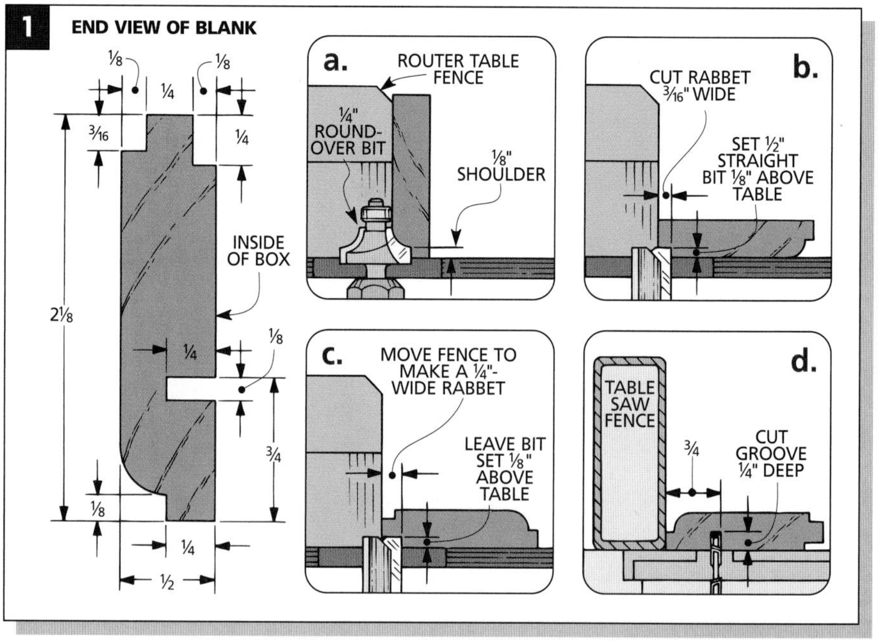
1
END VIEW OF BLANK
1/8
1/4
1/8
3/16
1/4
INSIDE OF BOX
2 1/8
1/4
1/8
3/4
1/8
1/4
1/2
a.
ROUTER TABLE FENCE
1/4" ROUND-OVER BIT
1/8" SHOULDER
b.
CUT RABBET 3/16" WIDE
SET 1/2" STRAIGHT BIT 1/8" ABOVE TABLE
c.
MOVE FENCE TO MAKE A 1/4"-WIDE RABBET
LEAVE BIT SET 1/8" ABOVE TABLE
d.
TABLE SAW FENCE
3/4
CUT GROOVE 1/4" DEEP

FRONT, BACK, & SIDES

With the details cut on the long blank, the next step is to cut the front (A), back (A), and side pieces (B) to finished length. To make sure the box ends up square, you want to cut the opposite sides of the box to exactly the same length.

AUXILIARY FENCE. To do this, first attach an auxiliary fence to the miter gauge. This fence helps support these small workpieces. Then cut the front, back, and side pieces to rough length. I cut the front and back to right around 6" *(Fig. 2)*. And the two side pieces are cut to a rough length of 5".

TRIM TO SIZE. Once the pieces have been cut to their rough lengths, attach a stop block to the fence *(Fig. 3)*. Now, tilt the table saw blade to 45° and trim off one end of all four pieces. (As you make these cuts, you will also cut a kerf in the fence that's used to set up the next cut.)

To cut the workpieces to final length, measure from the long-point of the mitered end and mark the length *(Fig. 2)*. Then adjust the position of the stop block by laying one workpiece against the fence until the mark aligns with the edge of the kerf in the fence *(Fig. 3a)*. Now you can clamp the stop block in place and miter the pieces to finished length.

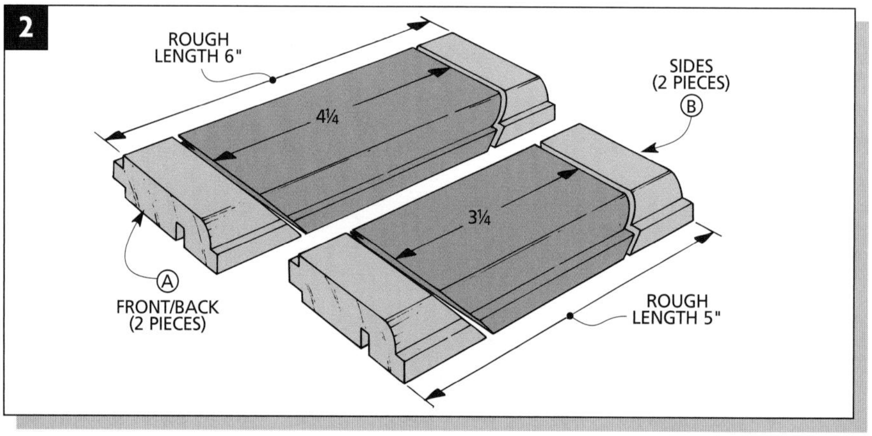
2
ROUGH LENGTH 6"
4 1/4
SIDES (2 PIECES)
B
3 1/4
A
FRONT/BACK (2 PIECES)
ROUGH LENGTH 5"

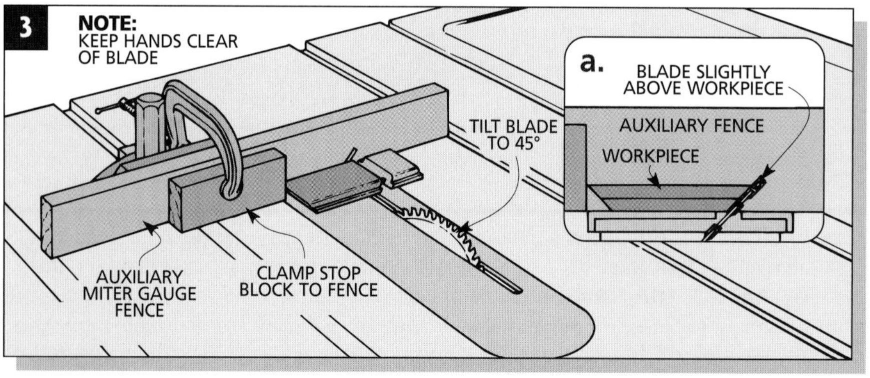
3
NOTE: KEEP HANDS CLEAR OF BLADE
TILT BLADE TO 45°
AUXILIARY MITER GAUGE FENCE
CLAMP STOP BLOCK TO FENCE
a.
BLADE SLIGHTLY ABOVE WORKPIECE
AUXILIARY FENCE
WORKPIECE

ASSEMBLY

Once the front, back, and side pieces are mitered to length, you can make the bottom of the Music Box.

BOTTOM. The bottom (C) is a piece of solid wood that's resawn and planed down to fit the 1/8"-wide grooves in the sides. (See the tips for making thin stock in the Technique articles on pages 65 and 96.)

To determine the length and width of the bottom, dry-assemble the box, holding it together with a rubber band.

Now, measure the inside dimensions, and add the depth of the grooves on all four sides, less 1/16" to provide extra clearance during assembly.

KEYWIND HOLE. Before assembly, holes have to be drilled in the bottom and one of the sides to accommodate the music works. (A kit with all the hardware you'll need and your choice of four different music movements is available from *Woodsmith Project Supplies.* See page 126.) To make the alignment of a shut-off pin and the movement as simple as possible, start by drilling an oversize hole ($1/2$" dia.) in the bottom (C) for the keywind stem to pass through *(Fig. 4).*

SHUT-OFF ARM AND PIN. The music movement has a wire shut-off arm that moves to start or stop the music. On the Music Box, this arm is activated with a shut-off pin that acts as a switch when the lid is opened or closed.

To mount this pin, drill a $1/8$"-dia. hole in one of the side pieces (B). This hole is located $3/4$" from the long point of the miter and centered on the top edge of the side piece *(Fig. 5a).* To allow room to connect the pin to the wire arm, drill a recess on the inside face of the side piece with a $1/2$"-dia. Forstner bit *(Fig. 5).*

MOUNTING HOLES. Now, dry-assemble the box again, putting the pin in place and attaching it to the wire arm. Then, center the movement in the box and mark the location of the two mounting holes *(Fig. 4).* Disassemble the box and drill $1/8$" mounting holes.

GLUE-UP. Finally, apply glue to the mitered ends and reassemble the box with the bottom (C) in place *(Fig. 6).* (Make sure that the movement's pin and arm are securely connected.)

LID

With the box complete and the music works installed, you can begin working on the lid. It's just a $1/2$"-thick piece of stock that's been dressed up a bit.

The lid (D) is cut to the same dimensions as the outside of the box *(Fig. 7).* (In my case, that was $3^1/4$" x $4^1/4$".)

Then I dressed up the lid with a small piece of walnut burl veneer and a thin solid-wood inlay strip. (Another option for dressing up the box lid is the chip-carved version shown in the Designer's Notebook on page 109.)

VENEER. The first step is to glue the walnut burl veneer to the top of the lid *(Fig. 7).* (For a quick way to apply the paper-backed veneer I ended up using, see the Technique box on the next page.)

ROUND OVER EDGES. Once the glue is dry, the next step is to round over the top

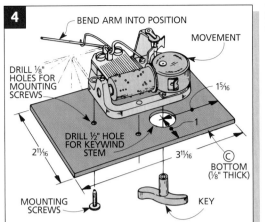

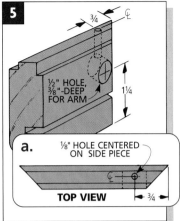

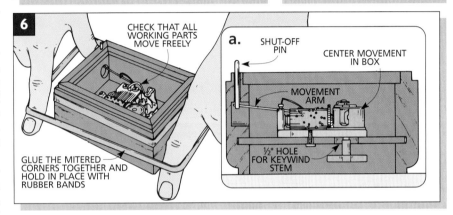

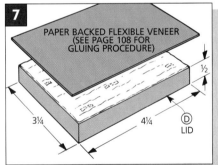

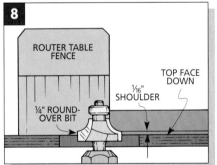

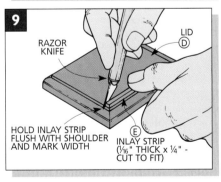

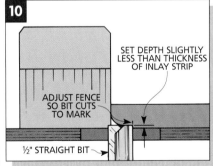

edges of the lid. To do this, I used a $1/4$" roundover bit on the router table *(Fig. 8).* And I adjusted the height of the bit to produce a $1/16$" shoulder.

CUT RABBET FOR INLAY. With the roundover complete, I routed a small rabbet around the edge of the veneer for

the inlay strip. First, use the inlay to mark the width of the rabbet on the lid *(Fig. 9).*

Next, adjust a $1/2$" straight bit to cut a rabbet slightly shallower than the thickness of the inlay *(Fig. 10).* (The strip is sanded flush later.) Now, adjust the fence so the bit cuts just up to the width mark.

INLAY STRIPS. After the rabbets were cut, I mitered the ends of the inlay strips (E) with a chisel. (For sources of solid-wood inlay strips, go to page 126.) To guide the chisel at 45°, I made a simple cutting jig *(Fig. 11)*.

To install the inlay, miter one end. Then temporarily tape this piece in place.

Next, mark the short point of the miter with a knife *(Fig. 12)*. Align this mark in the jig and cut it to length.

Finally, glue the inlay strips in place and sand them flush with the veneer.

FINISHING TOUCHES

Finally, to complete the Music Box assembly, all that's left is to attach the lid and drop in a dust shield.

HINGES. The lid is attached to the box with two small butt hinges. To mount these hinges, I chiseled out two shallow mortises in the top edge of the back piece *(Fig. 13)*. Each mortise is the same length as the hinge and as deep as the hinge knuckle *(Fig. 13a)*.

Next, position the hinge flush with the inside edge of the mortise *(Fig. 13a)*. Mark the hole locations, drill pilot holes with an 18-gauge brad in a hand drill, and screw the hinges in place.

To locate the pilot holes in the lid, fold the hinge closed and stick a piece of carpet tape on the top side of each hinge *(Fig. 13)*. Then press the lid down on top of the hinges.

Now open the lid, mark the screw hole locations, and drill the pilot holes.

FINISH AND DUST COVER. Before applying the finish, I removed the music works and the hinges. Then I sprayed on two coats of a lacquer wood finish.

Finally, cut a 1/8"-thick dust cover from acrylic plastic to rest on the inner lip. ■

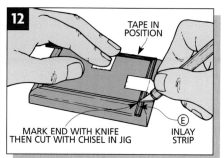

11 — JIG FOR MITERING INLAY STRIPS / CUT CHANNEL TO WIDTH OF INLAY / 45° MITER / GLUE 3/4"-THICK STOCK TO HARDBOARD BASE

12 — TAPE IN POSITION / MARK END WITH KNIFE THEN CUT WITH CHISEL IN JIG / (E) INLAY STRIP

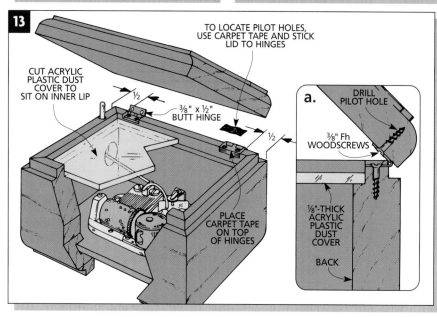

13 — CUT ACRYLIC PLASTIC DUST COVER TO SIT ON INNER LIP / TO LOCATE PILOT HOLES, USE CARPET TAPE AND STICK LID TO HINGES / 1/2 / 3/8" x 1/2" BUTT HINGE / 1/2 / PLACE CARPET TAPE ON TOP OF HINGES

a. DRILL PILOT HOLE / 3/8" Fh WOODSCREWS / 1/8"-THICK ACRYLIC PLASTIC DUST COVER / BACK

TECHNIQUE .... *Ironing Veneer*

When making the Music Box, I wanted to dress up the lid with a piece of walnut burl veneer.

PAPER-BACKED VENEER. I used a paper-backed flexible veneer. The paper helps keep the veneer flat and intact.

GLUING ON VENEER. I used yellow glue because I didn't want to buy a can of contact cement for such a small project. Since I didn't want to wait 24 hours for the glue to dry, I came up with a technique for speeding up the drying time — I used an electric clothes iron. The heat causes the water in the glue to evaporate quickly.

IRON. Before applying the veneer, turn the iron to a medium heat setting. If your iron has steam holes, make sure the steam setting is turned off. And to keep from getting glue on the base of the iron,

you may want to cover it with a sheet of aluminum foil (see drawing).

While the iron is warming up, I cut the veneer so it's slightly larger than the workpiece. Then apply glue, using just enough to "butter" the surface, so the grain pattern just shows through.

TACK ONE CORNER. Once the glue is applied evenly, all that's left is to iron down the veneer. To do this, start by placing the paper-backed veneer on the glued workpiece (see drawing). Then, to keep the veneer from moving on me, I place the iron over one corner until the veneer stays put.

Now, with the corner "tacked down," move the iron

slowly back and forth across the piece until the glue is set.

Note: Leaving the iron in one place may cause the veneer to burn.

Finally, flip the workpiece over and, using a sharp razor knife, trim the veneer flush with the sides.

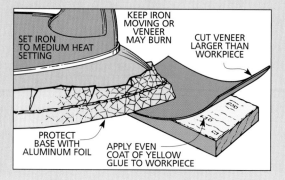

KEEP IRON MOVING OR VENEER MAY BURN / CUT VENEER LARGER THAN WORKPIECE / SET IRON TO MEDIUM HEAT SETTING / PROTECT BASE WITH ALUMINUM FOIL / APPLY EVEN COAT OF YELLOW GLUE TO WORKPIECE

DESIGNER'S NOTEBOOK

Dress up the lid with a simple chip-carved panel. If you're new to chip carving, the secret to success is to recess the lid for an insert. Then you can practice carving the design, before installing the insert in the lid.

CARVED LID

FULL-SIZE PATTERN

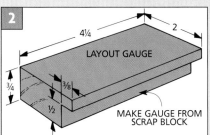

LAYOUT GAUGE

4¼

2

¾

⅜

½

MAKE GAUGE FROM SCRAP BLOCK

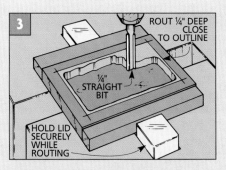

ROUT ¼" DEEP CLOSE TO OUTLINE

¼" STRAIGHT BIT

HOLD LID SECURELY WHILE ROUTING

■ The Carved Lid is built a little differently than the regular lid. The lid accepts a drop-in carved panel (F). This way I could carve the design a few times on a long workpiece, then cut out the one that looked the best and fit it in the lid recess.

■ The carved panel (F) has a simple design. I carved the design *(Fig. 1)* in a ¼"-thick strip of basswood (2½" x 12"). It's a soft, almost grainless wood that carves easily. (See Sources, page 126.)

■ To make the carved panel, I transferred the full-size pattern onto the blank. (As mentioned, the blank is over-size so that I could lay out the pattern three or four times, in case I needed to carve extras.) Hold the carving knife (see Sources, page 126) at a 65° angle and plunge the tip into the panel *(Step 1* at right). Now use your thumb as a pivot and pull the knife along the line.

■ To remove the chip, spin the workpiece around, hold the knife at the same angle and pull the knife toward you *(Step 2).* To complete the carved panel, all the remaining cuts will be exactly the same. If needed, carve a few extra panels.

■ Next, I made a gauge to lay out the outline of the recess *(Fig. 2).*

■ Once you've finished making the gauge, use it to lay out the recess on the top of the ½"-thick lid *(Fig. 3).*

■ With the layout complete, the next step is to rout a ¼"-deep recess to accept the carving *(Fig. 4).* To do this, use a ¼" straight bit and rout close to the line.

■ Now, to get a crisp shoulder around the recess, I used a sharp chisel to cut to the layout line. Here again I used the layout gauge, but this time the gauge is used as a support for the chisel *(Fig. 4).*

1 *Holding the knife at a steep (65°) angle, plunge the tip of the knife into the workpiece. Then, using your thumb as a pivot, pull the knife along the outline.*

2 *The second cut will remove the chip. To make this cut, spin the workpiece around. Hold the knife at the same angle as before and pull it toward you.*

To get the insert to fit tightly, angle the chisel so that you are undercutting the sides of the recess slightly *(Fig. 4a).*

■ Once you've finished chiseling the recess to the line, rout a ¼" roundover with a ⅟₁₆" shoulder around the four edges of the lid *(Fig. 5a).*

■ All that's left is to cut the panel to fit the recess and glue it in place *(Fig. 5).*

MATERIALS LIST

NEW PART
F Carved Panel (1)   ½ x 2½ - 3½
Note: Do not need part E.

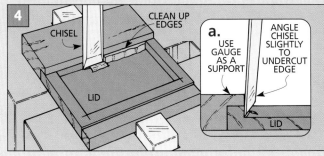

CLEAN UP EDGES

CHISEL

LID

a. USE GAUGE AS A SUPPORT

ANGLE CHISEL SLIGHTLY TO UNDERCUT EDGE

LID

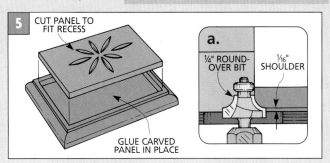

CUT PANEL TO FIT RECESS

a.

¼" ROUND-OVER BIT

⅟₁₆" SHOULDER

GLUE CARVED PANEL IN PLACE

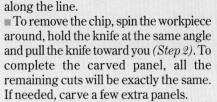

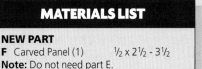

Candle Centerpiece

Make this beautiful centerpiece in just one weekend. It adds a warm glow to any table setting.
And changing the look is as easy as changing the color of the candles or varying the block heights.

When I first saw this centerpiece, I immediately thought "X's or O's." But despite its similarity to a certain popular children's game, the design makes an extremely striking and elegant candle holder.

ONE WEEKEND. The centerpiece is simple enough that it can be built easily in a weekend. The base is just a square of hardwood. The candle cups are all cut from one long blank, then drilled assembly-line fashion. And because it's such a simple project, there are a number of ways to customize it.

CUP HEIGHTS. The first way to change the look of the centerpiece is by simply varying the heights of the candle cups. The one shown above uses cups that are all the same height. But by combining taller and shorter cups, you can change the look of the centerpiece in a variety of ways. The Designer's Notebook on page 112 shows how easy this is to do and has some ideas to get you started.

In fact, you may want to make some extra candle cups of various heights to keep on hand so you can change the look of the centerpiece for different occasions. (Each cup is just held in place by a screw through the bottom.)

And of course, you can also mix and match different types of woods to create interesting looks. (I made my cups from cherry and used maple for the base.)

TEALIGHTS. The centerpiece uses "tealight" candles. They are safe to use in this project because the candles are contained in glass or aluminum cups. Plus the holes in the candle cups are drilled shallow enough that the candle wick (and flame) stay above the top of the cup.

These tealights can be found in all types of stores and in all kinds of colors and scents. This provides you with another way to customize the centerpiece. Choose colors that complement a table setting. Or light scented candles to enhance the ambience of a party.

BASE

The base of this centerpiece really couldn't be much simpler. It's just a square block of wood with an inset grid made up of thin wood strips.

I started out by cutting a square base (A) out of $\frac{3}{4}$"-thick stock (*Fig. 1*). Then, to hold the dividers that will be added later, two pairs of slots are cut into the top surface of the base at right angles.

These slots are cut on a table saw, using a dado blade (*Fig. 2*). All four slots are identical, so you only have to worry about setting up the rip fence on your table saw one time. The important thing here is not the distance from each slot to the edge of the base, but the distance *between* the slots. The square in the center of the base needs to be 2$\frac{1}{4}$" square to match the candle cups that will be added later (*Fig. 2a*). And don't forget to rotate the workpiece between passes.

DIVIDERS. The grid that sits on top of the base is made up of eight individual pieces. These are all the same width and thickness, but there are three different lengths (*Fig. 1*). Since these pieces are rather small, I found it easiest to cut one

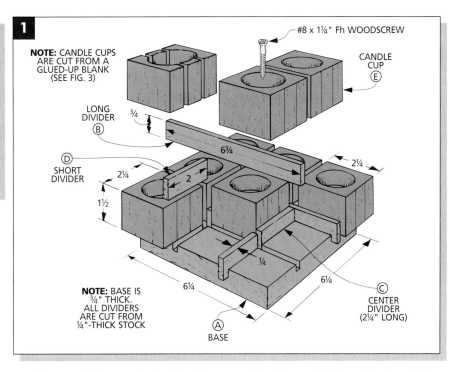

long blank and then cut the dividers from it. (For help with resawing thin stock, see the Technique article on page 65.)

First, the two long dividers (B) are glued in place. Then the two center dividers (C) are glued in between the long dividers. Finally, the four short dividers (D) are glued in place. That's all there is to the base. Now it's time to start work on the candle cups.

CANDLE CUPS

Each candle cup (E) is actually a block glued up from three layers of $\frac{3}{4}$"-thick stock (*Fig. 1*). But instead of trying to glue up each block individually, it's much easier, not to mention quicker, to glue

up three long strips into a blank and then cut the blocks from this blank.

I cut the strips for my blank about 3" wide. This way, you can glue them up without having to worry whether or not they're exactly aligned. Then after the glue is dry, the blank is squared up to its final dimensions (2$\frac{1}{4}$" square). The next step is cutting the individual blocks from the squared blank.

CUT TO LENGTH. After determining the height for the cups (*Fig. 1* and the Designer's Notebook on page 112), you can cut them to length. To get identical lengths, try clamping a scrap block to your rip fence to serve as a stop (*Fig. 3*). This prevents the cutoff cup from being trapped between the blade and fence.

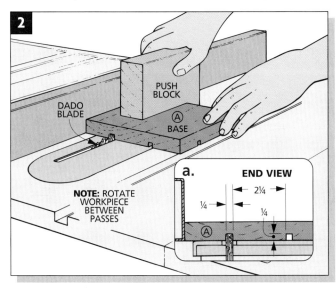

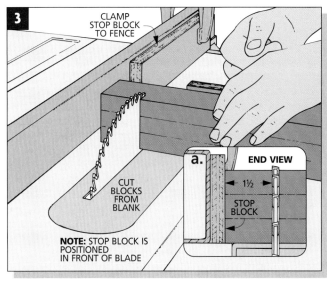

DRILL HOLES. Once all nine blocks have been cut, you're ready to drill the holes for the tealight candles. Using a Forstner bit, I drilled a $1\frac{5}{8}$"-dia. hole $\frac{5}{8}$" deep in the end of each block *(Fig. 4a)*. There's nothing complicated about this, but a couple of simple tips can make the process go more smoothly.

First, after centering a block under the bit, clamp a fence and stop block to the drill press table *(Fig. 4)*. This makes it a snap to position the remaining blocks.

Second, because you're drilling a large hole into end grain, you want to minimize the heat caused by friction to avoid burning the wood (and your drill bit). So I set my drill press to its slowest speed and used light pressure while drilling.

Note: Before you begin drilling the holes, it's a good idea to check the height of the candles you'll place in the centerpiece. You may need to adjust the depth of the holes so they are slightly *shallower* than the height of the candles.

After drilling the holes for the tealight candles, the next step is to drill a countersunk shank hole centered in the bottom of each cup for a mounting screw.

FINISH AND ASSEMBLY. Before assembling the cups and base, I applied a finish to all the pieces. Then just screw the blocks in place *(Fig. 5)*. (Use short screws so they don't poke through the base.) To create a uniform appearance, I oriented the candle cups so the joint lines were running in the same direction. ∎

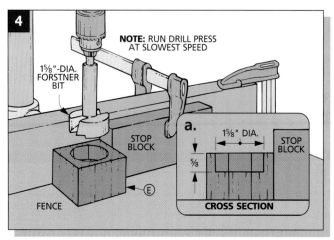

4 NOTE: RUN DRILL PRESS AT SLOWEST SPEED

$1\frac{5}{8}$"-DIA. FORSTNER BIT

STOP BLOCK

a. $1\frac{5}{8}$" DIA. STOP BLOCK

$\frac{5}{8}$

FENCE

E

CROSS SECTION

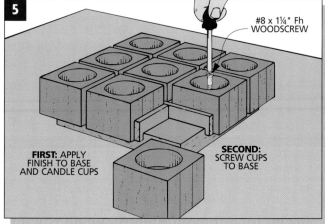

5 #8 x $1\frac{1}{4}$" Fh WOODSCREW

FIRST: APPLY FINISH TO BASE AND CANDLE CUPS

SECOND: SCREW CUPS TO BASE

DESIGNER'S NOTEBOOK

You can create a variety of striking arrangements by making candle cups of different heights.

CONSTRUCTION NOTES:

■ By mixing candle cups of different heights, you can change the look of the centerpiece. If you make several cups of various heights, you can mix and match them in different combinations.

■ To make the pyramid arrangement shown in the drawing, I made four regular cups (E). For the center I made a tall cup (F) that is $2\frac{1}{2}$" high. Finally, I made four medium cups (G) that are 2" high.

■ Even though the cups are different heights, the holes are all drilled to the same depth ($\frac{5}{8}$" in my case).

■ You'll also need longer screws to secure the taller blocks. The tall cups require $2\frac{1}{4}$"-long screws and the medium cups need $1\frac{3}{4}$"-long screws.

■ To make a stairstep design, you'll need three cups of each height. Arrange them from short to tall on the base.

MATERIALS LIST		
NEW PARTS		
F Tall Candle Cups	$2\frac{1}{4}$ x $2\frac{1}{4}$ - $2\frac{1}{2}$	
G Medium Candle Cups	$2\frac{1}{4}$ x $2\frac{1}{4}$ - 2	

HARDWARE SUPPLIES
No. 8 x $1\frac{3}{4}$" Fh woodscrews
No. 8 x $2\frac{1}{4}$" Fh woodscrews

Note: You can mix part E with the tall and medium candle cups as desired, so quantities of cups and screws will vary depending on your arrangement.

TALL & MEDIUM CUPS

Arch-Top Clock

With just two pieces, two screws and a clockwork, the toughest part of this project is trying to decide on the customization options. Change the type of wood or clockworks, or paint on a faux stone finish.

This Arch-Top Clock drew lots of attention when I first set it on my desk. But not nearly as much as when I lined up a half dozen of them like a row of dominoes.

The unusual thing was that all the clocks had the same basic design — but each one looked remarkably different. That's because I used different types of woods and finishes for each clock. You can see some of these examples in the Designer's Notebook on page 115.

Besides being an ideal project to experiment with different materials, another nice thing about this clock is that it doesn't require a large, expensive bit to make an opening for the clockwork. All it takes is a guide bushing for your router (more about that in a moment) and a simple shop-made template.

Once you have the template in hand, you can gear up to make any number of clocks quickly and easily.

GUIDE BUSHING. A guide bushing works somewhat like the bearing on a router bit. On a router bit, the bearing is meant to ride against the edge of the workpiece, so the bit follows the contour of the workpiece. A bushing, on the other hand, is meant to ride against a template that's attached to the workpiece. The bushing fits into the base of your router, around the shank of the bit. A collar on the body of the guide bushing extends below the router base and rides against the template. (Bushings are available through most woodworking stores and catalogs. See Sources on page 126.)

CLOCKWORK. The clockwork I used is a $2^3/_4$" fitup. This means the outside diameter of the clockwork is $2^3/_4$". But the back of the clock is slightly smaller in diameter. So after you rout out the hole to fit the back of the clock, the mechanism just press-fits into the hole. The lip around the outside of the mechanism then rests on the surface of the body. (See page 126 for sources of clockworks.)

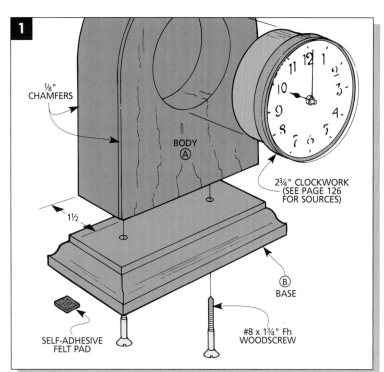

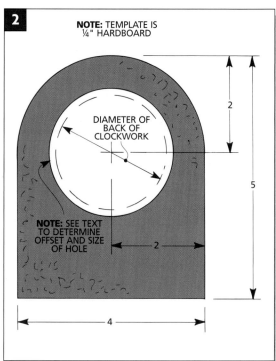

MATERIALS LIST

WOOD

A	Body (1)	1½ x 4 - 5½ rough
B	Base (1)	¾ MDF - 2½ x 5

HARDWARE SUPPLIES
(2) No. 8 x 1¾" Fh woodscrews
(1) 2¾"-dia. quartz fitup clockwork
(4) Self-adhesive felt pads

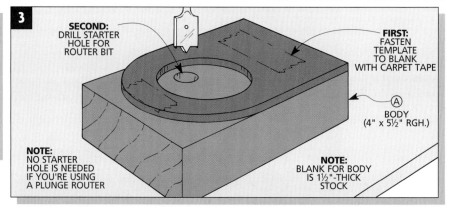

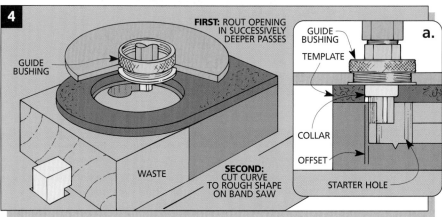

BODY

To allow room to recess the clockwork, the body (A) of the clock is 1½" thick *(Fig. 1)*. After cutting a blank to rough size, you can make a template.

TEMPLATE. The template is a piece of ¼" hardboard. It serves as a guide as you cut the arch on the body and when routing the opening for the clockwork.

The curve on the template is the identical shape and size of the arch on the body of the clock *(Fig. 2)*. But the hole in the template is larger than the diameter of the clockwork.

That's because the opening is routed using a metal guide bushing that attaches to the base of your router *(Fig. 4)*.

A collar on the bushing extends below the base of the router and rides against the template. So the bit doesn't cut right up next to the edge *(Fig. 4a)*. To compensate for this offset, the hole in the template needs to be larger than the diameter of the clockwork.

To determine the size of this hole, start by measuring the outside diameter of the guide bushing. Then subtract the size of the bit and add this figure to the diameter of the clockwork. For example, with a ⅝"-dia. bushing and a ½" straight bit, add ⅛" to the diameter of the back of

the clockwork (2⅜" for mine) and cut a 2½"-dia. hole in the template.

ROUT OPENING. After sticking the template to the body (A) with carpet tape, drill a starter hole for the router bit. Then you're ready to rout the opening for the clockwork *(Figs. 3 and 4)*. What you want is to make the opening deep enough so the lip around the front of the clock-work fits tight against the body. (In my case, that was ³⁄₄" deep.)

SHAPE TOP. Once the opening is routed, trace around the top of the template. Then remove the template and cut the top to rough shape on the band saw. Then you can sand the body to final shape (see the Shop Tip at right).

CHAMFERS. All that's left to complete the body of the clock is to chamfer the front and back edges.

Note: Leave the bottom edges square so the body of the clock will fit tight against the base.

BASE

The body of the clock sits on a base (B) made from ³⁄₄"-thick medium-density fiberboard (MDF) *(Fig. 5)*. I routed a ¼" Roman ogee profile around the base.

FINISH. It's easiest to apply a finish before assembling the clock. The Designer's Notebook below shows some interesting options I tried.

ASSEMBLY. Finally, it's just a matter of screwing the base to the body. After pressing the clockwork into the opening, apply self-adhesive felt pads to each corner of the base to protect the surface the clock rests on *(Fig. 1)*. ■

SHOP TIP .... Flush Trim Sander

To sand the top of the clock to match the template, I used a flush trim sander in my drill press.

This sander has a disc that rides against the template to guide the sanding drum (like the bearing on a flush trim router bit). Clamp a piece of plywood with a hole in it to the drill press to provide clearance for the sander (see detail).

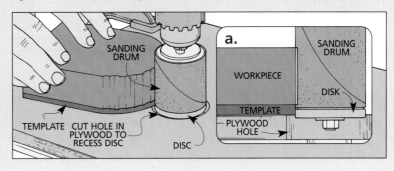

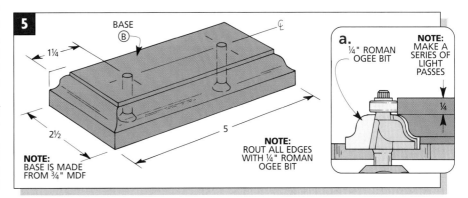

DESIGNER'S NOTEBOOK

Customize the clock with a faux stone finish, different types of wood, or a different clockwork.

CUSTOMIZED CLOCKS

■ Get different looks with various types of wood or by applying a specialty paint. (If you paint the clock, use MDF for the body so wood grain won't show through.)

■ Special spray paints give the appearance and texture of stone (left photo below). Some of these products involve applying a single coat. Others have you spray a lighter base coat with a darker second coat to get this effect.

■ For the look of marble (right clock in left photo), I applied a marbleizing paint. Applying this paint involves a couple of unusual techniques.

First, two base colors are swirled together in a dish to create a two-tone effect. This mixture is dabbed on with a sponge. Then the dark "veins" in the marble are made by applying a third color with a feather.

■ Both of these finishes require a top coat for protection, such as a clear acrylic or polyurethane. (You can find these paints at hobby stores.)

■ The photo below shows the clock with changes to the materials. On the left is the original cherry clock, but with a different clock fitup for a more contemporay look.

■ The body of the clock on the right is spalted maple. The black base and clockwork highlight the colors in the body.

Accessory Box

Contoured and contemporary, this striking black box is highlighted by a panel of bird's-eye maple in the lid. The elegance continues on the inside with leather linings and a convenient mirror.

Not long ago, while visiting a friend, I noticed that he kept an old dish on top of his dresser. It held tie tacks, watches, and other jewelry, an old pocketknife, a few keys, and some scraps of paper. And every night, he emptied whatever else was in his pockets into it. It certainly didn't look very attractive. In fact, it was a bit of an eyesore. That's why I built this Accessory Box for him.

As I was designing it, I knew I wanted it to be more than just a square box with a lid. So I tried to come up with some interesting design features.

Perhaps the most striking is the contrast between the figured maple in the lid and the black of the box. The maple is a piece of veneer glued to a hardboard backing. The panel is then cut to fit into an opening in the lid frame.

STAINED WOOD. And to provide the contrast, the rest of the box is a rich black. But it's not ebony, as you might think. Instead, the box was built out of walnut that has been "ebonized" — stained black.

I used an aniline dye to do this. It's a powdered dye that you mix with water to get the color you need. Application is also quite easy. I've provided more details about this on page 123.

INSIDE. The inside of the box is as attractive as the outside. There's a mirror on the inside of the lid that's "framed" with leather. Plus, leather is used to line the bottom of the box. Working with leather may be new to you, but again, I learned a few tricks that I've included in the Technique article on page 125.

CURVES AND HINGES. But that's not all. The techniques that go into building this box make for an interesting project. As I mentioned before, this isn't a traditional, square box; the sides have a curve cut into them. So do the front and back. Also, you won't see any hinges. Instead, the lid pivots open on small, hidden pins.

But even so, there isn't anything to building this Accessory Box that makes it especially difficult.

DIVIDERS. If you need to organize a lot of smaller items inside the box, you can easily make a set of removable dividers. This is covered in the Designer's Notebook on page 124.

EXPLODED VIEW

OVERALL DIMENSIONS:
10½"W x 8½"D x 2¾"H

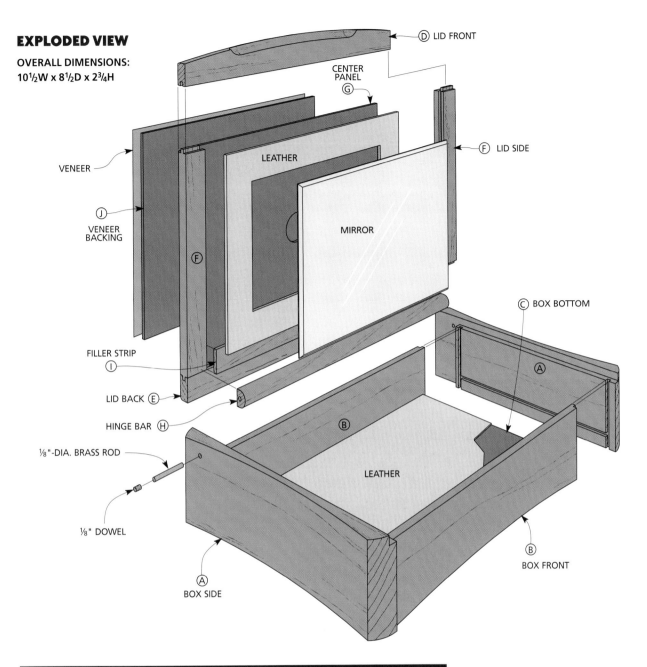

D LID FRONT

CENTER PANEL
G

F LID SIDE

VENEER

J

VENEER BACKING

LEATHER

MIRROR

C BOX BOTTOM

A

FILLER STRIP
I

LID BACK E

HINGE BAR H

B

⅛"-DIA. BRASS ROD

LEATHER

B

BOX FRONT

⅛" DOWEL

A

BOX SIDE

MATERIALS LIST

WOOD

A	Box Sides (2)	¾ x 2½ - 8¼
B	Box Front/Back (2)	¼ x 2¼ - 9¼
C	Box Bottom (1)	⅛ hdbd. - 6⅝ x 9¼
D	Lid Front (1)	½ x 1¼ rough - 9½
E	Lid Back (1)	½ x ¾ - 9½
F	Lid Sides (2)	½ x ¾ - 7
G	Center Panel (1)	⅛ hdbd. - 7 x 8¼
H	Hinge Bar (1)	½ x ⅜ - 9½

I	Filler Strip (1)	⅛ x ¾ - 8
J	Veneer Backing (1)	⅛ hdbd. - 6¾ x 8

HARDWARE SUPPLIES

(3) 7" x 10" leather (rough)
(1) 5" x 7" mirror
(1) 8" x 9" figured veneer (rough)
(1) ⅛"-dia. x 3" (rough) brass rod
(2) ⅛" dowel x ¼"

CUTTING DIAGRAM

¾ x 5 - 48 WALNUT (1.7 Bd. Ft.)

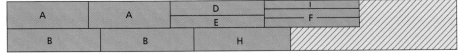

ALSO NEED: ONE 12" x 24" PIECE OF ⅛" HARDBOARD FOR PARTS C, G, AND J

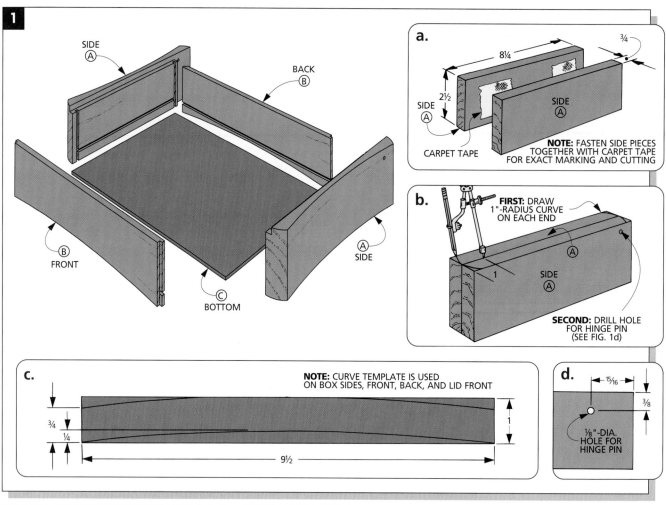

1

SIDE
(A)

BACK
(B)

(B)
FRONT

SIDE
(A)

(C)
BOTTOM

a.

8¼

¾

2½

SIDE
(A)

SIDE
(A)

CARPET TAPE

NOTE: FASTEN SIDE PIECES TOGETHER WITH CARPET TAPE FOR EXACT MARKING AND CUTTING

b.

FIRST: DRAW 1"-RADIUS CURVE ON EACH END

(A)

1

SIDE
(A)

SECOND: DRILL HOLE FOR HINGE PIN (SEE FIG. 1d)

c.

NOTE: CURVE TEMPLATE IS USED ON BOX SIDES, FRONT, BACK, AND LID FRONT

¾
¼

1

9½

d.

15/16

3/8

⅛"-DIA. HOLE FOR HINGE PIN

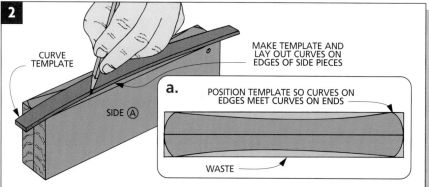

2

CURVE TEMPLATE

MAKE TEMPLATE AND LAY OUT CURVES ON EDGES OF SIDE PIECES

SIDE (A)

a. POSITION TEMPLATE SO CURVES ON EDGES MEET CURVES ON ENDS

WASTE

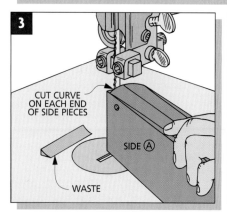

3

CUT CURVE ON EACH END OF SIDE PIECES

SIDE (A)

WASTE

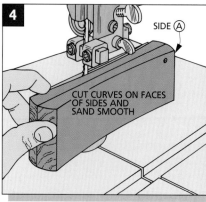

4

SIDE (A)

CUT CURVES ON FACES OF SIDES AND SAND SMOOTH

BOX

To build the Accessory Box, I started with the two sides (A) *(Fig. 1)*. These pieces are cut from ¾"-thick stock. After cutting them to size, the first thing I did was to fasten them together with carpet tape with their edges flush *(Fig. 1a)*. This simple step makes a lot of sense for a number of reasons.

First off, I drilled the ⅛" holes for the lid's hinge pin *(Fig. 1d)*. Having the sides taped together ensures that the holes end up perfectly aligned.

CURVES. Then, when you're laying out the curves on the side pieces, having them taped together creates a larger surface to work with. The 1" radius on each end of the side pieces can be drawn at the same time to ensure the pieces are mirror images *(Fig. 1b)*. And it's easier to lay out the long curves, too *(Fig. 2)*.

To draw the long curves on the sides, I made a simple template out of ¼" hardboard *(Fig. 1c)*. But I intentionally cut the template a little longer (9½") than the side pieces. This way, the template can

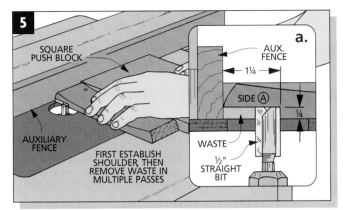

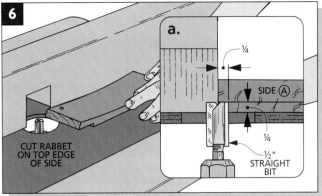

be used again later to draw the curves on the box front, back, and lid.

When laying out the long curves, position the template so it connects with the curves on the ends *(Figs. 2 and 2a)*. Then cut all the curves on the band saw and sand them smooth *(Figs. 3 and 4)*. Here again, I found that having these pieces taped together made it easier to keep the pieces flat on the table while making the cuts.

JOINERY. Now the two side pieces can be separated so the joinery can be cut. (To separate the pieces, you may need to work a putty knife between them.)

I routed all the joints on the router table. When working with small pieces, I like using the router table instead of the table saw. Plus, a straight bit in the router makes nice, clean cuts that give you dadoes and grooves with perfectly flat, square bottoms.

The first thing to do is rout a rabbet on the back inside face of each side piece *(Fig. 5)*. What you end up with here is a wide rabbet that provides clearance for the lid to open between the sides.

To cut this rabbet, I used a $^1/_2$" straight bit raised $^1/_4$" *(Fig. 5a)*. But before you begin, there are a couple of things to do to ensure a safe, square cut. First, the bit opening on the fence needs to be covered by an auxiliary fence so the piece won't tip into the opening.

Also, I squared up a scrap piece and used it to push the sides through the bit. This scrap piece holds the sides square to the fence, but it also backs up the cut, so there's less chance of chipout.

When routing the rabbet, I established the shoulder with the first pass *(Fig. 5a)*. Then I made several more passes to remove the remaining waste.

With the wide rabbet cut on the back end, next I cut a smaller rabbet along the top edge of each side. This rabbet will support the lid of the box. To cut this rabbet,

the height of the bit doesn't change, but you'll need to remove the auxiliary fence and reset the router fence so only $^1/_4$" of the bit is exposed *(Fig. 6)*.

To complete the sides of the box, there are just two more steps. First, dadoes are routed to hold the front and back pieces. Then a groove is cut for the bottom of the box.

DADOES. The dadoes in the front and back of the sides accept tongues routed later on the front and back pieces. To rout the dadoes, I switched over to a $^1/_8$" straight bit in the router table and used a scrap push block as I had earlier *(Fig. 7)*.

The only odd thing here is that these dadoes aren't the same distance from each end. The dado in front stops $^1/_4$" from the end, while the one in back stops $1^3/_8$" from the end because of the wide rabbet in back *(Fig. 7a)*.

GROOVES. Finally, to complete the sides, I routed a $^1/_8$" x $^1/_8$" groove in each side piece to accept the $^1/_8$" hardboard that will be used for the bottom of the box *(Fig. 8)*. I didn't want these grooves to be visible from the front, so I "stopped" them — that is, the groove runs only from the dado in front to the dado in back *(Fig. 8b)*. This involves using a couple of stop blocks to control the length of the cut *(Fig. 8)*. (For more on setting up a router table to cut a stopped groove, see the Technique article on page 120.)

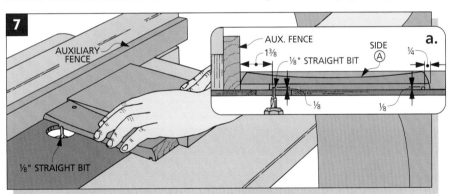

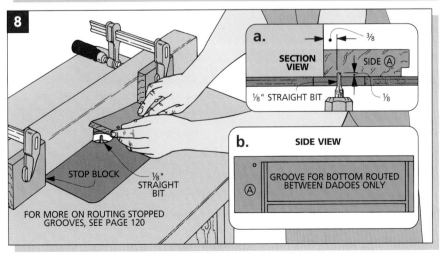

TECHNIQUE .... *Stopped Grooves*

Cutting a groove along the entire length of a workpiece isn't usually a problem. Just push the piece into the bit. But how do you accurately cut a groove that has to stop short of the ends of a workpiece (a stopped groove)?

That's the challenge I faced when I began cutting the groove on the sides of the Accessory Box. This groove stops at each end at the dado for the front and back of the box. This way, it won't be visible when the box is assembled.

The solution I came up with is to use a couple of stop blocks clamped to my router table fence. Placing one on either side of the bit limits the length of the groove (*Fig. 1*). And setting up the stop blocks is quite simple.

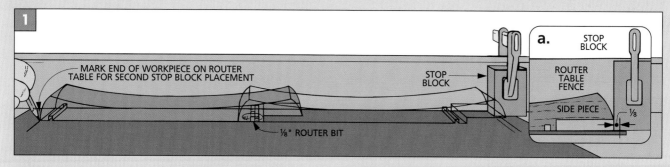

1

MARK END OF WORKPIECE ON ROUTER TABLE FOR SECOND STOP BLOCK PLACEMENT

STOP BLOCK

⅛" ROUTER BIT

a. STOP BLOCK

ROUTER TABLE FENCE

SIDE PIECE

⅛

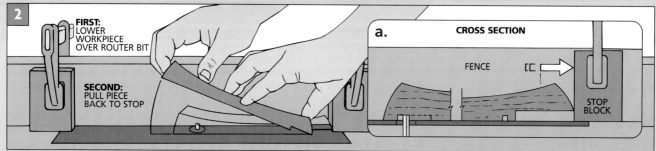

2

FIRST: LOWER WORKPIECE OVER ROUTER BIT

SECOND: PULL PIECE BACK TO STOP

a. CROSS SECTION

FENCE

STOP BLOCK

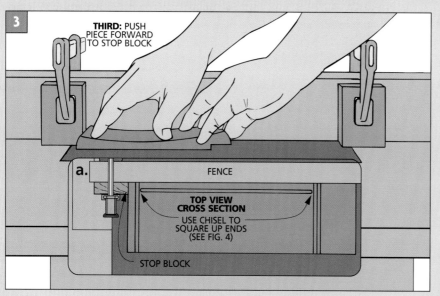

3

THIRD: PUSH PIECE FORWARD TO STOP BLOCK

a. FENCE

TOP VIEW CROSS SECTION
USE CHISEL TO SQUARE UP ENDS (SEE FIG. 4)

STOP BLOCK

I started by setting the height of my router bit. Then I adjusted the router table fence so it was the proper distance away from the bit (³⁄₈" in this case).

STOP BLOCKS. To set up the stop blocks, place one of the side pieces against the fence so that the dado at one end of the piece fits over the router bit. Then make a mark on your router table at the opposite end of the workpiece.

Now drop the other dado over the router bit and mark the other end of the workpiece on the table.

These marks serve as guides for attaching your stop blocks. Just to be safe, I placed my stop blocks about ⅛" in from the marks (*Fig. 1a*). That way I can't cut too far past the stopping points.

To rout the groove, carefully lower the workpiece down over the rotating bit (*Figs. 2 and 2a*). Now pull the workpiece back until it hits the first stop.

Then start pushing the workpiece forward until it hits the other stop (*Figs. 3 and 3a*). Finally, I used a chisel to clean up the ends of the groove (*Fig. 4*).

Note: You'll have to readjust the stop blocks in order to cut the groove on the other side of the box.

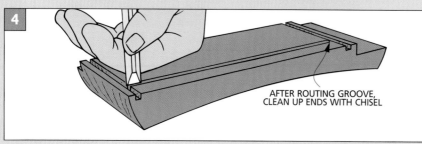

4

AFTER ROUTING GROOVE, CLEAN UP ENDS WITH CHISEL

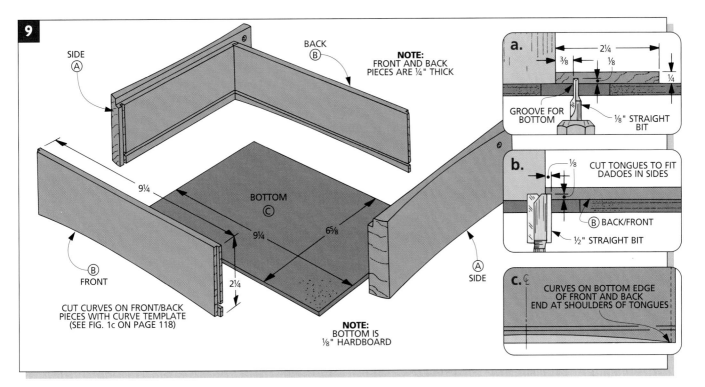

9

SIDE Ⓐ

BACK Ⓑ

NOTE:
FRONT AND BACK
PIECES ARE ¼" THICK

9¼

BOTTOM Ⓒ

9¼   6⅝

Ⓑ
FRONT

2¼

CUT CURVES ON FRONT/BACK
PIECES WITH CURVE TEMPLATE
(SEE FIG. 1c ON PAGE 118)

Ⓐ
SIDE

NOTE:
BOTTOM IS
⅛" HARDBOARD

a.   2¼   ⅜   ⅛   ¼

GROOVE FOR
BOTTOM

⅛" STRAIGHT
BIT

b.   ⅛

CUT TONGUES TO FIT
DADOES IN SIDES

Ⓑ BACK/FRONT

½" STRAIGHT BIT

c. ℄

CURVES ON BOTTOM EDGE
OF FRONT AND BACK
END AT SHOULDERS OF TONGUES

FRONT AND BACK. With the sides complete, I worked on the front (B) and back (B) of the box. These pieces are only ¼" thick *(Fig. 9)*. A ⅛" x ⅛" groove is routed to hold the bottom *(Fig. 9a)*. Then rout a tongue on each end to fit in the dadoes in the sides *(Fig. 9b)*.

The last step is to lay out a curve on the bottom of these pieces *(Fig. 9c)*. (Use the template for the curves on the sides.)

The curves on the front and back pieces end at the shoulders of the tongues on the ends *(Fig. 9c)*. And they're cut and sanded just like the curves on the sides. Just make sure the top of the curve ends up below the groove for the bottom.

ASSEMBLY. After cutting the curves, I dry-assembled the box and cut a ⅛" hardboard bottom (C) to fit in the grooves in the box. Then the box can be glued up.

LID

Now that the box is complete, you can turn your attention to the frame and veneered-panel lid.

FRAME. To begin, I cut all the frame pieces to size *(Fig. 10)*. The front (D), back (E), and sides (F) are all cut from ½"-thick stock. But the front is a little wider (1¼") than the other pieces so that a curve can be cut on it later.

The next step is to cut grooves to hold the ⅛" hardboard panel *(Fig. 10a)*. These grooves are cut slightly off-center to allow for both the veneered panel on

the outside and the leather trim and mirror on the inside.

With the grooves cut, stub tenons can be cut on each end of the lid's side pieces to line up with and fit the grooves in the front and back pieces *(Fig. 10b)*.

CENTER PANEL. Next up is the center panel (G). This is just a piece of ⅛" hardboard that the veneered panel, leather, and mirror will be attached to later.

To determine the size of the panel, dry-assemble the lid and measure between the bottoms of the grooves.

Note: It's a good idea to drill a finger hole in the panel. Then, when test-fitting the veneered panel later, it will be easier to remove it from the frame to apply glue.

Now the lid can be assembled. But the frame of the lid is not complete quite yet. Its front edge still needs to be shaped.

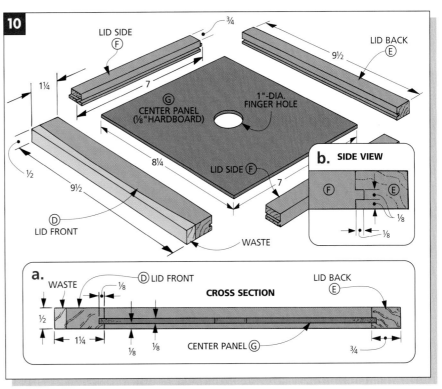

10

LID SIDE Ⓕ

¾

LID BACK Ⓔ

9½

1¼

7

CENTER PANEL
(⅛"HARDBOARD)
Ⓖ

1"-DIA.
FINGER HOLE

½

9½

Ⓓ
LID FRONT

8¼

LID SIDE Ⓕ

7

WASTE

b.   **SIDE VIEW**

Ⓕ   Ⓔ

⅛   ⅛

a. WASTE   Ⓓ LID FRONT

⅛

CROSS SECTION

LID BACK
Ⓔ

½

1¼   ⅛   ⅛

CENTER PANEL Ⓖ

¾

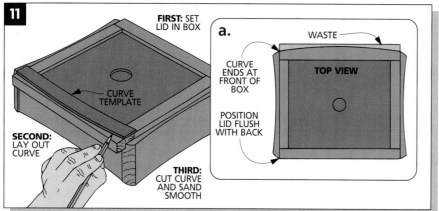

11

FIRST: SET LID IN BOX

CURVE TEMPLATE

SECOND: LAY OUT CURVE

THIRD: CUT CURVE AND SAND SMOOTH

a.

WASTE

TOP VIEW

CURVE ENDS AT FRONT OF BOX

POSITION LID FLUSH WITH BACK

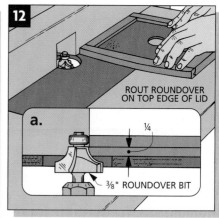

12

ROUT ROUNDOVER ON TOP EDGE OF LID

a.

$\frac{1}{4}$

$\frac{3}{8}$" ROUNDOVER BIT

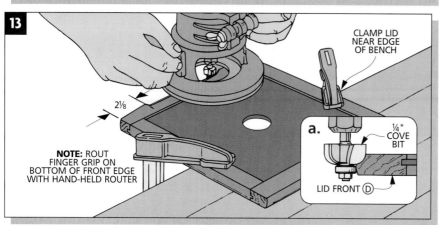

13

CLAMP LID NEAR EDGE OF BENCH

$2\frac{1}{8}$

NOTE: ROUT FINGER GRIP ON BOTTOM OF FRONT EDGE WITH HAND-HELD ROUTER

a.

$\frac{1}{4}$" COVE BIT

LID FRONT ⓓ

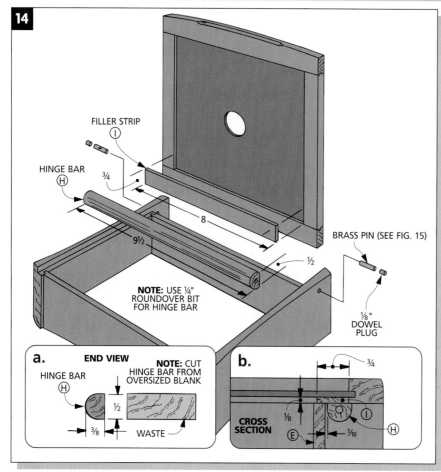

14

FILLER STRIP ①

HINGE BAR ⓗ

$\frac{3}{4}$

8

$9\frac{1}{2}$

$\frac{1}{2}$

BRASS PIN (SEE FIG. 15)

NOTE: USE $\frac{1}{4}$" ROUNDOVER BIT FOR HINGE BAR

$\frac{1}{8}$" DOWEL PLUG

a. END VIEW

HINGE BAR ⓗ

NOTE: CUT HINGE BAR FROM OVERSIZED BLANK

$\frac{1}{2}$

$\frac{3}{8}$

WASTE

b.

$\frac{3}{4}$

$\frac{1}{8}$

CROSS SECTION

ⓔ

$\frac{1}{16}$

①

ⓗ

LID CURVE

To reflect the curves in the sides of the box, the front of the lid is also curved. But on the lid, this is an outward curve, in contrast to the inward curve of the sides. And roundovers are routed on each edge. I started with the curve on the front.

To lay out this curve, you'll need to set the lid in the box. The back of the lid should be flush with the backs of the side pieces *(Fig. 11a)*. Then the template used earlier can be positioned so the curve ends up flush with the front of the box *(Fig. 11)*. Trace around the template and cut out the curve on the band saw.

After the curve had been cut out and sanded smooth, I rounded over the four top edges of the frame slightly *(Fig. 12)*. To do this, I used a $\frac{3}{8}$" roundover bit set to make a $\frac{1}{4}$"-deep cut *(Fig. 12a)*.

Finally, I added a finger grip to the bottom front edge of the lid *(Fig. 13)*. This can be done easily with a hand-held router and a $\frac{1}{4}$" cove bit *(Fig. 13a)*. The cove stops $2\frac{1}{8}$" from each end. I just clamped the lid to the edge of the bench, marked the start and stop points, and carefully routed between the marks.

At this point, the frame of the lid is complete, and now is a good time to sand it smooth. But the lid still needs to be attached to the box, so I turned my attention to adding the hinge bar.

HINGE BAR. What's a bit unusual here is that the lid doesn't use a typical metal hinge. Instead, it pivots open and closed on a pair of $\frac{1}{8}$"-dia. brass pins *(Fig. 14)*. These pins fit through the holes in the sides into a small hinge bar, which is attached to the lid.

The hinge bar (H) is just a $\frac{1}{2}$"-thick piece cut to match the length of the lid. One edge is rounded over to provide clearance as the lid is opened *(Fig. 14b)*. But to rout the roundover safely, I started with a 2"-wide blank *(Fig. 14a)*. Then after using a ¼" roundover bit to shape the edge, I ripped a ⅜"-wide (tall) hinge bar from the blank.

FILLER STRIP. But the hinge bar can't be glued to the lid quite yet. First, a filler strip (I) needs to be added to support the hinge bar *(Figs. 14 and 14b)*.

The thickness of this strip is what's important. It should match the shoulder inside the frame so that when the strip is glued in place, it will be flush with the face of the lid and provide a level surface to glue the hinge bar to *(Fig. 14b)*.

ATTACHING HINGE BAR. With the filler strip glued in place, the hinge bar can be glued to the lid. But its position is important. With the lid in position, the bar should be ¹⁄₁₆" from the back (E) of the box *(Fig. 14b)*. (I cut a couple of ¹⁄₁₆"-thick shims to help position the bar.)

FINISHING. In order to get into all the recesses of the box and lid, I applied a finish before attaching the lid. (Applying the stain at this point also keeps the stain

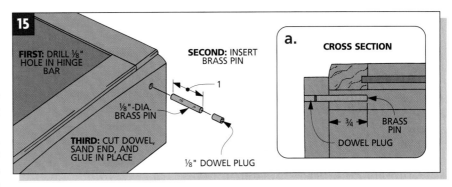

from getting on the veneered panel added later.) This is a two-step process. First, I stained the wood to make it look like ebony. (This is covered in the Finishing box below.) Then I applied a few coats of a wipe-on finish as a top coat.

ATTACHING THE LID. Now you can attach the lid to the box. The first step is to drill a ⅛" hole in the hinge bar for the pin *(Fig. 15)*. To do this, I set the lid in place and used the hole in the box sides to guide the bit. The goal is to drill a hole in the bar that's ¾" deep *(Fig. 15a)*.

The lid pivots on two ⅛"-dia. brass pins cut 1" long *(Fig. 15)*. (You can find brass rods at hobby shops.) Then the hole is plugged with a short length of ⅛"-dia. dowel. But if you cut and trim the plugs after you glue them in, you will mar the finish already on the box.

So instead, simply cut the plug to length so you can push it in flush with the surface. Then sand the end smooth and push the plug in place. Now all that's needed is a little "spot finishing" to make the plug disappear.

FINISHING . . . . *Ebonizing Wood*

When I was selecting materials for the Accessory Box, I came across the bird's-eye maple veneer that I used on the lid. And I decided that to really set off the maple, the box should be a deep black ebony — without actually using ebony.

For one thing, ebony is an exotic hardwood that's not always readily available. That means it's also expensive. Plus it's difficult to work with. So I did what many woodworkers have traditionally done to mimic the look of ebony — I "ebonized" a different species of wood.

START DARK. When I'm going to ebonize a project, I give myself a head start on the darkening process by choosing a dark-colored wood. (I used walnut for the Accessory Box.) You can ebonize any wood, but obviously a darker wood gets black more quickly.

ANILINE DYE

The process of ebonizing is as easy as applying a stain. I mix up a fairly concentrated, black aniline dye. I like to use a water-based dye because it's the easiest to work with and the most lightfast.

But there's something to be aware of. Because you're putting water on the wood, the grain will tend to "raise." (Small fibers in the wood will swell and "fuzz up" the surface of the wood.) So you need to take pre-emptive action by raising the grain before applying the stain. This is done by simply wetting the surface of the wood slightly. A couple of passes with a damp sponge is all that's needed. Then, when the wood has dried overnight, lightly sand back the raised "whiskers."

APPLICATION

If you haven't worked with aniline dye before, it comes in powder form that needs to be mixed with water. For the Accessory Box, I used three teaspoons of powdered dye in a quart of hot water. (Since the dye is water-based, use a glass jar. A metal can may rust.)

Before applying the stain, strain it into another jar to remove any undissolved chunks of the dye. (Cheesecloth or a coffee filter works well for this.)

To apply the dye, brush a heavy coat on the wood. Try to keep a wet edge. Otherwise the lap marks may show. Since the idea is to get the wood as dark as possible, I don't bother to wipe off the excess. In fact, you may want to apply a couple of coats.

SHINY TO DULL. When the stain goes on, the color is shiny and even. As the water evaporates, you may be in for a shock. The color will become flat and dull. (The color might even change some.) Don't worry, you haven't done anything wrong. When you apply a top coat, the sheen will be restored.

DESIGNER'S NOTEBOOK

Dividers will keep the contents of the box organized.

CONSTRUCTION NOTES:

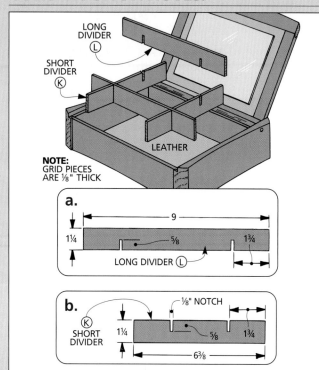

LONG DIVIDER (L)

SHORT DIVIDER (K)

LEATHER

NOTE: GRID PIECES ARE ⅛" THICK

a.

9

1¼

⅝

1¾

LONG DIVIDER (L)

b.

⅛" NOTCH

(K) SHORT DIVIDER

1¼

⅝

1¾

6⅜

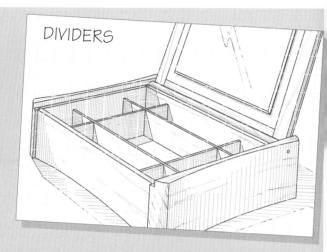

DIVIDERS

■ If you want to provide smaller spaces inside the box to organize jewelry, add dividers.

These simple dividers have just four interlocking pieces: two short dividers (K) and two long dividers (L) (see drawing). The pieces are all ⅛" thick and 1¼" tall (wide). Only their lengths are different (details 'a' and 'b' in drawing).

■ To join the dividers, I cut a pair of ⅛"-wide notches ⅝" deep in each piece (details 'a' and 'b' in drawing).

■ Then, I ebonized the dividers the same as the box.

■ Finally, "lock" the dividers together, and set them inside the box.

MATERIALS LIST		
WOOD		
K Short Dividers (2)		⅛ x 1¼ - 6⅜
L Long Dividers (2)		⅛ x 1¼ - 9

VENEERED PANEL

Now the lid is ready for the highlight, the veneered panel *(Fig. 16)*. I used contact cement to glue a piece of bird's-eye maple to a ⅛" hardboard backing (J) *(Fig. 16a)*. (Both the veneer and backing are oversize at this point.)

After the veneer was glued on, I trimmed the panel to fit the opening in the lid. Once it's cut to size, apply a finish, and glue the panel in place.

LEATHER AND MIRROR. The next things to add are the leather linings *(Fig. 16)*. I lined the inside of the box and lid. Plus, I covered the hardboard underside with leather. (This makes a nice surface to touch when picking up the box.)

The leather pieces for the box are simply cut to size and glued in place. There are some tricks to getting the best results here, so I've included those in the Technique article on the next page.

For the leather that's glued into the lid, I cut an opening in the center so it looks like a 1"-wide frame *(Fig. 16)*. That's because I added a mirror and wanted to attach it directly to the center panel (G). (I used silicone sealant to do this.) ■

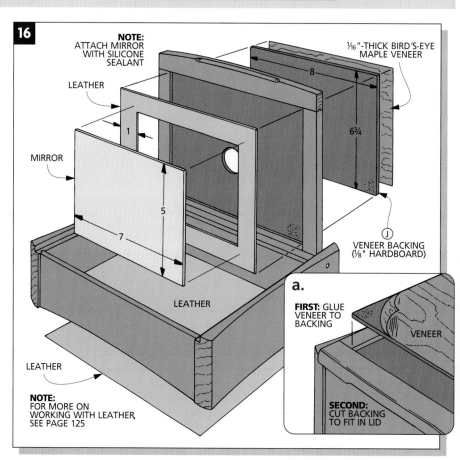

16

NOTE: ATTACH MIRROR WITH SILICONE SEALANT

LEATHER

MIRROR

1

5

7

1/16"-THICK BIRD'S-EYE MAPLE VENEER

8

6¾

(J) VENEER BACKING (⅛" HARDBOARD)

LEATHER

LEATHER

NOTE: FOR MORE ON WORKING WITH LEATHER, SEE PAGE 125

a.

FIRST: GLUE VENEER TO BACKING

VENEER

SECOND: CUT BACKING TO FIT IN LID

Cutting and fitting the leather for the Accessory Box can be a little tricky. Unlike wood, leather can stretch as you work with it, making it difficult to get straight, square cuts. (You can find leather at many fabric stores. I used a gray suede to line my box.)

TEMPLATES

To get a good fit, it's important to cut the leather to the exact size the first time. So I made some templates out of hardboard. They start oversize, then are trimmed until they fit. The only problem is getting the template out of the box once you get it to the right size. To do this, I glued on a small handle *(Fig. 1)*.

I made one template for the two pieces of leather on the bottom of the box (one inside and one on the outside).

For the lid, I needed two templates: one for the outside edge and another for the inside cutout. You won't need handles here, because of the hole in the lid.

For the inside template, don't try to match the exact dimensions of the mirror. In fact, the template should be smaller than the mirror. That's because a little bit of leather should extend under the mirror to prevent any gaps between the leather and mirror. The silicone sealant used to mount the mirror will fill the gap between the mirror and the center panel.

CUTTING

To cut the leather, I used a utility knife with a new blade. I held the template firmly in place and then made several passes on each side until I cut all the way through the leather *(Fig. 2)*.

Keep the back end of the knife low and don't apply too much pressure. Also try to avoid "pulling" the knife through the cuts or else you might tear the leather.

Note: It's a good idea to place a piece of posterboard or cardboard underneath the leather before you start cutting. It provides a firm surface for the knife and protects your table or benchtop.

GLUE

With the leather cut, I glued it in place. But I used liquid hide glue rather than yellow glue (see below). I applied the glue to the box instead of the leather to avoid accidentally getting adhesive on the good side of the leather.

Finally, to get the leather into the corners on the inside of the box, I used the end of a steel ruler.

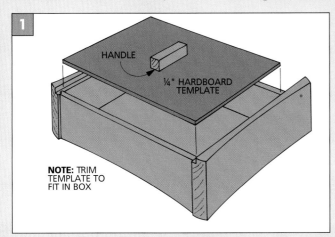

HANDLE

¼" HARDBOARD TEMPLATE

NOTE: TRIM TEMPLATE TO FIT IN BOX

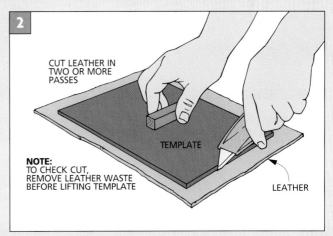

CUT LEATHER IN TWO OR MORE PASSES

TEMPLATE

NOTE: TO CHECK CUT, REMOVE LEATHER WASTE BEFORE LIFTING TEMPLATE

LEATHER

LIQUID HIDE GLUE

When gluing the leather to the Accessory Box, I didn't want the glue to set up before I could get the leather in place. To avoid this problem, I used liquid hide glue.

TWO TYPES. As its name suggests, hide glue is made from boiled-down animal hides. And there are two kinds available — traditional and liquid.

Traditional hide glue requires melting dry granules in hot water and then keeping the mixture warm to keep it liquid. Traditional hide glue sets up quickly, which is not what I wanted when attaching the leather.

SLOW SET-UP. The other kind of hide glue is liquid hide glue. It comes ready-mixed in a bottle, like regular yellow or

white glue (see photo). The difference between liquid and traditional hide glues is that liquid hide glue has an additive that keeps it fluid in the bottle. A result of this additive is that liquid hide glue sets up rather slowly compared to synthetic glues. (You'll have up to 10 minutes of "open time" before the glue starts to grab.) This gives you plenty of time to position the leather exactly where you want it.

BRUSH ON. To get an even coating, I poured the liquid hide glue into a jar and used a brush to apply it to the box.

If you can't find hardware locally, we've tried to find mail order sources with toll-free phone numbers and web sites (see box at right).

MAIL ORDER SOURCES

Some of the most important "tools" you can have in your shop are mail order catalogs. The ones listed below are filled with special hardware, tools, finishes, lumber, and supplies that can't be found at a local hardware store or home center. You should be able to find many of the supplies for the projects in this book in these catalogs.

It's amazing what you can learn about woodworking by looking through these catalogs. If they're not currently in your shop, you should have them sent to you. Most are also on the web and offer online ordering

Note: The information below was current when this book was printed. August Home Publishing does not guarantee these products will be available nor endorse any specific mail order company, catalog, or product.

THE WOODSMITH STORE

10320 Hickman Road
Clive, IA 50325
800-835-5084
www.woodsmithstore.com
Our own retail store with all kinds of tools and hardware including carving supplies, toy parts, clockworks, finishes, scroll saw blades, adhesives, and more. We don't have a catalog, but we do send out items mail order.

ROCKLER WOODWORKING & HARDWARE

4365 Willow Drive
Medina, MN 55340
800-279-4441
www.rockler.com
A very good hardware catalog with lots of toy parts like wooden pegs, dowels, and wheels. You'll also find hinges, finishes, veneers and veneering supplies, and inlay strips.

BOB MORGAN WOODWORKING

P.O. Box 35
Westport, KY 40077
502-225-5855
www.morganwood.com
Veneer is the business here. Find what you want in the online catalog.

KLINGSPOR'S WOODWORKING SHOP

P.O. Box 3737
Hickory, NC 28603-3737
800-228-0000
www.woodworkingshop.com
Widely known as a premier source for all types of sanding and finishing supplies. They also have plenty of quality tools and supplies.

KLOCKIT

P.O. Box 636
Lake Geneva, WI 53147-0636
800-556-2548
www.klockit.com
As the name says, a source for all kinds of clock parts. Plus they offer night light lamps and fixtures.

LEE VALLEY TOOLS

P.O. Box 1780
Ogdensburg, NY 13669-6780
800-871-8158
www.leevalley.com
Several catalogs actually, with hardware and finishing supplies. A good source of carving supplies, adhesives, wooden axle pins and wheels, brass shim stock, and hinges.

CHERRY TREE

P.O. Box 369
Belmont, OH 43718
800-848-4363
www.cherrytree-online.com
A great source for all kinds of toy parts. They specialize in craft hardware such as lamp parts, music box movements, clock fitups, mirrors, small hinges, and finishing supplies.

WOODCRAFT

560 Airport Industrial Park
Parkersburg, WV 26102-1686
800-225-1153
www.woodcraft.com
Just about everything for the woodworker including carving tools, toy parts, felt pads, mirrors, Weldon countersinks, scroll saw blades, flush trim sanders, finishes, veneers.

INDEX

AUGUST HOME
PUBLISHING COMPANY

President & Publisher: Donald B. Peschke
Executive Editor: Douglas L. Hicks
Project Manager/Senior Editor: Craig L. Ruegsegger
Creative Director: Ted Kralicek
Art Director: Doug Flint
Senior Graphic Designers: Robin Friend, Chris Glowacki
Associate Editor: Joel Hess
Editorial Intern: Cindy Thurmond
Graphic Designers: Jonathan Eike, Vu Nguyen

Designer's Notebook Illustrator: Chris Glowacki
Photographer: Crayola England
Electronic Production: Douglas M. Lidster
Production: Troy Clark, Minniette Johnson
Project Designers: Chris Fitch, Ryan Mimick, Ken Munkel, Kent Welsh
Project Builders: Steve Curtis, Steve Johnson
Magazine Editors: Terry Strohman, Tim Robertson
Contributing Editors: Vincent S. Ancona, Phil Huber, Brian McCallum,
Bryan Nelson, Ted Raife
Magazine Art Directors: Todd Lambirth, Cary Christensen
Contributing Illustrators: Harlan Clark, Mark Higdon, David Kreyling,
Erich Lage, Roger Reiland, Kurt Schultz, Cinda Shambaugh, Dirk Ver Steeg

Corporate V.P., Finance: Mary Scheve
Controller: Robin Hutchinson
Production Director: George Chmielarz
Project Supplies: Bob Baker
New Media Manager: Gordon Gaippe

For subscription information about
Woodsmith and *ShopNotes* magazines, please write:
August Home Publishing Co.
2200 Grand Ave.
Des Moines, IA 50312
800-333-5075
www.augusthome.com/customwoodworking

Woodsmith® and *ShopNotes*® are registered trademarks of August Home
Publishing Co.

OXmoor House®

Oxmoor House, Inc.
Book Division of Southern Progress Corporation
P.O. Box 2463, Birmingham, Alabama 35201

ISBN: 0-8487-2693-6
Printed in the United States of America

To order additional publications, call 1-800-765-6400.
For more books to enrich your life, visit **oxmoorhouse.com**